Praise fo...

"The field of parenting books is cro... unique, workable program that wil... the value of effort and money wh... about a variety of careers. And while all this is going on, the program gives you step-by-step guidance that will best insure the development of a loving and fulfilling interaction. *Earn It, Learn It* is packed with concrete learning ideas for your child and even has icons that help you and your child immediately identify the time and effort that may be required for a learning experience. In short, this book is a program that is enjoyable, concise, doable, and bound to help your child learn about money, careers, and effort."

—Foster W. Cline, MD, cofounder of the Love and Logic Institute
and coauthor of the Parenting with Love and Logic series

"In *Earn It, Learn It*, Alisa T. Weinstein introduces a revolutionary program for teaching children about the connection between work and money, without employing the old chores-for-cash methods that rarely work. Weinstein's program addresses the sense of entitlement that so many of today's children have by instilling a sense of responsibility for their own wealth and career choices through creative play. When children realize they can be a marine biologist, toy designer, or disc jockey—and earn money for it—their motivation and enthusiasm for work will soar!"

—Susan Heim, coauthor/editor, Chicken Soup for the Soul series

"For parents who want more from allowance day, *Earn It, Learn It* is a clever and fun way to teach your kids the true value of money. They'll learn not only that it doesn't grow on trees, but that you have to work for it, too—an invaluable lesson for 'the great recession' generation."

—Jen Singer, author of *You're a Good Mom (and Your Kids Aren't So Bad Either)*

"I think *Earn It, Learn It* is a great book introducing creative ways of teaching kids how money works in the world they live in! Great concept, great lessons, and every family can implement these ideas."

—Lori Mackey, founder of Prosperity4Kids.com

"Taking charge of your finances is empowering and can be key in creating and maintaining a fulfilling life. *Earn It, Learn It* helps kids uncover this key early on, giving them a head start to controlling their own destinies."

—Marianna Olszewski, bestselling author of *Live It, Love it, Earn it: A Woman's Guide to Financial Freedom*

"This book is truly revolutionary! Alisa T. Weinstein has done a monumental job of giving parents a clear, simple, and detailed model for teaching children about earning money for doing things they enjoy and quite possibly even love doing. I highly recommend this book both as a parenting coach and as someone who created a life out of doing what she loves."

—Carrie Contey, PhD, speaker, author, early parenting coach

"The Earn My Keep philosophy is so creative and innovative and I love the message it promotes: that hard work and money earned have value—a notion that seems to have lost its strength for our youth over the past couple decades. This book is an essential tool for every parent. It provides parents with a resource (and step-by-step guide) to help promote these values, and increase the amount of quality connection time with their children. Alisa T. Weinstein's writing style makes the book easy to understand and follow—it is clear that she is a mom who can empathize will all those challenges of parenting."

—Allison K. Chase, PhD, clinical psychologist specializing in children, adolescents, and families

Praise from Parents* for *Earn It, Learn It* & the Earn My Keep Allowance Program

"I have never seen anything like *Earn It, Learn It*. I love the way it teaches about earning money through work."

"I was having such a difficult time teaching my kids the value of money before. But Earn My Keep is not only effective, it's creative, fun, and easy too!"

"This gives my kids an opportunity to feel special and important, much more so than cleaning their rooms or brushing their teeth!"

"I couldn't believe how my child took to this. It really makes his imagination work and he puts a lot of thought into it. It boosts his self-confidence and gets the whole family involved. There's lots of family laughing. When I started, I had no idea how much fun it would end up being for my child!"

"Earn My Keep offers a broader perspective than chores alone because it couples responsibility and accountability with discovery and experiences, just like a real career."

"I was so surprised by how much my daughter enjoys the program…not only while doing it, but in the days and weeks that have followed. She told all her friends about it, and can't wait for her next 'job.'"

"This is different than just doing chores and helping mommy around the house. This gives my child confidence to act like a mini-professional. My five-year-old son, who is only interested in sports and cars and trains, told me he was going to be the best Librarian there is! I've never been so surprised! He took his job very seriously, and loved every minute."

"For my kids, *Earn It, Learn It* is about learning a new job and being given some responsibility, which I think is as important as teaching them about the value of money."

---

* Feedback compiled from a preliminary nationwide research study, as well as a nationwide research study run by an independent market research firm.

"My daughter now understands how important and fulfilling jobs are to all of us, adults as well as children."

"*Earn It, Learn It* is a wonderful way to teach about the value of money, and to interact with your children to help them explore their natural talents."

"Earn My Keep is a very gratifying experience for me and my son. That's the sweetest part. I was really surprised when we started, but it's so cool to watch him work toward something. I noticed that he was not as quick to spend the money he earns. He plans on saving it for the baseball cards that cost $50 per pack. If I had just given money to him, he would have spent it on junk!"

"It continues to amaze me the way in which my daughter totally changed the way she wraps her brain around things to formulate a plan of her own. And then we work it out together. And she feels great about it because these are her ideas at work."

"Children with ADHD do well when large tasks are divided into smaller, manageable steps. The tasks in *Earn It, Learn It* are short and easy, giving my son a real sense of accomplishment in a short period of time, which makes us both feel great!"

"Earn My Keep helped my daughter see that my job is not all snacks and meetings, but work that requires good manners and knowledge. I know of nothing else that could drive that lesson home any better. And for once I didn't have to nag!"

"I have four children, all at different levels. While smart in many areas, my eleven-year-old is grades behind in reading. I often worried about the options available for someone like him. The *Earn It, Learn It* career list excited us both. Now he knows that in life there are so many choices that play to his strengths!"

"My family already has an allowance program in place, but that hasn't stopped me from loving *Earn It, Learn It*. The activities are a fun new way to get a conversation going about some great careers, while spending good, quality time together."

"Earn My Keep shows kids that working for your money is rewarding, but it can also be fun. My child learned that careers are rewarding in more than a monetary way."

"Not only does *Earn It, Learn It* motivate kids, it teaches several skills along the way. In one week alone my daughters learned about telling time and brainstorming ideas, and exercised their public speaking skills. These are invaluable lessons they will utilize even in school. An added bonus is the family memories we share together!"

Earn It,
Learn It

Earn It, Learn It

Teach Your Child the Value of Money, Work, and Time Well Spent

ALISA T. WEINSTEIN

founder of Earn My Keep, LLC

Foreword by Linda E. Jessup, RN, MPH, FNP,
founder of the Parent Encouragement Program (PEP, Inc.)

 sourcebooks

Published by Sourcebooks, Inc.
P.O. Box 4410, Naperville, Illinois 60567-4410
(630) 961-3900
Fax: (630) 961-2168
www.sourcebooks.com

Library of Congress Cataloging-in-Publication Data

Weinstein, Alisa T.
    Earn it, learn it : teach your child the value of money, work, and time well spent / by Alisa T.
Weinstein. — 1st ed.
       p. cm.
    1. Finance, Personal. 2. Occupations. 3. Professions. I. Title.
    HG179.W435 2011
    332.024--dc22
                                            2010039355

            Printed and bound in the United States of America.
                  VP 10 9 8 7 6 5 4 3 2 1

To Mia (who loves lip balm)
and Derek (who eats it).

Contents

Foreword xvii

Part I: The Story 1

Introduction: The Battle of the Lip Balm 3

Chapter 1: Getting Started with Earn My Keep 9

Chapter 2: Insider Tips for the Ultimate Experience 25

Chapter 3: FAQs 31

Part 2: The Careers 43

Accountant 45

Acquisitions Editor 51

Archaeologist 57

Astronomer 63

Banker 69

Buyer 75

Chef 81

Contractor 87

Copywriter 93

Costume Designer 99

Curator 105

Dietitian 111

Diplomat 117

Disc Jockey 123

Entomologist 129

Environmental Planner 135

Event Planner 141

Geneticist 147

Geologist 153

Guest Relations Manager 159

Horticulturist 165

Human Resources Manager. 171

Interior Designer. 177

Investigator 183

Journalist. 189

Judge. 195

Land Surveyor. 201

Librarian 207

Linguist. 213

Marine Biologist 219

Market Researcher. 225

Meteorologist 231

Musician 237

Nurse Practitioner 243

Outdoor Adventure Guide 249

Paleontologist 255

Photographer. 261

Producer 267

Project Manager 273

Publicist 279

Social Activist 285

Toy Designer. 291

Translator 297

Transportation Engineer 303

Travel Agent 309

TV Writer 315

Urban Planner. 321

UX Researcher. 327

Zoologist. 333

Create-Your-Own!. 339

Part 3: The Bonus Stuff 343

Earn My Keep Cash 344

Sample Thank-you Note 346

Astronomer, Contractor, Paleontologist & Toy Designer:
    Play-dough Recipe 347

Accountant: Income Tax Return 348

Accountant: Budget Plan. 349

Copywriter: TV Script. 350

Copywriter: Radio Script. 351

Costume Designer: Pieces List. 352

Guest Relations Manager: Feedback Card 353

Human Resources Manager: Wellness Program Enrollment Form 354

Investigator: Search Warrant 355

Judge: Family Constitution 356

Judge: Adoption Petition. 357

Market Researcher: Moderator's Guide 358

Market Researcher: In-Depth Interview Questionnaire 360

Meteorologist: Symbol Story 361

Nurse Practitioner: Medical History Questionnaire. 362

Outdoor Adventure Guide: Campfire Recipe 363

Producer: Consent and Release Agreement 364

Project Manager: Project Delivery Plan 365

Publicist: Press Release. 366

Social Activist: Letter to the Editor 367

TV Writer: Script 368

Urban Planner: Census Form 371

Acknowledgments. 373

About the Author 377

Icon Legend 379

Foreword

We are living in an era of entitlement, a term used to describe a strange malaise gripping many of our youth. Children from a surprising variety of socioeconomic groups, who have been given too much with little or no effort on their part, clearly feel they deserve to have what they want, when they want it. The symptoms of these "gimmies" are easy to recognize—the insatiable craving for more stuff while showing less appreciation, less interest, and less valuing for what they already have.

Experts have noticed that children showing signs of entitlement often have more difficulty relating in healthy ways with others. In addition, they are frequently medicated for more stress-, depression-, and anxiety-related conditions than peers unaffected by this condition. It's all too easy for a child to slip into this state of entitlement.

Fortunately, a delightful antidote to much of that risk has sprung from the frisky imagination of Alisa T. Weinstein, a mother of two with a background in marketing and enough energy to light a small city. In today's society of high commerce and consumption, children between the ages of four and twelve have few ways to earn, learn, or become discerning about money. But the alternative allowance program featured in *Earn it, Learn It* provides us with multiple opportunities to teach children in this age group to work for, value, and handle money wisely.

In this book, Ms. Weinstein addresses some of the knottiest questions parents have about these issues. She deals straightforwardly with common parental concerns about allowances, and the flexibility of this approach can be tailored to any parent's convictions on the subject.

Ms. Weinstein recognizes that the motivation to "get" can be harnessed. It can be used to reach much more substantive goals and to teach vital values that build character, competence, and solid social connections in the bargain.

Children generally possess only a narrow range of ideas about the broad spectrum of career opportunities that exist in the world. They yearn to know more about the fascinating kinds of work adults love to do. If only they could find someone to make the introductions.

This book offers kids a full "dress-up box" of real-life vocations to try on. Each profession, such as Zoologist, Musician, Meteorologist, or Outdoor Adventure Guide, is introduced by an enthusiastic expert in that field. Since children learn best experientially, they suddenly have at their fingertips engaging opportunities to explore the multitude of interesting careers that keep our society humming along productively, artistically, and scientifically. The ability to envision an exciting future for themselves explodes with each new possibility.

For many harried parents, finding ways to connect with their kids at certain ages can be difficult at best. As your child checks the day's weather, learns to measure rain or snowfall, and provides the family with a daily weather report, the whole family will benefit from her discoveries and contributions. Children's regular family responsibilities, such as caring for family pets, learning to make tasty sandwiches, or organizing the bookcase in the family room, also take on greater meaning as the child recognizes the value of good work—and possibly the connection to being a Meteorologist, Zoologist, Chef, and Librarian.

"Finding the time" is probably the biggest obstacle parents identify in their lives. *Earn It, Learn It* will hand you a treasure chest of manageable ways to be involved with your child that fit into workable chunks of time. You will find many of these experiences to be as eye-opening and as irresistible as your child does. Suddenly quality time becomes so easy to achieve you will both want to go back for more on a frequent basis.

You will be amazed at how hard your children are willing to work, how self-motivated, resourceful, and dedicated they can become, how excited they will be to progress and finally accomplish these tasks. Becoming a competent producer and generous contributor, rather than just a consumer, supplies a deep level of satisfaction that sticks to children's intellectual, emotional, and moral ribs longer—and nourishes them better—than just getting "stuff." Appreciation grows as kids develop a recognition of the effort and care others exert on *their* behalf. From this fertile mix, their confidence and self-respect will flourish.

There's gold—and a bit of genius—in these pages. As our culture dumbs down a lot of learning experiences for children, the program in *Earn It, Learn It* helps us all wise up. So cut way back on the overgiving of gifts and treats. Instead, read, share, get involved with, and enjoy these rich opportunities together. Perhaps the best part of all is that your child's relationship with you and others will grow and flourish as you venture along with your mini-professional.

Linda E. Jessup, RN, MPH, FNP, certified Adlerian parent educator, founder of the Parent Encouragement Program (PEP, Inc.)

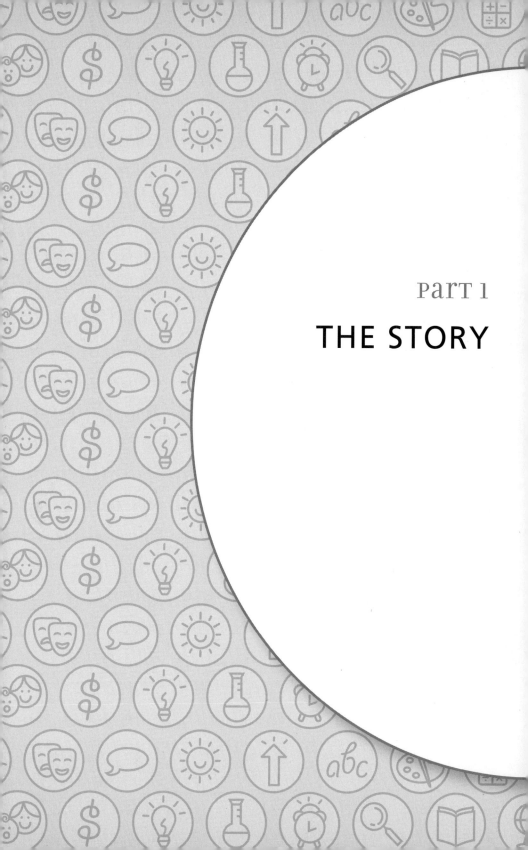

Part 1

THE STORY

The Battle of the Lip Balm

So there we were, in Target, my four-year-old's resolve growing stronger with every passing second. A waxy, glittery, cotton-candy-pink Lip Smackers lip balm was calling her name. How dare I say no?

But I did. And in a moment of spontaneous genius I also said we'd go home and hunt down every last lip balm hidden in every last purse and pocket she owned. Once we'd done so, of course she'd see she didn't need that new one. Right?

Thirteen lip balms later (I counted twice to be sure), it seemed I was wrong. She still had to have that tube of glittery bliss. So much for genius. But I just couldn't and wouldn't budge. She's four, for Pete's sake.

"Mia, I'm not buying you any more lip balm. You want it? Get a job."

And so she did.

• • •

If you don't believe in paying allowance for chores, this program is for you. If you do believe in paying allowance for chores, this program is for you. If you want your child to really, truly, undeniably understand that money doesn't grow on trees—and you want to teach it in a way that's engaging, enlightening, enriching, and (dare I say it?) fun—throw everything you thought you knew about allowance out the window. Because it's very, very possible that this program can kick-start your kid's appreciation for money, work, and time well spent.

I'll bet my lip balm on it.

Cutest Little Professionals Ever

The short of it is that allowance is a tricky subject.

I didn't want Mia to earn money for doing things like making her bed or setting the table—these are tasks we undertake because we're members of the same family, living under the same roof. One day she'll take out the garbage because it's full and stinky and simply needs to be moved to the garage, pronto, not because I'm waving a $5 bill at the door upon her return.

Yet I did want her to learn the value of money. That it does not, in fact, grow on trees. That the Target fairy does not come into my room every night and say, "Alisa, here is $552.36. Buy your daughter as many items from the dress-up aisle as she wants. And a new AquaDoodle. Those are really fun."

But how to get my message across? The answer hit me as soon as "Get a job" tumbled out of my mouth: Mia was going to take on true professional tasks. She was going to do more than earn. She was going to learn. Explore. Experience. And she was going to have an absolute ball in the process.

I grabbed a sticky note and started scribbling out a plan (one day to be called "Earn My Keep") in which Mia tried on all sorts of careers: Astronomer, Photographer, Toy Designer—with tasks tailored for her current social, emotional, and academic level (read: something I could squeeze in between three loads of laundry, two work deadlines, and one fifteen-month-old who liked to stick forks in our electric sockets).

So what happened? In the literal sense, she chose a career. We agreed to a task. She completed the task. And I paid her. But in the bigger-picture sense? She learned how to respect the money she earned, better appreciate the money Mom and Dad earn, and start to define what she may (or may not) want to do as a grown-up. All wrapped in some way-cool quality time I managed to eke out of an already packed schedule.

The fact is, what started out as an education in reality quickly revealed so much more: that exploration is the key to self-discovery. That the way to make a life is to do something you love. And that spending one week's pay on that aforementioned coveted lip balm is perhaps the most satisfying feeling a four-year-old has ever known.

SO WHAT IS Earn MY KeeP?

Earn My Keep is an easy-to-do parent/child program that helps kids ages four to twelve earn money for exploring and experiencing real careers. Kids pick a task from one of fifty career profiles, complete it within a set amount of time, and earn a set amount of money.

Not Your Mother's Allowance Program

So here's a pretty incredible fact: allowance has been the go-to means of teaching American kids fiscal responsibility for more than one hundred years. Even more incredible: it hasn't changed since its inception.[1] But allowance basics—earning for doing chores or for doing nothing at all—offer little more than change in a piggy bank and groans of "Do I have to?!" In the end, kids either think money falls from the sky or making their bed is automatic cause for payment (neither of which has been known to fatten a wallet in the real world).

Think about how you learned about money. Do you remember? Was it effective? Are you replicating the same lessons with your kid? And even if the "chore chart" is working as well for your child as it did for you, is it working as hard as it could be? Teaching kids that "hard work equals money earned" is a meaningful real-world lesson. But adding an education in finding passion and purpose in life, introducing the concept that hard work can also be work loved—that's pretty tasty icing on the cake.

There's also that elephant-in-the-room question: where are you now, financially speaking? Earn My Keep was born in one of America's worst recessions—a time when my husband and I were paying for our own overspending. And heaven knows, I didn't want my children to repeat our mistakes.

---

1 I couldn't believe it myself. But it's in black-and-white in the *Encyclopedia of Children and Childhood in History and Society*, in an article called "Allowances" by Lisa Jacobson: parents started doling out allowance way back in the early twentieth century, when children's purchases of (wait, this will shock you) movie tickets, candy, and toys raised concerns about their spending habits. (And we thought we had nothing in common with our great-grandparents.)

The first step, I thought, was making that aforementioned critical connection between hard work, self-satisfaction, and money earned. Enter Earn My Keep, the allowance program that allows you to:

o Differentiate between things we do as productive family members (making the bed, clearing the dishes) and things we do to pay our (eventual) bills.

o Expose your child to art, culture, creative thinking, history, language, literature, manners, math, money management, public speaking, research, science, and social responsibility—without your kid even realizing it.

o Introduce a whole bunch of career opportunities and the idea that passion and job satisfaction exist—a major component to achieving a better quality of life in adulthood.

o Teach your child that we depend on each other to make the world work, and how accepting that responsibility can make the world a better place (the Horticulturist grows the strawberries, which the Dietitian uses to make a healthy treat, which the Chef decides to serve in his or her restaurant, which the Accountant determines is too expensive—you know the price of organic food).

o Get that deep-down yummy feeling that comes from satisfying a child's curiosity about the adult world.

o And, most importantly, connect with your kid, promote a lifelong love of learning, and introduce the above-mentioned and all-important fiscal understanding.

Creatively Challenged? Time Crunched? Budget Tied? Bring It On!

So by now you may be wearing a quizzical look that falls somewhere between confused, skeptical, and "this chick is out of her mind." (My husband, Adam, wore the same look when he first learned about my grand plan for his daughter.) But rest assured, the Earn My Keep allowance program is not only doable, it's the kind of thing you'll actually look forward to doing. Better yet, your kid will too.

If you still need convincing, let's start with the creative aspect. As in, you don't need to have a creative bone in your body to look like a hero to your child. Why?

The brainstorming has been done for you. Inside this handy-dandy guide are more than nine hundred fifty activities that bring amazing careers to life for your kid—no thinking necessary. But if you do happen to love thinking outside the (crayon) box, then no holds are barred. Consider Earn My Keep a starting point for wherever you want the experience to go.

Now, the time issue. Yes, Earn My Keep eats more minutes than making a bed or cleaning a playroom. But depending on the tasks you choose, not much more. Within every career there are twenty tasks (give or take)—some can be done while snuggling at bedtime, while shopping for groceries, even while tackling tasks your child may already do. (Got a fish tank? Sounds like a Marine Biologist to me!) The point is, you have complete control over how much time and attention you give this program—and that can change with every career.

What's even more amazing is that the busier and more stressed-out you are, the more Earn My Keep can work for you. Rather than adding one more item to your never-ending to-do list, it packs so many of our (sometimes out-of-reach) parenting priorities into one nice, neat, deliciously easy-to-implement package.

And finally, a word for my budget-conscious brethren: I hear you. That's why Earn My Keep is bursting with responsibilities that cost nil, zip, zero, or can be completed using items you find in your own home. And a great tip? You'd be surprised how many professionals are willing to talk with children for free. All you have to do is ask.

Yes, That Bed Will Still Get Made

And thus stands the first of many questions from my husband: if you're paying Mia to be a Paleontologist, who's going to make her bed? Set the table? Feed the dog? (That's funny he said that. We don't have a dog.) My answer was pretty simple: She is. No one pays me for making my bed and setting the table. Well, I receive love and adoration from my family, yes. But still. Can't buy lip balm with it.

That's another inherent benefit of Earn My Keep: this is the real deal. Kids dig the truth. They may not dig the responsibilities we have in life "just because." (Frankly, neither do we.) But those tasks become a lot less daunting when everyone tackles them with the same outlook. I minded making my own bed less when

I realized it was motivating Mia to make her own bed more. Not that she jumps at the task every day. But over time, she's realizing that "Putting my pillows where they belong" is code for: "We all pitch in around here."

And now a much-deserved note on the aforementioned authenticity: every Earn My Keep career profile comes with its own Earn My Keep Expert. These guys and gals are responsible for bringing their profession to life for your child. And let's give them a heartfelt round of applause for their participation. Because while I'm pretty good at turning adult-level tasks into kid-friendly ones, I doubt my affinity for ladybugs would classify me as an Entomologist, my four whitewater rafting adventures as an Outdoor Adventure Guide, or my stash of '80s mixed tapes as a Disc Jockey. (More detail about the Experts' indispensable help to come!)

Can't-Miss Career Exploration

The Earn My Keep Experts inspired career profiles so chock-full of fun things to do, your family can enjoy exploring them, even if the allowance portion of the program isn't your thing.

CHAPTER 1

Getting Started with Earn My Keep

So you're ready to jump, feet first, into Earn My Keep. Begin with Quick Start! on page 10. But then dive into this chapter and the next for heaps of tips and guidance on how to get the most from the program.

"Kids? Say Hello to Earn My Keep!"

How will you introduce Earn My Keep to your child? I had it easy—Mia had not yet begun another kind of allowance program. One morning she woke up, was given a choice of ten careers and got to work as a Market Researcher (she picked her dad's job first—he swelled with pride for at least a week). Over time, I matter-of-factly introduced "making the bed" and "setting the table." Yes, she questioned the difference between "just-because jobs" and "Earn My Keep jobs." But that simply opened more discussion about why Mom and Dad work, and why she was "working" too. Reality education at its best.

But what about your situation? If your kid has been getting an allowance for doing chores, your best bet is to just come clean. "Honey, I've been reading this

MAKE IT OFFICIAL

Kick off your Earn My Keep experience with new places for your kid to store his hard-earned allowance, like a new wallet for money to spend, an empty (clean) spaghetti sauce jar for money to save, and a repurposed shoebox for money to donate.

book about this new program. You earn allowance by doing real adult jobs like [insert a few from Part 2 that would pique interest here]. We can even start with my job! We'll do it together." Any child who's been earning money for chores is going to jump at the chance to try something he sees as more fun. (Want to do Earn My Keep *and* pay your child for chores? See the FAQ on page 31.)

If your kid has been getting allowance for doing nothing at all, your best bet is to…uhhh…just come clean. "Honey, I've been reading this book about this new program. You earn allowance by doing real adult jobs like [insert a few 100% irresistible careers from Part 2 here]. We can even start with my job! We'll do it together." The fact is, children are crazy-intrigued by the adult world. Capitalize on that, and you'll find yourself with a willing participant.

All that said, let's get earning!

QUICK START!

1. Select a career (like Chef, on the next page) with your child.
2. Pick a task (or multiple tasks) from the career's profile (such as the sandwich one, circled on the next page) and set a deadline for finishing that career. (You could pick one task, two tasks, ten—what matters is that you define your kid's responsibilities and the date by which the career's work needs to be completed.)
3. Pay your child for the effort.

Chef

Oh, your favorite meal—you know what ingredients go in, how long it takes to cook (and how long it takes to eat!). Let's just say that, afterward, you're one satisfied customer. Chefs get to work with every ingredient imaginable to create their customers' favorite meals, right to order. Talk about a tasty career!

Jump In

o ① 🌐 🔍 Use the library or the Web to report about the history of the sandwich, including the Earl of Sandwich (yes, a real person!). Then make and enjoy your own sandwich, filled with your absolute favorite things.

o ② 🎨 Pick up a blank apron and/or chef's hat at a craft store and decorate it with fabric markers, paints, rhinestones—whatever you wish.

o ③ 🔍 🙂 Find an area restaurant that orders food from a local farmer. Then eat there—it's a great way to support your local economy.

CHEFS:

- Create meals in restaurants
- Experiment with all different kinds of foods
- Plate food in appealing ways
- Ensure health and safety code standards are met

TWO THINGS TO KEEP IN MIND

1. Begin with what you know. Consider starting with your own career (or a similar one that's on the list). Kids love to learn about their parents' professions, and the resulting positive experience whets the appetite for more.

2. Choose only ONE Level 1 task the first time you try Earn My Keep. The program's tasks are all designated as Level 1, 2, or 3 (more about this in the following section). As you'd figure, Level 1s are the easiest, and you should start there no matter your child's age, ability, or interest. Why? You'll deliver a feeling of accomplishment right off the bat. And the more you and your kid feel good about the program, the more likely you'll both want to continue. Then, when you and your child—and your schedule—can handle it, you may decide to add more tasks and/or Level 2s and 3s. Just remember: there's nothing wrong with *always* doing only one or two Level 1 tasks. You'll be happily surprised at how little time it takes to make a big difference.

Understanding the Icons

Attached to all the Earn My Keep tasks are Earn My Keep icons. If you're a planner, they're fun and helpful. If you're not a planner, they're still fun and helpful. (For easy reference, a condensed version of this list is printed on the last page of the book.) Here's what the icons mean:

LEVEL IT! ICONS

These so-not-scientific levels indicate the balance between the time and effort (yours and/or your kid's) needed to complete a task.

① LeveL 1

Can be done in one quick sitting. Can be done with just you and your child. Can be done with stuff you've got on hand. Can be done while dinner is cooking, in the car, at meals, even bedtime.

② LeveL 2

Can be uncomplicated, but may require a few days to complete. Can involve concepts younger children may not be able to grasp. Can involve more, or different, family members. Can involve leaving your home. Basically, the minute you get in a car or pull out the full-monty art supply bin, you've hit a Level 2 task.

③ LeveL 3

Can require a few days (or more) to complete. Can involve concepts younger children may not be able to grasp. Can involve leaving your home, field-trip style. Can involve more, or different, family members and friends—even people you and your child have never met before!

LeveL IT! DIsclaImer

The rankings of 1, 2, and 3 are meant to be fluid. For example, a Level 1 task becomes a Level 2 task if you need to go to the library, instead of researching online from home. Or, a Level 1 task may become a Level 3 task if you're dealing with interruptions such as bathroom breaks, phone calls, or pulling now-twenty-month-olds off the dining room table (the chandelier is NOT a toy!). Level 1, 2, and 3 will be different for each individual child—what's a 2 for one kid may be a 3 for another. And, finally, if you expect your child to complete three Level 1 tasks in one week, you may find you've created a Level 4!

LEARN IT! ICONS

These icons indicate the topics and skills introduced or reinforced through task exploration—every task has at least one.

 ArT

Encompasses professional and museum-style art, as well as arts-n-crafts- and construct-and-build-type projects.

 creative THINKING

Involves creation of original ideas and/or problem solving.

Librarians are amazing! You can ask them anything. Some public library systems even have chats where you can "talk" with a real Librarian online, in real time. This is all good to know if your child needs a little boost on a "report," "list," "describe," or "define" type of task.

 cULTUre

Includes world, national, neighborhood, and family culture.

 HISTOrY

Covers ancient, not-so-ancient, family, and even personal past.

 LanGuaGe

Encompasses both written and spoken expression.

LITERATURE

Includes books, plays, screenplays—any written work.

manners

Covers the use of respect and kindness when requesting, delegating, and managing.

MaTH

Incorporates basic math concepts taught in most elementary schools, like addition, subtraction, fractions, decimals, and spatial relations.

💲 MONEY MANAGEMENT

Includes basic money concepts, like the value of currency, as well as budgeting and comparison shopping.

💬 PUBLIC SPEAKING

Involves speaking with new people, or presenting to a larger number of friends and/or family members.

🔍 RESEARCH

Covers library and Web info and fact-finding searches, observing and recording of experiments, investigating, and even interviewing.

⚗️ SCIENCE

Encompasses scientific thought and observation, as well as the good old-fashioned experiment.

⏰ TIME MANAGEMENT

Includes anything with a time component for task completion.

NURTURE IT! ICONS

Bringing out the best in our kids can be as simple as nurturing a few important relationships with their elders, their community, and their planet. As such, you'll find at least one Intergenerational icon and at least one Social Responsibility icon in every profile (sometimes even within the same task).

Educational experts find that tasks like those in Earn My Keep give parents the opportunity to enhance their kids' development. For example: Creative Thinking tasks bolster how information is processed (cognitive development). Manners tasks foster healthy reactions to others, better regulation of emotions, and the desire to act morally and ethically (social-emotional development). Public Speaking tasks encourage self-expression (language development). And Art tasks strengthen a child's fine-motor skills (physical development).

INTERGENERATIONAL

These tasks strengthen ties between your child and an older generation—a mission ever more important if distance separates you from your parents, or you have waited longer to start your family. The older the parents, the older the grandparents, thus shortening the amount of time they have to spoil their grandchildren (and, yes, impart wisdom). Older neighbors, other family members, and friends, too, have much to offer the younger ones in their lives.

To find these tasks, look for the Intergenerational icon and the words "someone from an older generation" in the task itself. If you don't live near anyone who fits the bill, modify—many tasks can be done together over the phone or via webcam. And actually, you can turn any task in the book into an Intergenerational one, simply by asking someone a generation or two older than your child to take over the Mom or Dad role.

SOCIAL RESPONSIBILITY

These tasks foster your child's sense of environmental and social responsibility the Earn My Keep way. Real professionals apply these principles in their jobs—pick a Social Responsibility task and your kid can, too!

UP IT! ICONS

Up It! icons indicate a way for you to make a task more challenging for an older child, or give a task you've already done a new twist. Good to note: sometimes a task has only one Up It!, but sometimes there's more than one. If a task has more than one Up It!, they may not be sequential. Meaning, sometimes you do need to do the first Up It! to do the second, but sometimes you don't. Give the list a quick read before making your selection.

AGE RANGE DISCLAIMER

Why aren't there any "suggested age" icons on any of the Earn My Keep tasks? Because the same task can be done by a four-year-old and a twelve-year-old—it all depends on the level of difficulty you set for your child. Plus, not every kid can do the same task at the same age. So by not limiting the tasks to specific ages, you're more able to tailor the program for your child's personal academic, emotional, and social level. And (yes, there's more!), not specifying age ranges enables you to use the same task for two different children at the same time!

Understanding the Lingo

Earn My Keep's language is as flexible as it comes:

o "Report," "List," "Describe," and "Define" mean what you want them to mean. For younger children, these would be verbal tasks. Older children can write out their work or even use a computer. For kids in the middle, try a little of both!

o "Research" indicates using the library or Internet. But a word of caution: information found online is not always true, so look for reputable sources, like those from universities or government entities. It's also sometimes hard to find kid-level info. Your local public Librarian is an amazing resource, as is your child's school Librarian or Media Center Expert.

Speaking of language, you'll notice that while Part 1 of the book talks to adults, Parts 2 and 3 speak directly to kids. Why? Program set-up (Part 1) is clearly parental domain. But program-in-action is all about empowering your child (notice it's Earn My Keep, not Earn Your Keep). Because the profiles speak directly to your child as a peer, he feels respected, thus nurturing the desire to act like a real professional and take ownership of his fiscal independence.

○ "List two, three, or four…" "Pick one, two, or three…" "…for two, three, or four days…" means to choose one of those numbers. Younger children may be more comfortable with the lowest number; older ones, on the higher range. And feel free to raise the number even more if your kid could use a good (but attainable) challenge.

○ "Mom or Dad" can mean "Just Mom" or "Step-Dad" or "My Other Mom" or even "Grandpa"! While the terms "Mom" and "Dad" are used throughout the book, caregivers come in every shape, size, and title. Whatever role you play in your child's life, substitute in the book as you see fit. (This goes the same for the likes of "Big Sis" and "Little Bro," too.)

Trust The Experts

An Earn My Keep Expert helped build every profile. So whether your kid picks Transportation Engineer, Urban Planner, or Linguist, rest assured she's doing just what the pros do to earn money. Almost. 1) Every Expert has his own take on how to do his own job; 2) some professional tasks are impossible to re-create on a child's level, require access to more advanced equipment, or are simply too time-consuming for even SuperParent to conquer; and 3) in some cases the program suspends reality for a dose of kid-level fun, specifically sprinkled in to promote a love of learning, encourage creativity, and spark the imagination!

Understanding the Career Profiles

While no two professions are exactly the same, their profiles in this book certainly share some similar characteristics. You'll find the same structure used for each career profile so it's easy to jump from career to career, week to week. Here's what's in each one:

Introduction: Makes a connection between what your kid does every day, and how that could translate into a career he loves (during Earn My Keep and beyond!).

Bulleted Definition: Defines what it is the Experts do.

Jump In: Includes tasks that provide an overview of the profession (like "Shadow a…" and "Visit a…").

Interview: Introduces the unique nuances of each career, in the Experts' own words.

Bio: Highlights exactly how the Expert became an Expert. Some earned formal degrees. Others fell into their careers. Either way, it's a great introduction to how real people become real professionals.

Awesomeness: Gives the Experts a chance to shout to the world: MY JOB IS AWESOME BECAUSE…(I often think about the fun argument that would ensue if all the Experts were in the same room: "My job's the best." "No, *my* job's the best." "No, MY job's the best!!")

Did You Know?: Delivers a cool career-oriented fact.

Career Crossing: Reinforces the idea that we're all connected—that we all take part in making the world go 'round. Each Expert notes five professionals without whom she would be unable to get part of her job done. Asterisks (*) note careers you'll find as profiles in the book.

Some profiles suggest you take advantage of the examples and photocopy-able work sheets found in Part 3: The Bonus Stuff. That's because, depending on the task, your child may benefit from seeing a real-world example (like TV Writer's TV Script), or enjoy a bit of extra "oomph" from a fill-in work sheet (like Nurse Practitioner's Medical History Questionnaire). Language like "An example can be found on page such-and-such" will show up in the task itself, and direct you to that specific Expert-inspired and approved "bonus."

Downloadable versions of the photocopy-able work sheets can also be found at EarnMyKeep.com.

Also keep your eyes out for the occasional "So You Want to…" This is a mega-task, incorporating lots of mini-tasks into one—your child will see a project through from start to finish. An example: Guest Relations Manager's profile includes individual tasks such as welcoming guests and handling concerns, but the

"So You Want to…Make a Guest Feel Welcome" task incorporates them both for a more comprehensive career experience.

So How Much Should Your Little Earner Earn?

Earn My Keep addresses the value of money in connection with the work done to earn it. But when it comes to the value of money at the toy store—exactly how many dolls or trucks or scooters an allowance can buy—you know your family much better than I. The amount you pay your child and how you recommend he organize his earnings is all up to you.

You can start by defining what your child's allowance is expected to cover. Little things like toys and treats? Or more, like school lunches? School supplies? Activities with friends? Then consider if you'd also like your child to save and/or donate any of his earnings. You may need to up the allowance amount to cover additions like these.

Many financial experts recommend paying $1 for every year of a child's age (a seven-year-old would then earn $7), or $1 for every year he's been in school, starting with kindergarten (so a third grader would earn $4). They also suggest asking around the neighborhood—while we wouldn't typically advocate "doing what your friends are doing," your child would most certainly appreciate earning a similar amount as his buddies.

And then what percentage goes to savings and/or donations? Some families prefer a system that replicates their own real-world percentages (say, 25 percent to savings, and 10 percent to charity). Other families save half, keep half, and donate time (instead of money) to charitable organizations and causes. In our family, right now, Mia's allowance is for little extras only. She earns $2 for every completed Earn My Keep career—one dollar as a bill, the other in coins. The bill (50 percent) goes into her "save" envelope (we use the front of the envelope like a check register, updating her balance the fancy way—with a pen). Then ten cents (5 percent) goes into her "donate" envelope (same check-register thing). The rest goes into her wallet, ready to be spent.

No matter which path you choose, though, experts do recommend allowing your kid to (take a deep breath here) make some financial mistakes (yes, even after you've taught her otherwise). If she chooses, let her blow her entire allowance the second it hits her hands. And then let her regret that she doesn't have money for the very next thing she covets. This will hurt you both, yes (oh, the tears! the puppy dog eyes!), but stand firm. Resist the urge to replenish what she's just spent. (Also resist the urge to say "I told you so.") Problem solve with her on ways to resist impulse buying in the future. And then get to planning your next Earn My Keep experience!

You may find it helpful to do a few money-oriented tasks and/or careers when you begin the program, especially with children who've never handled money before. Check out Banker (page 69), which has tasks like opening a real-life savings account, and Accountant (page 45), which has tasks like calculating sales tax (this one is particularly helpful when explaining why that $2 mini bubble machine your son's been saving for actually costs $2.12 at the register).

Why does Earn My Keep have fifty jobs, instead of fifty-two (for every week in the year)? Four beautiful words: two weeks' paid vacation!

Also to consider: it's fabulous our children are earning money. But their payroll comes from us. What if there aren't extra funds in the family budget to donate to your worthy cause? Never fear.

There's always the option of reallocating money from your kid-related budget items (like school supplies) to your child's allowance (and then expecting her to purchase these items herself). Or try this approach:

Start with pretend money you can buy from discount websites, such as www. OrientalTrading.com, or money you make yourself, like EMK Cash, which you can photocopy from pages 344 and 345 or download from EarnMyKeep.com.

Then invest, say, $15 or $20 into a shopping trip to your local dollar store or the $1 bin at a craft or discount store—you can snag great little toys and games. Put stickers on them with prices you make up (like $1, $2, and $5) and store the items in a big, attractive box or displayed nicely on a closet shelf. "Pay" your child for the task(s) he completes, then allow him to "go shopping" at your in-home store.

You could also put dollar amounts on one-on-one activities that further promote the ever-elusive parent/kid quality time (not that you could ever really put a price on such wonderful things): a visit to the zoo, a ball game, a mini-sleepover in the backyard—compile the list with your child and she'll be even more eager to participate.

AND WHEN SHOULD YOUR LITTLE EARNER GET PAID?

Taking a cue again from the real world, it's time to set up the best day of the week (or every two weeks or every month): PAYDAY! If you're working outside the home, and receive payment on a regular basis, consider matching your kid's pay dates with your own—imagine how much he'd love getting paid the same day Mom or Dad does!

Or maybe you'd like to pay your Earn My Keeper every Friday, so she's got a little extra cash to spend over the weekend. Or maybe you'd prefer doling money out on Mondays, which nurtures your child's ability to save through the whole week, and then the weekend, too. (Though if your kid is challenged by fiscal restraint, it may be best to pay closer to when spending takes place. Then consider sliding that day back bit by bit, month by month, as his money skills improve.)

The day you pay also depends on what your child's allowance is for—if it's purely for "extras" (like toys or activities with friends), the end of the week may work great. But if you're also including things like school lunches, Sundays may be better.

Basically, there's tons of ways to set your family's Payday. Here's some examples:

One career a week = Payday every Friday

One career every two weeks = Payday every other Sunday

Two careers every two weeks = Payday every other Monday

One career every month = Payday the last day of the month

More important than the day of the week, though, is consistency. Like adults, kids need to know what to expect: a certain amount of money delivered on a certain day on a regular basis. So, just like I knew how long it would take me to save for that lovely, new water heater (really, it's gorgeous), Mia has to save for her next big purchase (which right now is a new Barbie...no, a label maker...no, a souvenir when we visit her grandparents...). This means while the level and/or number of tasks you pick can change with every career (ebbing and flowing based on everything else you've got going on), expectations (task completion) and Payday stay the same. (For more on Earn My Keep's flexibility, see Chapter 2.)

THE JOY OF SUCCESS

Rumor has it that the fun of being a parent is watching our kids succeed. (It's also being able to watch the occasional cartoon without feeling like you're too old to be watching cartoons. But I digress.) This means it's OK to help success happen.

Of course, an older child can be expected to tackle his Earn My Keep tasks on his own. But feel free to enjoy checking on his progress, discussing any stumbling blocks, and encouraging him to find his own solutions. For the younger child you'll do the same, just in real-time while she does her task. Remember, what you're paying your child to do is to learn what we, too, get paid for: effort and commitment. (Yes, adults also get paid for the end result, but if your child's very best hand-made Musician ukulele sounds more like a wailing cat, and she put her heart and soul into the creation of said wailing cat-instrument, then by golly, she's earned her keep.)

chapter 2

Insider Tips for the Ultimate Experience

T his chapter outlines a few great things to know—tidbits that will deepen the experience for you and your child (or, as you'll read below, children).

There's Flexible, and There's Earn My Keep Flexible

The Earn My Keep program works with one child or multiple children, during obligation-free weeks and crazy-busy ones, and with a career change every week, every two weeks—even every month. Just get into a consistent groove (to bolster that fiscal understanding), and shape the program as you see fit.

For instance, Earn My Keep's varied tasks allow you to keep your child's learning style in mind: some tasks are good for active kids; others work better for more reserved children. You can base your level of participation and supervision on your child's developmental and academic age (older children can be encouraged to do some tasks on their own). And with about twenty tasks per career, your child can Earn My Keep over and over again, with an entirely new experience every time.

SOLVE THE SIBLING DILEMMA

If you have more than one kid of Earn My Keep–age, start by having each child work from the same career profile (if you're able to do two different careers at the same time *and* keep your sanity, I bow at your feet). Then:

o Give each child the same task, adjusted for age and ability. So, say you have the option of "List one, two, or three…," you could have the younger child list one, and the older child list three. (Avoid "But he took what I said for my list!" by having them work independently, as opposed to together.)

o Or give each child a different task within the same career. This works well if your children have completely different learning styles and/or interests.

o Or have your kids work together, on the same task, and split the earnings (everyone splits the work, and therefore, the payment). And what career doesn't employ teamwork to get the job done? Note: I'm not saying to use this option every week (we all need a break from our fellow partners now and then). Another note: The kids could tackle two tasks together, and therefore earn their regular amount.

FOLLOW WHAT'S IN THE BONUS STUFF…OR NOT

Remember those extra examples and work sheets (the bonus material found in Part 3: The Bonus Stuff)? In regard to the work sheets (and true to Earn My Keep–form), you can choose to use them exactly as they are, or as a springboard to create your own versions. If you do use one from the book, make sure to photocopy the original rather than write directly in the book. This way, you can use the sheet over and over again! (Or solve this problem by downloading a clean one from EarnMyKeep.com.)

WORK EARN MY KEEP INTO LIFE AS YOU KNOW IT

It's easy to incorporate Earn My Keep into your family's lifestyle for exponential benefits. For example, select careers that correspond with destination vacations (Travel Agent), family announcements (Publicist), or spring cleaning (Project Manager).

Or coordinate your career choice with your child's school lesson plans and finally be able to answer: "Yes, you WILL use what you learn in school when you're out of school!"

Let's Boost That Paycheck!

Did the little Miss hit another birthday? Consider a raise. Or did she do an outstanding job making a Land Surveyor compass? Offer a bonus. Remember how adults appreciate these payroll gifts, and extend the love to your little professional.

Who Says If It's Fun, It's Not Work?

Certainly not our Experts, who all love their careers (even with the not-so-lovable parts like rush deadlines and billing). So while it may be hard at first to pay your Event Planner for organizing a lovely tea party for her grandma, aunt, and cousins, just keep repeating your new mantra: "I'm fostering passion and life-long career satisfaction…I'm fostering passion and life-long career satisfaction…"

> ### REMEMBER:
> ### EFFORT, IMPORTANT.
> ### RESULT, NOT SO MUCH
>
> Your child is an acting professional, not an actual professional! The final result of his effort is not nearly as important as the effort that created it. What you're looking for is a result that fits your child's abilities—one that shows he tried his best.

New Experiences, Inspired Here

Earn My Keep's careers can also be these fun, engaging tools that help your kid try new foods, participate more in school, follow directions—wherever she could use some encouragement.

Here's an example: let's say you have a finicky eater. Perhaps she'd give new foods a try if doing so makes her a professional. Like tasting three different kinds of grapes (Geneticist). Checking out the layers of a hard-boiled egg (Geologist). Putting together food service for a TV production (Producer). Testing the quality of a private-label brand yogurt (Buyer). And so on and so on.

Or let's say your child is uncomfortable speaking up in class, addressing adults, or making new friends. You could agree to a Shadow task, where your child will be role-playing as a mini-professional, thus lowering the intimidation factor of speaking to someone new. Plus, it gives him something cool to discuss on the playground the next day.

Earn My Keep is also a great way to help children step out of their comfort zones: kids who love science may love being Environmental Planners (not just Meteorologists). Those who love math may love being Interior Designers (not just Bankers). Those who love to tell stories may love being Copywriters (not just Journalists). Even some of the career titles themselves may be unfamiliar (ever met a UX Researcher before?!). Just start with what feels natural, then push the envelope. Exploration of new things is one of the best parts!

CREATE A CREATE-YOUR-OWN!

If your child has an interest in a career beyond the book's forty-nine, head straight to the fiftieth: **Create-Your-Own!**. There you'll find ways to explore any profession your kid can dream up. This may even be one of the first places you visit—some classic kid-favorite careers aren't blown out as profiles. (And sidenote: why no Astronaut, Firefighter, or Policeman? Because kids are already role-playing these careers at home. And/or they'd be too dangerous to emulate Earn My Keep–style—we do NOT want actual Firefighters showing up after your little one decides putting out a real fire would be a great way to earn his keep!)

The Art of Shadowing an Expert

It's the mother of all Earn My Keep tasks: "Shadow a [CAREER NAME HERE]." This is the kind of experience your kid will be thinking about, talking about, dreaming about for ages—just like she loves Take Your Child to Work Day, and how we loved visiting our folks' offices when we were kids.

Making a Shadow task happen can be as easy as asking a family member, friend, or neighbor. It can also mean contacting a complete stranger. Either way, it's worth the effort to try at least once. And this goes for any aged child. Whether four, seven, or eleven (or even your age!), getting the inside scoop on how to do any job is pretty cool. (Note that the only reason why Shadow tasks are marked Level 3 is because they involve quite a bit of coordination on your part.)

For those Experts who may elicit the question "Where am I *ever* going to find one of those?!", there are some helpful hints next to the task description. The phone book and Internet search engines are also great resources.

This is your kid's opportunity to dress, act, and think professionally. And this means showing appreciation professionally, too. Every Shadow task is completed only when your child mails or emails a thank-you note to his Expert. This offers your kid a chance to reflect on what he enjoyed, something new he learned, and how he appreciates the time the Expert took with him. A sample hand-written-style thank-you note can be found on page 346.

(Want more tips on how to complete Shadow tasks? See page 39.)

WHY DOESN'T EVERY CAREER HAVE A SHADOW TASK?

Unfortunately, not every career lends itself to this kind of kid-friendly experience. Curators, for example, are responsible for irreplaceable artifacts and may not be able to give kids that kind of backstage tour. Judges' days are typically so scheduled, they don't often open to this kind of free time. That said, you may happen to have a connection with an Expert in your kid's chosen profession who'd be happy to be shadowed!

CHAPTER 3

FAQs

D o I think I've explained everything there is to know about using Earn My Keep? You'd better believe it. Do I think you'll have questions before you even get started? You'd better believe it. Do I think little surprises will crop up when you actually put the program in motion? You…get the point.

The Philosophy

Q: *Isn't it odd to pay my child for spending time with me?*

Sure does feel that way at first, doesn't it? I went through the same thing. It's quite a shift to earn allowance for having fun and family bonding. But whenever someone questions, "*This* is what you're paying your child to do?!", I always come back to the same place: "Well, why not?"

Just because Mia's having fun doesn't mean she's not learning or exerting effort. Just because we're spending time together doesn't mean the money she earns is worth any less at the store. And she's very aware her Earn My Keep jobs are not the same as plain ol' arts-n-crafts projects we do just for fun. Earn My Keep tasks require real focus, commitment, and follow-through. Arts-n-crafts projects can be abandoned as soon as a neighbor stops by.

So if you, too, feel odd paying your child to Earn My Keep, remind yourself what you're really investing in: time spent engaging your child in a world she finds fascinating, with the added bonus of an education in fiscal understanding. Different, yes. But odd? Maybe not so much anymore!

Q: *How can I be certain my child is putting forth his "best effort"?*

You know when that tiny brow gets all scrunched up, and the tongue comes out the side of the mouth, and it looks as if your little one is almost in pain from thinking so hard? *That's* a child who's putting forth his best effort.

Not that Mia's brow furrows during every task she undertakes. Sometimes I notice the effort when I least expect it. For example, she happens to love playing dress-up (shocker for a little girl, I know). So being a Costume Designer came naturally. The big test showed up near the end. "Awww, Mom. Do I *have* to clean up??" Real Costume Designers leave dressing rooms neat and organized. Therefore, yes, Mia, you do too. It was that last bit that really made the task worthwhile for her.

So for the younger child, "effort" isn't necessarily the end result, but the process of following the task through to completion. For the older child, however, you actually do have a measuring stick: his schoolwork. Around fourth grade, you'll notice your child's teacher requiring more attention to be paid to the final result. Effort is always important, but marks are also based on proper spelling, correct answers, and presentation. Knowing this, check out the level to which your child is able to meet his teacher's criteria, and consider matching your expectations to that.

Q. *My kid is not making the bed or setting the table "just because." Now what?*

I don't like doing laundry. I don't even think if I got paid for it, I'd like doing it. So I don't expect Mia to tackle her household chore list with the same gusto every day/week/month, either. If your child is dragging her feet when it comes to these types of tasks (and you agree shoving her in a cardboard box stamped "all-expenses paid, one-way to Malaysia" is not an option), try these more practical (and lovingly constructive) approaches.

First, stay calm (OK, try to stay calm). Then borrow from financial and child developmental experts: Explain how being a part of a family is being a part of a team. That teamwork is a critical component to a happier family. And that helping to keep your home clean and organized, as opposed to dumping all the work on one or two people, is a way to show you respect and care about each other's feelings. (There are more ideas to be found in books and online, but these are good starting points.)

If all that doesn't work (and it very well might not), give Plan B, version 1, 2, or 3 a go:

○ Version 1: Consider starting small—for a few weeks, make setting the table the one household chore for which she's responsible, while also doing Earn My Keep. When she's got that chore down pat, add another.

○ Version 2: Lessen resistance by rotating chores every week, allowing "trades" (I'll make your bed tomorrow if you make mine today), and/or working together to get the job done.

○ Version 3: Remind your child that privileges come with responsibilities. And that failing to complete household responsibilities results in the loss of privileges, like watching TV, going to a sleepover, or talking on the phone. You're not engaging in a power struggle—you're simply stating the facts!

Q: *What if I still want to pay my child for household chores?*

Then you should continue to do so! You know what makes your family tick. But you can absolutely still benefit from Earn My Keep. Consider paying your kid for completing career tasks the way you would if he did an "over-and-above" kind of chore. Or don't even include money at all. So the fiscal understanding part won't come from Earn My Keep, but the wow-I-think-you're-super-cool-for-spending-this-time-with-me and the learning-about-all-these-amazing-adult-careers-is-the-best-thing-EVER parts totally will.

The Learning

Q: *Is it OK if my child does not understand (or care) about the money part?*

Absolutely. It makes sense to start an allowance program as soon as a kid begins to grasp the concept of money. But even in those first few years, fiscal understanding can remain a bit hazy. Don't let this deter either one of you. We don't wait to talk about the "potty" until our kids are ready to use it. We talk about it every time we change a diaper. Then one day BAM! Your three-year-old plants her tush on that big porcelain bowl and the whole family does a happy dance. Applying the same principle to fiscal understanding paves the way for a similar happy-dance experience!

Q: *What if my kid doesn't understand some of the words in the profile?*

Not only is that expected, that's great. Much of the industry language has been kid-ified and/or defined throughout the profiles—but not all of it. Kids love using adult-sounding words in conversation. It helps younger children learn the importance of context. And it creates even more dialogue between the two of you, which is never a bad thing. Remember, too, as kids get older, they'll grasp more and more of the language, which further promotes those fabulous feelings of self-confidence and accomplishment.

Q: *What if I don't want to follow what the tasks say?*

Fabulous! Add to the tasks. Subtract from them. Blend six of 'em together. The tasks are yours to do with what you will. So say your budding Archaeologist likes this one: "Find an object in your home that hasn't been seen or touched in many years (try looking in the basement, attic, or a hard-to-reach cabinet no one ever opens)." But your kid wants to do this at night, with all the lights off, holding a flashlight, wearing a hand-made adventure hat, and carrying a flyswatter. I say: go for it. You may find this kind of modification easier as you get into the program, but at any point, feel free to mix things up to your family's liking.

Q: How do I help my child when she tries and tries, but just doesn't grasp the task we picked (or can't find the answer, or...)?

What you decide to do all depends on why your child can't finish her task. If your kid truly doesn't understand the assignment, or is getting confused to the point of frustration (or tears!), consider modifying your final expectations or picking a totally different task. Explain to her that not understanding is by no means the same as failing—that even in the real world, adults sometimes need help when tackling new things (you can even throw in an example of when this recently happened to you!).

Now, if your kid understands the task, but every attempt at completion has fallen flat, you may still choose to pay her the full amount of her allowance. Or instead, you could emulate a real-world situation and deduct some (if adults only turn in half a report, pay may be docked, or evaluations may be less-than-stellar, resulting in a lower bonus or pay raise). What matters most is that payment reflects her effort, no matter the final result.

Q: How do I help my kid when he gets frustrated?

There's a difference between getting frustrated and giving up. If your child wants to give up, skip to the next FAQ. If your kid is frustrated, read on.

First, see if your child can work himself out of this situation on his own. Acknowledge that he's hit a challenge. Encourage him try to look at the task a different way. Or get him to suggest different people who may be able to help (watch his little mind come up with "local Librarian," "Cousin Josh," and "Aunt Debi"), and then ask them.

You can also let your kid take a break. Teach him that it's OK to stop mid-project sometimes. That adults often walk away from challenging assignments— just for a bit—to clear their minds and gain new perspectives. Of course, if your child waits too long, and doesn't complete his task by Payday, he won't earn his allowance. So make sure he understands that, too!

Q: *What do I do when my child wants to quit, period?*

The most important thing is that, at the very least, your kid finishes the career she's started. Do what you can to get her to that point, without doing the task for her. Ask what it is about the career she doesn't like. Discuss fun ways to modify her task. Engage her in creating the final result. And remind her that the only way she'll earn that pocket change is to be the best Earn My Keeper you know she can be.

Afterward, take some time to reevaluate how important your child's understanding of fiscal matters is to you, at this moment in time. Could you come back to Earn My Keep in a few months? Or perhaps there's another method that works better for your family, and that's great, too.

The Facts of Life

Q: *We love the idea of Earn My Keep, but how can we fit it into our busy schedule?*

So on top of school and practice and play dates and homework and dinner and bath and bed, I'm suggesting you add on something else?! Without question, many kids' lives today are so jam-packed, it seems nearly impossible (if not even unwise!) to throw on any more commitments. Fortunately, this book is packed with tons of Level 1 tasks—definitely start with those until you feel your child can handle a bit more.

Even more fortunately, the range of tasks in Earn My Keep was designed with this challenge in mind. If your child is bogged down with homework, try skipping over tasks with cues such as "report," "define," or "list." Instead, try out something that's more hands-on and/or active (like constructing something or interviewing someone). This fosters a different kind of learning, and relieves that "Earn My Keep-as-homework" feeling. Along these lines, create more interest in the schoolwork or extracurricular activities your kid does have by selecting careers and tasks that complement what he's already doing—building upon the world as he knows it ups the program's benefits and makes the time you do choose to put toward it even more worthwhile.

Q: *What if my family is unable to do Earn My Keep every week?*

We now know experts say the only way for allowance to truly teach fiscal understanding is to do it consistently—a premise that certainly supports the authentic nature of Earn My Keep. (If we decide to just not work the third week of every month, I sincerely doubt we'd keep our jobs, much less get a paycheck!) That said, this doesn't mean you need to do a new career every week. You could stretch the deadline for one task across two weeks. Or pick more extensive tasks, or even more than one task, and give your child three or four weeks to complete it (or them). You'd then simply identify your family's Payday, and how much your earner earns, based on this schedule. And remember: the program has a year's worth of careers with two weeks' paid vacation built in—if you and your kid ever need a break, feel free to take a week off!

Another tip? Consider doing Earn My Keep at the same day and time every week—sort of like scheduling "me" time. Only it's "me and you" time.

Q: *My child and I agreed to tasks we can't complete by the deadline. Now what?*

Who hasn't needed an extended deadline at work? All sorts of unforeseen challenges can pop up in the most unwelcome way: ear infections, pop quizzes, taking on a project too big for the time allotted—the key is to handle this professionally. Help your child identify why you can't complete the work on time and agree to an alternate deadline. Or keep the same deadline but lessen your expectations for the final product. The real world recognizes we're all human. But a real boss would still expect work to get done.

The Good Problem

Q: *My kid always wants to do the same career. How do I get him to try something different?*

The beauty of the program is, by the sheer number of tasks and flexibility of language, you can theoretically do the same profession over and over and never have the same experience. However, this does defeat the purpose of exposing our kids to lots of different paths and experiences. So I offer two suggestions: one, point out the Career Crossing sidebar—perhaps your child will be intrigued by a career that is closely tied to his one true love. If it's in the book, you can turn to page such-and-such. If it's not in the book, use Create-Your-Own! (on page 339) for guidance on how to emulate the career experience. Or two, do the beloved profile, then a new one, then the beloved one, then a new one, then the beloved one—where every other week Junior is trying something new.

Q: *What if my child wants to do more than one career a week?*

No sooner has your kid finished being a Translator or Contractor or Diplomat, is she asking to Earn My Keep again. Truly, that's fantastic. But we adults know it takes time to earn money, and isn't patience a virtue? At most, I'd recommend one career per week. This not only saves your disposable income, but buys you the time you need to fold laundry, make school lunches, organize science projects, please your boss, make it to practice, get dinner on the table, and collapse!

Q: *My four-to-twelve-year-old loves Earn My Keep. What do I offer her jealous older sibling?*

What a wonderful switch (aren't the younger ones typically jealous of the older ones?!). That said, Earn My Keep was not intended to start World War III. The reason why the program is recommended up to age twelve is that teen thing: at some point, kids are going to want to babysit and mow lawns and take on money-making jobs outside of the home. However, if you've got an older child who wants to try Earn My Keep, and you're ready and willing to dish out those teen-level allowances, here are a few ways to go about it:

o Expect more. Many of the program's tasks can be done by older kids, with more extensive expectations for the final result. Use her current schoolwork as a guide to upping current tasks to appropriately challenging levels. You can even ask one of your kid's teachers for guidance. Bet he'd be glad to help.

o Allow lengthier time spans for more in-depth exploration. Start with a shadow task, then tackle three or four in the same career, with a final report and/ or presentation after a full month. Payment would then be larger, but your child would be expected to make her money last longer, thus upping the fiscal understanding portion of the program.

o Write a letter to: Shana Drehs, Senior Editor Extraordinaire, Sourcebooks, 1935 Brookdale Road, Suite 139, Naperville, IL, 60563. Title it: "I want *Earn It, Learn It for Teens.*" She'll get the idea.

The Shadow Tasks

Q: *My child wants to shadow an Expert, but I'm having trouble finding one who's available. Should I still pay my kid?*

Ultimately this is up to you. But my opinion is no, you shouldn't pay your child for trying to find an Expert. Without the actual shadowing interaction, he's not learning anything about the career. Fortunately, the profiles are stocked with Level 1 tasks (the quickest and easiest of all the tasks). So even at the last minute, it's easy to pick a substitute activity that can be done lickety-split. I can't say your child won't be disappointed, but this may fuel enthusiasm to find a different Expert for a different career next time.

Q: I found a willing and excited Expert for my child to shadow, but he's not available when we want to do his career (read: this week!). What do I do?

Wait for him. The chance to spend time with an actual Expert is truly a gift for your kid, and the fact that you have a willing participant who can volunteer his time is fantastic. Depending on when the Expert is available, you can choose to do the same career twice in a short time span or pick different careers until the week of your scheduled shadowing. If you choose to do different careers, consider doing ones that complement your Expert's profession. Check out the Career Crossing list on his page (or even ask him!) for professionals with whom he works. If the career's in the book, it'll have an asterisk. If not, you can use Create-Your-Own! (page 339) as a guide. Either way, your child will get a sense of the Expert's place in "the bigger picture," and will more likely have some great questions for him when you finally are together.

Did you know chocolate chip sea stars aren't edible? That genes tell stories? Or that a plumb bob is not a piece of fruit or a person? I sure didn't until Mia and I started this program. It is my sincere wish that you and yours use Earn My Keep far beyond the pages of this book. And that when your child asks if there's really such thing as a money tree, you smile and enthusiastically answer "Yes— and now you've got the power to grow one yourself!"

Q: We had an appointment scheduled to shadow an Expert, but it got canceled (for any number of fabulous reasons). Do I still pay my child?

Here, too, I'd say no, you shouldn't pay. Earn My Keep earnings are based on doing something to earn them. That said, you're definitely left in a pickle that needs to be solved. Some ideas:

o Reschedule the appointment for another week and select a substitute task from the same career. (No reason she can't do the same career twice.)

o Reschedule the appointment for another week and select a substitute task from a different career.

o Ask your Expert if he has a colleague who could take his place on short notice.

o Find another Expert on your own. Though, personally, I'd be wiped from the first effort and would probably just do a substitute task that week!

Expect your child to be disappointed when an appointment falls through—this is a very exciting Earn My Keep task. In fact, whenever you set up a Shadow task, consider letting your child know cancellation or postponement may happen. And even more important: include your kid when deciding your "next step." This is not only a great way to diffuse the letdown, but to teach "Plan Bs"—an invaluable skill in the game of life. Learning to look at disappointment as a surmountable challenge will only better prepare her for those real-life challenges we face everyday!

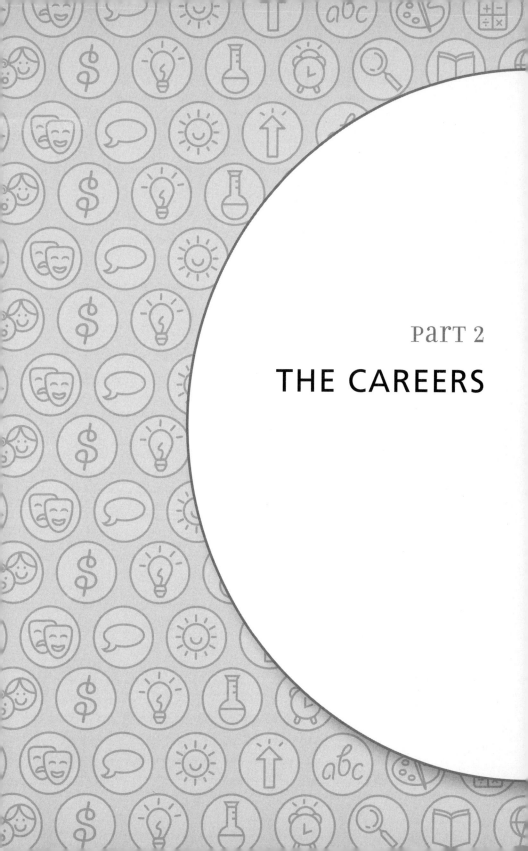

part 2

THE CAREERS

Accountant

S hopping for your best friend's birthday present is no easy task—what you *want* to get (tickets for two to Disney) and what you can *afford* to get (a t-shirt that says "Disney") are two different things. Fortunately, the Accountant in you knows sticking to a budget is how dreams really do come true.

Jump In

○ ① 🎭 🌐 🔍 Visit the library or Internet to report about "trade and barter" (when did it originate? what's great about it? not so great?). Then try it out with Mom or Dad.

○ ② 🎨 🎭 🌐 🖩 🔍 Make your own abacus using hints and guides from a library book or online site. This fun counting tool was created way before the invention of the calculator (and what Accountant doesn't use a calculator?).

⬆① 🎭 🌐 🔍 Report about the history of the abacus.

⬆① 🖩 💲 Use your abacus to add up the cost of your favorite field trip (the zoo? a ballet? a ball game?). First list what you pay for, and its cost: one admission ($10?), one bucket of peanuts ($7?), one juice box ($3?), one souvenir hat ($14?). Then use the abacus to determine your field trip's price tag.

○ ③ 🔤 ☀ 💬 Shadow an Accountant—she can show you some of the forms she uses to do your parents' taxes! Mail or email a thank-you note afterward.

ACCOUNTANTS:

- Prepare income tax returns for individuals and businesses
- Perform audits, which means reviewing companies' financial reports
- Handle bookkeeping for small businesses, including payroll (paying employees)
- Assist clients in budgeting for major expenses, like retirement or college tuition

SAYS JO RICE, CPA, CFP, PFS, RICE, VOWEL &
WYATT CPA, PLLC IN TULSA, OKLAHOMA

I love _developing plans that help people save money._

My biggest-on-the-job challenge is _the long hours (though I thrive on the pressure!)._

Audits make me _keep my clients honest._

My favorite tax refund is _the earned income credit, which helps lower-income families._

Managing my client's investments involves _being a good listener._

If I weren't an Accountant, I'd be _a Psychiatrist._

Prepare Taxes

○ ①($)(🔍) Check out a sales receipt to find your state's sales task.

(👕)①(🐾)(🏛)($) Ask someone from an older generation if he has a receipt for an item more than ten years old (like a car, major household appliance, or a piece of jewelry or art). Find the sales tax. Use the library or an online search to determine if the tax amount in the state the item was purchased in has changed over the years. If so, calculate what the item would cost today.

○ ①($)(🔍)(😊) Report about one, two, or three tax refunds available for people who do something great

Accountant Jo is a Certified Financial Planner (CFP) and Personal Financial Specialist (PFS) who specializes in taxes, small business accounting, and providing clients with financial planning advice. She began her accounting career at Arthur Andersen, one of the country's Big 8 public accounting firms, and has enjoyed owning her own company since 1977.

(say, adopting a child, donating to charity, or taking a working vacation)—the library and the Internet are great resources.

⬆①💡 Keep a list of two, three, or four "tax refunds" owed to your family for going above-and-beyond usual family responsibilities (Big Sis organized the linen closet without being asked? Mom woke up forty-five minutes early to surprise you with your favorite breakfast?). At the end of your list-making, dole out your "refunds" (big hugs? a back rub? first dibs on dessert?).

○ ①$🔍 Use the library or the Internet to list what taxes are for, who sets them, and what happens if they aren't paid.

⬆②$🧮 Set up a store that "sells" your favorite things (t-shirts? snow globes? nightlights?). Put a little sticker (or sticky note) on each item with its cost (10¢, 50¢, or $1). When customers (Mom? Dad? Grandma?) "buy" the item, use pen and paper (or a calculator) to calculate the sales tax (try using 5%) and add it to the selling price. (When all the items have been purchased, be sure to give all the money back!)

⬆①🧮$ Change the sales price to make your calculations a bit more complex. Say, 14¢, 66¢, and $1.27.

○ ①$🔍 Use the library or an online search to define two, three, or four of the items needed to complete a tax return: payroll stub, home mortgage interest statement, real estate tax statement, donation invoice.

⬆②🧮$ Prepare a tax return for your Earn My Keep earnings. (This will work so long as you've done at least one career already.) Photocopy the Income Tax Return work sheet on page 348, or download a copy at

EarnMyKeep.com, to help you calculate how much you'd owe the government in taxes (and then give Mom and Dad a big hug for not taking taxes out of your allowance!).

Monitor Spending

○ ② ▦ $ Develop a budget for a spectacular event (a birthday party? game night? third Tuesday of the month?). For a guide, photocopy the Budget Plan work sheet on page 349, or download a copy at EarnMyKeep.com.

> ⬆ ① 💡 ▦ $ Hold the event, then review your budgeting. Was the budget realistic? Do you see where you could've budgeted better? If there's a *surplus**, how will you spend it?

○ ② ▦ $ Create your own *stock*** — and then follow it for at least a week. First pick a sports team (your product) that plays more than two games in one week (try baseball, basketball, or hockey). Name your product with three initials (the Blue Sox could be: BSX). Their initial price is $10 a *share****—buy as many as you'd like (you can use photocopies of EMK Cash, found on page 344 and at EarnMyKeep.com). Then keep track of the team's record. Every win means the stock goes up $1; every loss means it goes down $1. At week's end, do you end up with a gain or a loss?

✳ **A surplus** is an amount that's more than what's needed.

✳✳ **Stocks** represent ownership in a company—the person who owns the highest percentage of a company's stock controls the company.

✳✳✳ **Shares** refer to how much of the stock one person owns—some companies are broken into millions of shares!

DID YOU KNOW?

Accountants are often asked to help Lawyers and Judges solve legal disputes—any case involving money!

Follow a real stock for three, four, or five days (now that you've got the hang of investing!). You'll find a daily list in your local paper with stock names and their low, high, and day's final price (or you can look online). Keep a record of how the stock performs, just like how some real Accountants help their clients manage their investments.

CAREER CROSSING

ACCOUNTANTS WORK WITH:

Attorneys

Bankers*

Benefit Plan Administrators

Insurance Agents

Investment Advisors

Acquisitions Editor

You laughed so hard, milk almost came out of your nose! It was the best story your best friend ever told, and you had to know if it was OK to share it with Mom and Dad. "Of course!" was the answer. And when Mom and Dad busted out laughing too, you proved you knew a good story when you heard one. Just like a real Acquisitions Editor!

ACQUISITIONS EDITORS:

- Develop ideas for books
- Acquire books from Authors and Literary Agents
- Guide a book through the entire publishing process
- Edit manuscripts
- Help manage cover and interior book design

Jump In

○ ① Use a library or online search to define "fiction" and "nonfiction." Then find an example of each at the library or at home. And then give a suggestion of how the fiction book could become nonfiction and vice versa.

○ ① Compare two, three, or four books, all about your favorite outdoor activity (look in your home library, the public library, or your local bookstore). List one, two, or three ways they're similar (besides the subject, of course). Then list one, two, or three ways each is unique.

① Dream up a new book on the same subject that's different from the ones you found. Maybe you'd prefer more pictures? Special tips? Expert interviews? Give your version a title, too.

② Make your book using arts-n-crafts materials you have at home.

SAYS SHANA DREHS, SENIOR EDITOR, SOURCEBOOKS IN NAPERVILLE, ILLINOIS

I love _the thrill of reading a manuscript for the first time._

My biggest on-the-job challenge is _accepting that one of my books may not sell as well as I'd like._

The first time I saw one of my books in a bookstore I _turned every copy face out so more people would see them._

Editing books is fun because _I learn new information (nonfiction) or lose myself in a new story (fiction)._

You can judge a book by its cover because _we put an enormous amount of energy into its design._

If I weren't an Acquisitions Editor, I'd be _another kind of Editor who misses editing books!_

○ ① 🌐 🔍 Use a library or Internet search to report about the publishing company of your favorite book (its name will be printed on the _copyright page_* and/or the back cover). Include details such as when the company was founded, where it is located, and one, two, or three of its best-selling titles.

*The **copyright page** is typically found in a book's beginning pages.

○ ② 📖 🔍 Listen to an audio version of one of your favorite books. (They have these at the library, and/ or downloadable online.) Report about the experience, in comparison to reading the book. Was it what you expected it to be?

Acquisitions Editor Shana graduated with a bachelor of arts degree in journalism and English from the University of Iowa. She worked at Random House for five years before moving to Sourcebooks. One of her most exciting moments in publishing was the first time a book she edited became a _New York Times_ bestseller!

○ ② 💡 📖 🔍 Study one, two, or three display tables in the children's section of your favorite bookstore. Report about what makes the books on the table the same (theme? Author?), why they may entice a customer to buy them, and one, two, or three ways you'd display the books differently.

○ ③ 🔤 ☼ 💬 Shadow an Acquisitions Editor. (Try using the phone book or Internet to find a publishing company or university press in your area.) She may even show you a manuscript she's editing! Mail or email a thank-you note immediately after your time together.

○ ③ 📖 💬 🔍 Attend a book signing. Ask your local library or bookstore about upcoming events. Afterward, report about the experience.

> **WHY DOES ACQUISITIONS EDITOR SHANA THINK HER CAREER IS AWESOME?**
>
> "I've loved to read since I was a little girl. And now I get to help make books that get other people excited about reading. It's the best career in the world!"

Acquire Book Projects

○ ① 💡 ☼ Ask two "Authors" (Mom and Grandma? Big Bro and your best friend?) to each tell you an idea for a children's book that involves frozen yogurt, space aliens, and shoelaces. Listen carefully. Then politely choose one book to "*acquire**,*" explaining one, two, or three reasons why you made that choice.

When you "acquire" an Author's book idea you have bought the rights to publish it.

An advance is money paid to Authors for the right to publish their manuscripts.

🔼 ① 💡 ☼ Negotiate a silly *advance*** for the right to publish the acquired book. (Publishing without an Author's approval is usually against the law!) You may want to offer one hug, but the Author wants three—how will you come to agreement so you're both happy?

○ ① 💡 🔤 Convince your Publisher (Mom or Dad) that she should print your favorite book (pretend the book hasn't yet been published). Include one, two, or three reasons why the book is unique (like no one's ever written a story about a coconut tree, or the Author grew up on an island) and one, two, or three reasons why readers will buy it. Acquisition Editors must prove to their Publishers that the books they want to acquire are worth the money, time, and effort to publish them.

○ ① 💡 🎨 ☀ 📊 💲 🔍 Prepare a cost estimate to produce a book about the most exciting thing that ever happened to someone from an older generation. First, get the story from him (remember to be polite). Together, decide how you'd make your book (construction paper? a string binding? stickers?). Then calculate the cost of all your materials.

DID YOU KNOW?

Some Acquisitions Editors acquire as many as forty books a year on all sorts of subjects, including cookbooks, "how to" books, and, of course, kids' books!

⬆ ② 🎨 💡 🎨 Make the book together. Use crafty materials or a computer program to create *The Most Exciting Thing That Ever, Ever, Ever Happened to [PERSON'S NAME HERE], Ever* book.

Edit Content

○ ① 💡 🔤 📖 List two, three, or four new titles for your favorite book, each for a different audience. So, say your book is geared toward boys. Create a new title for girls, for moms, and for teachers—ones that would attract each audience to buy the book.

⬆ ② 🎨 💡 Design a cover to go with one of your new titles using markers, crayons, and paper or a computer program.

○ ② 💡 🔤 📖 Imagine your favorite TV show or movie is being turned into a book. Write what readers will find on the back cover—those two or three sentences that sum up the story. Remember: what made the show or movie great may not be what makes the book great. Give that consideration when writing what goes on your back cover.

*A **manuscript** is an Author's typed story before it's printed into a book.*

○ ② ⑬ ⓐⓑⓒ Write a *manuscript** about the most amazing time you ever spent outdoors (family camping? first baseball game? learning to ride a bike?).

⇧ ② ✎ ⑬ ☺ Turn your manuscript into a real book, using environmentally friendly materials you find around your home. The cover could be a decorated brown grocery bag. The paper could be wrapping paper Mom never uses. Your ink could be those old bits of crayons you were going to throw out!

○ ③ ⑬ ⓐⓑⓒ ▦ Count the words on one page (or in one chapter) of your favorite book (yes, you can estimate). Then handwrite a version with half its original word count (yes, you can estimate again). You'll have to decide which text to keep and which to edit out. In your opinion, does it make the page or chapter better? Acquisition Editors ask Authors to stick to a set word count, so they know how much paper they'll need to print the book.

CAREER CROSSING

ACQUISITIONS EDITORS WORK WITH:

Authors

Cover Designers

Librarians*

Literary Agents

Publicists*

Archaeologist

There it was in the attic: a black box with a round tray attached on top. A long arm-like thing rested on the tray's edge. And next to the box were all these shiny, black, round disks in cardboard sleeves with names written on them: U2? Bon Jovi? Madonna?! Ah-hah, you Archaeologist, you, *that's* how people listened to music before CDs and iPods!

Jump In

- ① 🎭 🌐 🔍 🕐 Use a library book or online search to list one, two, or three ways our current culture has changed, based on choices people made during the Industrial Revolution. (Hint: Reuse, Repurpose, Recycle.) Archaeologists know we're more likely to make better decisions in the present when we learn about the past.

ARCHAEOLOGISTS:

- Use the scientific process to study culture
- Learn about people by looking at places they've lived and objects they've used
- Study trash (it's true!)

- ③ 🔤 ☀ 💬 Shadow an Archaeologist—they work at universities, anthropology museums, state and federal governmental offices, and in National Parks and Forests. You might even be able to help in the laboratory! After your time together, mail or email a thank-you note.

- ③ 🎭 🌐 🔍 Visit an archaeological site or exhibit at a National Park. (Try finding a park at www.nps.gov.) Before going, research the type of history you may learn about when you visit.

SAYS CAROL J. ELLICK, M.A., RPA,
OWNER, ARCHAEOLOGICAL AND CULTURAL EDUCATION
CONSULTANTS IN NORMAN, OKLAHOMA

I love *being the first to touch an object that hasn't been touched in hundreds of years.*

My biggest on-the-job challenge is *working outside when it's cold and wet.*

The longest I've ever worked on-site was *six months. Work stopped only because the area flooded!*

I once uncovered a site *that was seven thousand years old.*

What's gross? *Blowing my nose after working all day—dirt boogers!*

If I weren't an Archaeologist, I'd be *a Teacher.*

Excavate & Analyze Artifacts

○ ① 💡🔍⚗️ Find an object in your home that hasn't been seen or touched in many years (try looking in the basement, attic, or a hard-to-reach cabinet no one ever opens). Ask Mom or Dad how and when it was used. Report if you think others would've used it in the same way, and if the object could be used today and/or if it was replaced by a newer version.

This could be Mom's fondue pot, Dad's high school football jersey, even Big Sis's first shoes.

○ ① 🎨💡 Use markers, crayons, and pens to make a paper plate look like a piece of pottery. Cut the plate into five, nine, or twelve pieces, then try to put it back together (the more pieces you make, the harder this is!).

Imagine putting together a jigsaw puzzle without having the picture on the box. That's how Archaeologists put together the broken pottery they uncover!

⬆️ ① 💡 Remove one or two pieces before putting it back together.

(↑)(1)(⚗)(💡) Draw two pieces of "pottery," cut up the plates, mix up the pieces, and put them both back together.

o (2)(⚙)(🔍)(⚗) Visit the home of someone from an older generation. Look through each room, reporting about the shoes you see (you can pick them up, but put them back exactly how you found them). List the type of shoes, their purpose, and their storage location.

(↑)(1)(💡)(📖)(⚗) Make a guess about the owner's culture based on the shoes you found. Are there lots of athletic shoes that have worn soles, but still look clean? The owner may exercise indoors.

(↑)(1)(🔍)(⚗) Interview the shoes' owner. See if your guesses about the shoes' purposes and uses are right!

Study Culture

o (2)(💡)(🔍) Step outside your home—describe the building and its landscape (trees and grass? sidewalks and store fronts?). Do the same for one, two, or three more buildings next to your home. For each of the buildings, list a few things that are the same as your home, and a few things that are different.

Archaeologist Carol has been an Archaeologist for thirty years. She earned her bachelor's degree from The Evergreen State College and has worked on archaeological sites throughout the Western United States and in Japan. She loves fieldwork, but loves teaching kids about the archaeological process and other cultures even more. So she went back to school to earn her master's degree in education, enabling her to create archaeology and culture lesson plans for teachers and students.

WHY DOES ARCHAEOLOGIST CAROL THINK HER CAREER IS AWESOME?

"I get to do what I've always wanted to do: share new discoveries about past cultures with everyone!"

①①💡 List two, three, or four things the architecture and landscapes say about your community's culture. For example, if there are a lot of apartment buildings in your neighborhood, this may suggest you live in a busy area (apartment buildings are homes to many people).

○ ②💡 Draw a picture of your bedroom, as is, messy and all (you'll need to be in your room to draw an accurate picture). Then draw a second picture, showing where you think everything should be. Lastly, clean your room according to your picture. Archaeologists look at where items were left by past people (your first picture) to *infer**   how they used to live their lives (your second picture).

To infer means to make an informed decision based on what you see in front of you.

○ ②💡 Write a story about an ancient culture you create. What was the culture called? (You might call them the Mimi-Deedees.) Where did your culture's population live? What did they eat? What did they do for fun? Then list the rooms of their homes, plus one, two, or three objects found in each room. Also include what the object was used for—like how the Mimi-Deedees kept hair dryers in the kitchen to melt grilled cheese sandwiches!

DID YOU KNOW?

Archaeologists don't just study ancient pasts—they study yesterday, too. Those working on Le Projet du Garbage (the Garbage Project) study people's trash habits, to learn about who recycles!

①② Use an empty shoebox, popsicle sticks, toothpicks, yarn, doll furniture—whatever you can find around your home—to make a model of one the rooms described in your story.

Catalog Finds

○ ①⑨⊞⊙⊙ Ask Mom or Dad for two, three, or four artifacts of one of their favorite hobbies (so you could get a tennis racket, tennis ball, and visor). Use a ruler or tape measure to measure each artifact. If you have a scale, also weigh each artifact. Then identify what the artifacts, together, tell you about the hobby. (For example, holding a visor is just holding a visor. But when you hold it *with* a tennis ball and racket, you understand tennis is an outside sport—the visor blocks the sun!)

⬆①⊙⊞⊙ Create a chart with pen and paper, or on the computer, listing each artifact's measurements and weight.

⬆②⊙⊙⊙ Draw or photograph each artifact. Add your pictures to your chart with tape or glue. (If your database is on the computer and you drew your pictures, scan them in.)

CAREER CROSSING

ARCHAEOLOGISTS WORK WITH:

Artifact Analysts

Botanists

Geologists*

Graphic Designers

Illustrators

Maybe it was the evening you noticed the stars were particularly bright. Or that the moon was following your every move. Or that the days were getting shorter (and the nights longer!). That was the moment you became an Astronomer—a person who observes the planets, stars, and galaxies of our universe, without ever leaving Earth. Far out!

Jump In

○ ① 🎭 🌐 🎨 Interview someone from an older generation about where she was when man first walked on the moon. Did she see the broadcast live on television? Most TV sets were only black-and-white back then, and not every home had one!

○ ① 🔍 ⚗️ Use the library or the Internet to research our *solar system**. List how many *planets*** are in it, their names, and one, two, or three unique characteristics of each (like Earth is the only planet that supports life).

⬆️ ③ 🎨 ⚗️ Make a scale model of our solar system using store-bought or homemade play-dough. (Try the recipe on page 347.)

⬆️ ② 🎨 💡 Discover a planet! What will you name it? What is it like there? You can be scientific (atmosphere, temperature, etc.) or

ASTRONOMERS:

- Study objects in outer space
- Analyze data collected by telescopes
- Operate and maintain instruments
- Build new cameras

❋ **solar system** is a group of outer-space objects that orbit a star (in our case, the sun).

❋ **Planets** are round balls of rock or gas that orbit the sun. (Cool fact: astronomy had no definition for the term "planet" until 2005!)

says Marc Kassis, support Astronomer,
W.M. Keck Observatory in Kamuela, Hawaii

I love _proto-planetary disks around young stars._

My biggest on-the-job challenge is _instrument and telescope break-downs._

If I could name a star, it'd be _a red giant named Nancy Drew (at my daughter's insistence)._

The coolest thing I've ever seen in space is _the spectra of Orion Nebula objects—through an instrument I built!_

While my family is sleeping, I'm _reviewing data and fixing instrument problems._

If I weren't an Astronomer I'd be _sad because this is the best job in the universe!_

imaginary (aliens, space goo, etc.) or both. Then draw a picture of your planet or build one out of play-dough or clay.

o ③ 🔍 🧪 Visit a planetarium: a dome-shaped theater that shows incredible films about outer space. Report about two, three, or four new things you learned there.

o ③ 💬 🔍 🧪 Participate in a public viewing—that's when professional and amateur Astronomers bring their telescopes to dark sites and observe the night sky. Find area events by using Web searches or calling a local university's astronomy department or your local planetarium.

Operate & Maintain Instruments

o ① 🔍 🧪 Look in a library book or an online site to report about how Astronomers use an object's color to determine what it's made of, how fast it's moving, and its temperature.

(↑)(1)(⚗) Order a pair of diffraction-grating glasses (they're about $1 online). They separate light into its components, leaving a vision of beautiful stripes of color. You'll be amazed by what you see when you look through them at a lamp!

(↑)(1)(⚗) Hold a peacock feather in the sun—it's one of the few everyday objects that diffracts light, splitting it into its component colors for a beautiful, *iridescent** effect.

○ (1)(🔍)(⚗) Use a library or Internet search to define the purpose of a telescope. (Hint: It's not to magnify.)

(↑)(3)(🔧)(💡)(⚗) Build your own telescope using a kit. Many sell for under $15. If you can't find one in your local toy store, try searching online.

○ (1)(💡)(🔍)(⚗) Visit the library or the Web to report about spectroscopes. Can you figure out what spectroscopes have in common with rainbows?

(↑)(3)(🔧)(💡)(⚗) Build a spectroscope. An online search provides quite a few ways that use materials from around your home (such as a CD-ROM, a cardboard box, a cardboard tube, plastic film, and duct tape).

Astronomer Marc earned his bachelor of science degree in physics from Willamette University in Salem, Oregon. He became interested in astronomy while participating in a Research Experience for Undergraduates astronomy program in La Serena, Chile. He then earned a PhD in astronomy from Boston University where he built an instrument that is used at the NASA Infrared Telescope Facility on Mauna Kea!

*Iridescent objects' rainbow-like color changes, depending on how light hits it.

WHY DOES ASTRONOMER MARC THINK HIS CAREER IS AWESOME?

"I get to work with state-of-the-art technology while exploring the universe with Astronomers from all over the world!"

○ ② 💡 🔍 🕐 Report on how light pollution affects Astronomers (you'll find information in the library and online). List one, two, or three ways Astronomers can combat light pollution while working. Also list one, two, or three ways lowering light pollution is good for the environment.

Collect & Analyze Data

○ ① 🔍 ⚗ 🕐 Study the night sky, from the same location, for three, four, or five nights. Keep a log, noting what you see and what time you see it.

○ ① 🔍 ⚗ Grab a pair of binoculars (new? borrowed? secondhand?), wait until it gets dark, and look for Jupiter's *moons**: Callisto, Ganymede, Europa, and Io. A library or Internet search will explain where they typically appear.

○ ② 💡 🕐 Use markers and paper or a computer program to create an Activity Schedule for your day's projects. For instance, in the morning, you could build a telescope (either with materials you find around your home or a store-bought kit). Then you'd schedule

DID YOU KNOW?

Astronomers use telescopes during the day, too—it's how they capture information about solar flares and sunspots on the sun!

(But don't try this at home. Astronomers use very special telescopes specifically designed to protect their eyes from the sun's rays.)

Moons are natural satellites that orbit planets.

time after lunch to troubleshoot (is your telescope in proper working order? Anticipate problems and have the right tools on hand to fix them). Later, you'd watch the news or look online to determine the time of nightfall. Lastly, you could assign times for telescope availability—does Mom get to use it from 7:45 p.m. to 7:50 p.m.? Dad from 8:00 p.m. to 8:05 p.m.?

⬆ ① ☀ 💬 🕐 Put your Activity Schedule into action for one, two, or three days.

o ② 🔍 🧪 Stargaze. Pick a clear night and try to get as far from your home and streetlights as possible. Lay out a blanket (or just plop down in the grass) and see how many stars you can count.

🔼 ① 💡 🔍 🧪 Locate the Big and Little Dippers—it helps if you first read about their locations in a book or online.

🔼 ① 💡 🔍 🧪 Use a star map. Now that you know how to find the Big and Little Dippers, use the map to find one, two, or three constellations of your choice. Star maps are found in library books about stars.

🔼 ① 🔍 🧪 Use the library or an Internet search to report about one, two, or three constellations seen from the *Southern Hemisphere** (what you see in the sky sure is different down under!).

*The **Southern Hemisphere** is the part of Earth located below the Equator.

🔼 ① 🎭 🌍 🔍 Report about the way one, two, or three different cultures interpret the *constellations*****. Try: Greek, Inca, Indian, Chinese, or Western.

Constellations are star groupings perceived to resemble people, animals, or objects.

CAREER CROSSING

ASTRONOMERS WORK WITH:
Computer Software Programmers
Electrical Engineers
Machinists
Project Managers*
Purchasing Agents

Banker

I t's hot. It's sunny. And it's you and your best friend, waiting in line to buy two, icy-refreshing, fruit-flavored sno-cones. Suddenly, your buddy realizes he's short 25¢ and could he borrow a quarter from you? As any Banker would be, you're happy to lend one—with his promise to let you taste his flavor in return!

Jump In

○ (1) (🎭) (🌐) ($) (🔍) Use the library or an Internet search to report about one, two, or three of the following: one-, five-, ten-, twenty-, fifty- or one-hundred-dollar bill. Include who's on the front, what scene is on the back, and why.

(⬆) (2) (🎭) (🌐) (☀) ($) (💬) (🔍) Visit a bank and ask to see each of these in person. Also ask if you can see a two-dollar bill (yes, they exist) and a Susan B. Anthony dollar (it's a coin!).

○ (1) (🎭) (🌐) (🔍) Collect five, ten, or fifteen different state quarters from Mom, Dad, Grandma, under the couch, or wherever you can find them. Report about the symbol printed on each quarter and why it represents that state.

(⬆) (1) ($) (👁) Donate your quarters to your favorite charity when you're done with the task.

○ (2) (🐾) (👁) (🎭) ($) Create family currency for fun family-only things. Looking at real bills (and/or coins) for inspiration, use paper and markers, or a computer program, to create bills (and/or coins) with your family's

BANKERS:

- Lend money when people provide proof they can pay it back
- Grow money by paying people for every dollar they keep at the bank
- Protect money in ways much safer than under your mattress!

SAYS DAVE WINGERT, VICE PRESIDENT AND CASHIER, FARMERS SAVINGS BANK IN REMSEN, IOWA

I love _meeting with customers._

My biggest on-the-job challenge is _the stress of audits and examinations._

Brand-new dollar bills make me feel _uneasy, because they stick together!_

On my checks, there's _nothing fancy, but my wife, Pat, has pink roses on hers._

My favorite piece of American currency is _the $100 bill because it's the largest in circulation right now._

If I weren't a Banker, I'd be _a Teacher—they get three months off each year!_

name on them. You can even add pictures and sayings of your choice (such as *In [YOUR LAST NAME HERE] We Trust*).

⬆①💡$ Put your currency into circulation—post a chart listed with family activities and prices (waffles for dinner—$3? an extra bubbly bath—$7?). Pass out your money to family members. Let them buy what they want!

○ ②💡☀🧮$ Store currency in a vault—a safe, secure place for valuables (a shoebox hidden behind your favorite book on the bookshelf?). Write down how much money you have (this is called your "check register"). Invite each person in your family to make a withdrawal individually (they tell you how much they want, you go into your room to get it, and then write down the amount you've doled out). Ask Mom or Dad

This can be real money, board-game money, or even EMK Cash (on pages 344–345 and at EarnMyKeep.com).

to make a deposit, too (yes, write it down). At the end of the day, make sure the amount you have left in the vault is the amount stated on your check register.

○ ③ (abc) (☼) (☺) Shadow a Banker at work—maybe you'll get to see the inside of the vault! After your time together, mail or email a thank-you note.

Banker Dave graduated from the National Business Training School in Sioux City, Iowa, and became a Banker not far from the farm where he grew up. He married his childhood sweetheart, raised his family, and spent forty years with Farmers Savings Bank, where he now serves on the Board of Directors.

Oversee Transactions

○ ① (☼) (▦) (⑤) Start with the following (real or pretend): one $20 bill; two $10 bills; four $5 bills; ten $1 bills. Give change to a customer

You can do this with coins, too.

(Mom or Dad) in two, three, or four different ways. So, if Mom asks for $15, you could give her one $10 and one $5 or two $5s and five $1s.

○ ① (⑤) (🔍) Visit the library or the Web to report about the purpose of checking accounts and checkbooks. Then ask to see Mom's or Dad's checkbook (there's also a chance the account information is online).

(⬆) ② (✂) (💡) Decorate Mom or Dad's checkbook cover with stickers, markers, and/or glitter glue. (Alternate: Make your own checkbook and checkbook cover with paper, markers, and crayons.)

WHY DOES BANKER DAVE THINK HIS CAREER IS AWESOME?

"I get to help people work through their financial problems to really make a difference in their lives."

○ ② 💡 ⚙ ☼ 🖩 $ Create a checking account of kisses (or tickles? stickers?) for someone from an older generation. Tell him how many kisses he has in the "bank" and establish a (silly) penalty if he goes over (maybe "Bark like a dog"?). Spend fifteen, thirty, or forty-five minutes together, allowing him to use his kisses. If he *overdraws**, enforce the penalty!

*Someone who **overdraws** tries to take out more kisses (or, in the real world, money) than he owns.*

○ ② 🎭 ☼ 🖩 $ 💬 🔍 Use a library book or Internet search to report about savings accounts—then open one. This can be an account at your local bank, or money you start saving in your old piggy bank.

⬆ ① 🖩 $ Calculate how much *interest*** your first deposit will have earned by your next birthday. Your birthday in five years. In ten years. (Assume that you save $5 a month and you earn 1% a month in interest.)

***Interest** is the price to borrow money. In this case, the bank pays you to borrow the money you've deposited. Other times, it's you borrowing money from the bank.*

Make Loans

○ ① 💡 ☼ $ Decide whether or not to loan money to Mom or Dad. Set an appointment to discuss how much he needs, what the money will be used for, and when he intends to pay you back. Be a good listener and very polite, even if you turn his application down (in which case you'd offer good reason why you said no!).

DID YOU KNOW?

Every transaction, no matter how small, really adds up. Some Bankers will handle more than $30,000 in one day!

⬆ ② 💡 🖩 $ 🔍 Calculate how much interest he would owe you based on the amount and length of the loan. Look in your local paper or call your local bank to find out the day's real-life interest rate.

Keep Valuables Safe

○ ② 🐮 💡 😊 🔍 Visit the library or the Internet to report about the purpose of safe deposit boxes, including how Bankers ensure that the boxes are opened only by their owners. Then make your own using an old shoebox, construction paper, felt, glitter glue, paint, stickers—whatever you want. Fill it with your most cherished treasures and find a safe place to hide it.

👆 ② 🐮 💡 ☀ Create safe deposit boxes for each member of your household, giving each person one

These can be less detailed than the one you made for yourself.

of two "keys" (Mom gets your left "favorite sock," you keep the right? Little Bro gets your newest toy truck, you keep the oldest?).

👆 ② 💡 ☀ Put your safe deposit box system into action for two, three, or four days. First give everyone access to the boxes in order to put something valuable or special inside. Then store the boxes safely in your room. Only allow access if a box's owner shows you her "key" and you show her yours!

CAREER CROSSING

BANKERS WORK WITH:

Auditors

Bookkeepers

Receptionists

Software Vendors

Tellers

Every Mother's Day you treat Mom to something special (a card, homemade pancakes, even a gift you picked out yourself!). It's all about what Mom likes best. Buyers do the same for stores: thinking about what their customers would best like to buy, and filling their stores with these items. This makes their customers feel very special, indeed.

Jump In

- ① 💡 🌍 Make an inventory list of what you'd buy for a store filled only with things for someone from an older generation. Would it be her favorite movies on DVD? Her favorite type of clothing? Ingredients for her favorite recipe? Then share your list with her—bet your store would be her favorite place to shop!

- ③ ⓐⓑⓒ ☀ 💬 Shadow the owner of a local *Mom-and-Pop** store to get a firsthand look at how buying works. Afterward, mail or email a thank-you note.

Buyers:

- Buy products for stores to sell
- Meet with manufacturers and designers to negotiate prices (the less the Buyer pays for an item, the less the item may cost customers)
- Influence trends by deciding what people will want to buy at their stores

✳ A **Mom-and-Pop** store is a small business.

Analyze Markets

- ① 💡 Ask Mom or Dad to grab you the most uninteresting, unexciting item she can think of (a spoon? a garbage bag? the bath mat?). Then think quickly: your store just bought one million of 'em—list one, two, or three reasons why customers should still scramble to buy your item. (For example: it's winter and who couldn't use a new spoon for soup?!)

says ELIZABETH Mattes, Buyer, TJX Corporation, Maramaxx Division in Framingham, Massachusetts

I love _that I get to work with one of my favorite things: fashion!_

My biggest on-the-job challenge is _team members who don't have a "Can do!" attitude._

The first time I saw one of my buys in a store I _bought it._

I negotiate best when _I love the item I want to buy._

The farthest I've traveled for work is _Hong Kong._

If I weren't a Buyer I'd be a _Consumer Advocate._

○ ① 🔍 Find advertising in newspapers, on TV, or online for your most favorite book, game, or doll—from three different stores. Buyers are always aware of what the competition is doing.

⬆① 🖩 $ 🔍 Write down what each store is charging for the item. Now find one, two, or three coupons that may lower the *listed price** of the item—some of the advertising you found may even have coupons attached.

*The **listed price** is the advertised price.*

○ ① 💡 🔍 Pretend your home is your store—list one, two, or three each of the items your "customers" like most (fluffy pillows, toilet paper), use most (orange juice, toilet paper), and will need to be restocked soon (construction paper and, yes, toilet paper).

Buyer Elizabeth graduated with a business degree in marketing from the University of Massachusetts. From there she was recruited by Jordan Marsh for its Buyer training program, where she started as a Sales Manager, moved up to Assistant Buyer, and finally, Buyer—a career she's loved for two decades.

(⬆)(①)(💡)(▦)($)(🔍) Make recommendations of where Mom or Dad could buy the items that need restocking. Use the newspaper or Internet to compare prices and look for coupons.

○ (②)(💡)(🔍) Report about the window displays at your favorite store in your local mall. What items are featured? Is there a theme (such as seasonal, color, sale, or type of item)? Do similar stores have similar windows?

(⬆)(②)(🍪)(💡)(☀) Oversee the "building" of a window display for a store in your home. First, decide what you've "bought" to "sell" (stuffed animals? dress-up costumes? biking gear?). Work with a Window Designer (Mom? Dad?) to draw (or cut from magazines) pictures of your items, taping the pictures to one side of an available window. Jazz up your window with taped-up ribbon or little signs that say "On Sale."

○ (②)(💡)(🔍) Find a new product mentioned in a kids' news magazine or website (you probably have one in mind already). List one, two, or three product *trends** this hot item could kick-start. So let's say you found a new bake set that comes with animal-shaped cookie cutters. It could inspire the production of a kids' cookbook, stuffed animals, and coordinating kitchen aprons!

○ (②)(🔍) Walk around your favorite national store (like T.J.Maxx, Target, or Toys "R" Us), reporting about three, five, or seven customers you see. State their genders and two things in their carts, then make guesses on their ages,

> **WHY DOES BUYER LIZ THINK HER CAREER IS AWESOME?**
>
> "Every day is a different day. I get to decide what my department sells. I get to meet fascinating people and build relationships that have lasted twenty years. And I get to travel around the world looking for unique products that keep my customers coming back for more!"

✳ **A trend** is the "next big thing."

buying habits (impulse—just grabbed a pack of gum; planned—has a shopping list), and typical tastes (electronics—may listen to lots of music; sporting equipment—likes to stay healthy).

(⬆)(1)(💡) Review your customer list to better define your store's typical shopper. Were most people buying toilet paper and laundry detergent? Were they female? Mom-aged? That's who the Buyer is buying for!

Buy Products

○ (2)(🔍) Find one, two, or three *private-label** items at the grocery store. Private-label goods are manufactured exclusively for the *retailer***. Buyers ensure the final product meets the retailer's standards.

*Private-label merchandise used to be called "generic."

(⬆)(1)(🔍) Buy one *name-brand item**** and a private-label version of one of your favorite snacks—taste both to see if the private-label version measures up.

**A retailer is a business that sells goods to consumers.

○ (2)(💡)(☀)(▦)($) Ask Mom or Dad ("Toy & Game Manufacturer") to (1) open the toy closet, drawer, cabinet, box, plastic tub (or wherever it is you store your toys), and (2) write item prices on a big piece of paper (say, Big Toys, $10; Little Toys, $7; Video Games, $5; Puzzles, $3; Games, $3). You then use a set budget ($15? $20? $25?) to buy some of the Manufacturer's toys and games to sell at your toy store. (Keep your customers, like Little Sis, cousins, or friends in mind!)

***A name-brand item is sold under the manufacturer's name (like Dannon yogurt).

You can use real money (which you'd return to Mom or Dad afterward) or pretend money (like EMK Cash on pages 344–345 and at EarnMyKeep.com).

(⬆)(1)(🔍) Invite Little Sis, cousins, and/or friends to "buy" at your toy store. Which item is your best buy? Does an item not sell that you thought would?

- ② 💡 🔍 🗓 Use the library or the Internet to determine the environmental consciousness of one of America's largest manufacturers (try one that manufactures cars or toothpaste or bicycle helmets). List one, two, or three reasons why a Buyer may be more likely to buy products from a manufacturer that has an environmentally conscious reputation.

- ② 💡 🎭 Visit an ethnic supermarket—one that's new (or new-ish) to you. Pick three, four, or five items you think your customers (your family) would like to buy. Think about their preferences (Little Bro loves cheese, Big Sis loves noodles, Dad loves every kind of berry). At home, display your buys on the kitchen counter so your customers can see them. Then open 'em up and enjoy a snack together.

You can also look in the ethnic aisle in your local supermarket.

CAREER CROSSING

BUYERS WORK WITH:

Manufacturers

Merchandise Assistants

Merchandisers

Product Developers

Shipping Managers

Oh, your favorite meal—you know what ingredients go in, how long it takes to cook (and how long it takes to eat!). Let's just say that, afterward, you're one satisfied customer. Chefs get to work with every ingredient imaginable to create their customers' favorite meals, right to order. Talk about a tasty career!

Jump In

○ ① ⊕ ⊛ Use the library or the Web to report about the history of the sandwich, including the Earl of Sandwich (yes, a real person!). Then make and enjoy your own sandwich, filled with your absolute favorite things.

○ ② ⊛ Pick up a blank apron and/or chef's hat at a craft store and decorate it with fabric markers, paints, rhinestones—whatever you wish.

CHEFS:

- Create meals in restaurants
- Experiment with all different kinds of foods
- Plate food in appealing ways
- Ensure health and safety code standards are met

○ ③ ⊛ ⊛ Find an area restaurant that orders food from a local farmer. Then eat there—it's a great way to support your local economy.

○ ③ ⓐⓑⓒ ⊛ ⊙ Shadow the Chef at your favorite restaurant (call in advance to schedule a good time). Ask if he will demonstrate how to make your favorite dish. Afterward, send a card or email thanking him.

Apply Food Chemistry

○ ① ⊛ ⊛ Cook your favorite vegetable three different ways (try boiling, roasting, steaming, or sautéing). Report about the differences in color, texture, and flavor.

Remember to always wash your hands before working with food!

SAYS JEFF KAPLAN, RESTAURANT MANAGER AND CHEF,
SAWGRASS MARRIOTT GOLF RESORT & SPA
IN PONTE VEDRA BEACH, FLORIDA

I love *never knowing what food challenge to expect.*

My biggest on-the-job challenge is *making sure each guest has the perfect experience.*

My favorite thing to make is *seafood—any kind.*

The best compliment I ever received on my cooking was from *a guest who said I "make her feel like family."*

My favorite kitchen gadget is *my team!*

If I weren't a Chef I'd be *a Teacher.*

○ ②🔍🧪 Shake one cup of heavy cream in a tightly sealed jar for about ten minutes and wow! Fresh butter! (Tired of shaking that jar? Use an electric blender.) Then visit the library or the Web to report about the science behind what just happened.

○ ②💡🔍🧪 Change just one ingredient in a dish to alter it entirely. Try smoothies—first, use your blender to mix one cup of your favorite fruit, one cup of milk, and half a cup of ice cubes. Pour about a third into a glass. Into the blender throw half a cup of a different fruit, half a cup of milk, and a quarter cup of ice cubes. Blend, then pour half into a glass. Add one cup of plain-flavored yogurt to the blender, blend, then pour what's left into a glass. Do a taste-test of all three to see how they differ.

Chef Jeff has twenty-two years on-site technical training and experience in culinary arts. He has worked in dozens of hotel/ restaurant kitchens, from New York City, New York, to Miami, Florida, starting as a Prep Cook and working his way up to running his own kitchens!

Consider adding one tablespoon of sugar to one and one tablespoon of honey to another to see which is sweeter.

Create Meals & Menus

○ ① 🔍 Try a new food every day for three, four, or five days. Each can be eaten by itself, or incorporated into a recipe—your choice. You never know when the Chef in you will be inspired by a new flavor!

○ ② 💡 🎭 Serve your family an ethnic version of your favorite American meal: instead of mac 'n cheese, make pasta with marinara sauce (Italian); instead of chicken nuggets, make chicken stir fry (Chinese); instead of a hamburger, make kofta (Middle Eastern).

IMPORTANT

Stay safe! Never use a stove, oven, or other kitchen appliance without an adult's supervision.

○ ② 🖊 Start a file of your favorite recipes. Use a traditional file box and note cards, a three-ring binder, or a computer program.

⬆ ③ 🌐 🖐 Ask someone from an older generation to add one of her all-time favorite recipes to your file. Talk about its history. Then make the recipe—if you're able, make it together.

○ ③ 💡 🧮 ☼ 🕐 Pick a recipe, create a shopping list, go to the grocery store, choose the ingredients, come home, prepare the dish, and serve. (Be sure to help with clean-up afterward.)

○ ③ 💡 🕐 Visit a local farmer's market and make a dish using an ingredient purchased there.

Fill Orders

○ ① 🖊 💡 Help Mom or Dad "plate the food" for one, two, or three meals—this is how food is arranged to affect how customers feel when they see your dish. Just as you wouldn't want to eat a bruised apple, diners don't want to eat a meal that doesn't look yummy.

○ ② ⏲ Make two or three meal orders at the same time. (Try this with breakfast—meals can be simple, such as "cereal" and "toast".)

⇧ ① 💡 ☀ Cater to an unsatisfied customer (Mom? Dad?). Do you make a new dish? Offer a kiss and a hug?

○ ② ⏲ Prepare to cook prior to making a recipe. First, stock your cooking area with premeasured dry ingredients, measuring cups for wet ingredients, mixing bowls, spatulas and other utensils, and wash and prepare ingredients (keep perishable ingredients in the fridge until ready to use). Wait an hour. THEN make your dish.

⇧ ② 🔍 ⏲ Make this recipe again, but don't prepare ahead of time. Report the differences in the experience.

> **WHY DOES CHEF JEFF THINK HIS CAREER IS AWESOME?**
>
> "I have the opportunity to make people happy with my delicious creations!"

DID YOU KNOW?

Chefs prepare and serve food to celebrities, athletes, local heroes—imagine getting the opportunity to serve someone you admire!

Manage Inventory

○ ① 🗒 Determine the amount of each ingredient needed to make your favorite dinner meal for four (including a healthy dessert).

⇧ ① 🗒 Recalculate the amounts needed to make the meal for two and for six.

○ ① 🗒 $ Select a product (tomato soup? pumpernickel bread?), then visit two, three, or four grocery stores in-person or online to find which carries it at the best price.

(↑) (2) (▦) ($) Report if/how your stores' results change three, four, or five days later.

○ (2) (💡) (▦) ($) Set a price point (say, $10). Create and serve a dinner meal for your family that fits within it. Remember the value of coupons!

○ (3) (💡) (▦) ($) Plan two, three, or four days' worth of menus (breakfast, lunch, dinner, and one snack). Write down what items you have at home. Go shopping to fill in the rest, noting (on paper or in a computer program) how much each additional item costs. After your two, three, or four days, report how much of those items have been used up, and what you still have left. Can anything left over create a new meal? Did you run out of anything? Chefs monitor ingredient usage to help control costs over time.

(↑) (1) (🖐) Donate any extra *nonperish-able** items. Look for collection bins at your local grocery store.

*Nonperishable means it takes a long time for the food to spoil.

CAREER CROSSING

CHEFS WORK WITH:

Accountants*

Food Purveyors

Kitchen Managers

Pest Control Technicians

Purchasers

Undone doorknob? Unhung artwork? Unpainted bedroom? The minute you hear that toolbox open, you're there. In fact, fixing up your home sounds like an absolutely perfect way to spend an afternoon. And if you grow up to become a real Contractor, it's an absolutely perfect way to spend every day at work!

Jump In

○ ① 💡 🔍 Use the library or Internet to define "renovation," "addition," "remodel," and "new construction." Then make a list of which rooms in your home could benefit from each.

○ ② 💡 🔤 ☼ ▦ 💲 Visit a builder's supply store (you'll find addresses in the phone book) or a home improvement store. With a preset budget ($5?), add to your at-home inventory (screws? a new hammer?). Present your purchases and a note of appreciation to your favorite at-home Contractor (the one who changes light bulbs, washes crayon marks off walls, and un-clogs toilets!).

○ ③ 🔤 ☼ 💬 Shadow a Contractor—maybe he'll bring you on-site to check out one of his latest projects. Be sure to wear closed-toe shoes, so you don't injure yourself on any stray nails! After your time together, mail or email a thank-you note.

○ ③ 💬 💡 Get involved with a community group such as Habitat for Humanity. Even the youngest volunteers can help sponsor or build homes for neighbors in need.

contractors:

- Build homes and buildings
- Estimate how much it costs to build a structure
- Order building materials
- Coordinate and schedule subcontractors, like Painters and Electricians

says jason matthews, owner, high country renovators
in boone, north carolina

I love _interacting with different people, with different needs._

My biggest on-the-job challenge is _clients who don't pay their bills on time, because then I can't pay my suppliers and subcontractors._

My day starts at _6:30 am_ and ends at _5:00 pm._

The most unusual request I ever filled for a client was _stocking the fridge before they came into town._

One time I dropped a _hammer on my head! (It was on top of the ladder when I moved it.)_

If I weren't a Contractor, I'd be _a Teacher._

Prepare to Build

○ ① 💡 📖 Read *The Three Little Pigs* from a Contractor's point of view—define how the first two little pigs could have better built their individual homes (and no, "use bricks" is not allowed as an answer!).

○ ① 💡 🔍 Create a *materials list**, using library books or an Internet search, to update a classroom for your favorite teacher (let's say it's your Art Teacher). Your list should include specific flooring (that can withstand splattered paint), wall materials (that can showcase artwork), countertops (that hide glue stains), window count, and extras specific to that teacher's needs (like a sink).

* *Materials lists like these are called "schedules," like Flooring Schedule and Window Schedule.*

⬆ ① ☼ 💬 Give the list to your teacher.

○ ② 🔬 💡 Take a picture of your kitchen with a digital camera. Photocopy the picture in black and white, using the machine's settings to blow it up to 8″x10″-ish. Then use markers and pens to mark up the picture, turning the room into a Mad Scientist's laboratory. Maybe the sink needs to be bigger and deeper (to wash out gigantic tubes of goo). What about changes to the countertops? Ceiling? Number of electrical outlets?

Contractor Jason graduated with a bachelor's degree in construction management from East Carolina University. He's been in the construction industry for fifteen years. His first job was digging footers and pouring concrete—ten years later, he opened his own construction company!

○ ② 💡 🖩 $ 🔍 Estimate the cost to build a doll- or action-figure-sized house out of dried pasta. First define how big your house will be, how many types of pasta you'll want to incorporate (spirals for the chimney? elbows for the roof?), how many boxes of pasta you'll need, and how you'll affix them together (glue? the homemade play-dough recipe on page 347?). Then visit the grocery store or online shops to determine how much your pasta house will cost to construct.

🕐 ③ 🔬 💡 🖩 $ Build your house. Once done, revisit your estimate to see if you came within budget.

🕐 ① 🔬 💡 🖩 $ Make a change or addition to your house (Mom or Dad's choice). Does he want the house painted day-glo pink? If there is no money left in your budget (like for paint), do what real Contractors do: suggest a lower-cost alternative (one of Little Sis's pink stickers on the door?)

WHY DOES CONTRACTOR JASON THINK HIS CAREER IS AWESOME?

"I'm my own boss. If I want to see a baseball game or go fishing, I can go—so long as I have all my jobs in order!"

Construct & Install

○ ① 🛠️ 💡 📊 🔍 🧪 Construct the greatest pillow fort EVER! Start with bed pillows—stack 'em and see how long it takes a toddler, pet, or participating Mom or Dad to topple your fort. Add one, two, or three reinforcements, one at a time, testing each as you go (decorative pillows? sofa cushions? balled-up sleeping bags?).

○ ① 🛠️ 💡 📊 🧪 Grab your LEGOs, Lincoln Logs, Duplo blocks—whatever stacking toys you've got—to construct a prince or princess tower. How tall can you make it before it tumbles? Use a tape measure, measuring tape, or ruler to find out.

⬆️ ① 🛠️ 💡 📊 🧪 Rebuild your tower, using tactics that get it even taller. Add a base? Support posts?

○ ② 🛠️ 💡 Use an empty shoebox and other on-hand arts-n-crafts items to build [YOUR NAME]'s Train Depot. Include a waiting area, a ticket counter, and a platform for passengers to get on and off the train. Think about where your station's entrance(s) would best keep passengers moving quickly and safely.

○ ② 🛠️ 💡 Build a mini water theme park in a bathtub or sink: construct slides, pathways, and jungle gyms using plastic building materials (such as LEGOs, empty food containers, and/or household tubing) while the tub is

Be sure to clean your job site immediately after project completion. Contractors know the condition in which they leave a work area is as important as the work done there.

DID YOU KNOW?

Construction is really one big puzzle—a Contractor's job is to put the pieces together just-so, for an amazing finished product: a fort, a water theme park, even your home!

empty. Once you're ready, use a pitcher to pour water over your slides and jungle gyms—is your construction strong enough to withstand the flow? If not, make adjustments until it is.

○ ② 🎨 💡 🐢 Build a zoo using only materials you find outside (pebbles, rocks, tree bark, mulch, pine combs, dried acorns, leaves, twigs). Include exhibits for a lion, monkey, and hippopotamus. Think about their individual needs before building—then you'll know what you need to collect.

⬆️ ③ 💡 🎨 🔍 Visit the real zoo with someone from an older generation *before* building yours. Take notes on the animals' habitats for inspiration when you build at home (this is the kind of research Contractors do before building anything new!).

○ ③ 🎨 💡 🐢 Build a real birdhouse. Take a class at a local home improvement store, buy a kit in a store or online, or create one using materials you find at home.

⬆️ ① 🔍 🐢 Do research before you build, so you know what kind of birdhouse is most likely to attract your region's feathered friends.

CAREER CROSSING

CONTRACTORS WORK WITH:
Architects
Building Inspectors
Electricians
Plumbers
Structural Engineers

Copywriter

You taped a picture of that gotta-have-it toy to the fridge, hoping (praying) Dad would see it and say, "Wow! I should run out this instant to get my kid one of those!" You thought you were being clever—but you were actually being pretty good at advertising. Brush up your Copywriter skills and you may just get yourself that new toy yet!

Jump In

- ○ (1) 🎭 🌐 🔍 Use the Internet to uncover the cost of running a thirty-second Super Bowl ad in the 1970s, the 1990s, and last year. (Super Bowl ads are some of the most anticipated TV commercials all year!)

    ⬆ (1) 🎭 ✂ 🔍 Ask someone from an older generation about his favorite Super Bowl commercial—does he remember the product, message, and story line? If you can, go online and see if you can find it together (thanks to the Internet, this can even be done long-distance).

- ○ (1) 🎭 😊 Watch one well-known *Public Service Announcement (PSA)** (try www.YouTube.com). Bet Mom or Dad remember a few from their childhood. Discuss the commercial's main message—what were viewers supposed to learn?

COPYWRITERS:

- Persuade an audience to buy a product or service
- Write advertisements, marketing pieces (like brochures), and websites
- Oversee the production of TV and radio spots
- Use creativity and imagination to get people to pay attention to messages

PSAs work to positively change behavior, not sell a product or service.

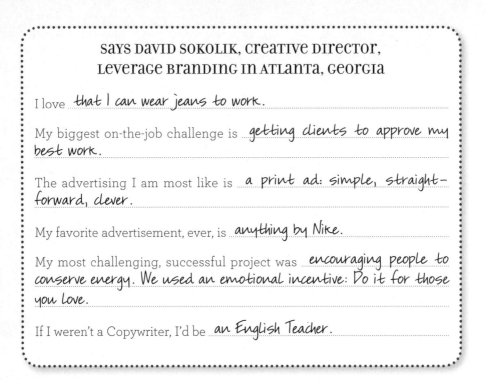

SAYS DAVID SOKOLIK, CREATIVE DIRECTOR,
LEVERAGE BRANDING IN ATLANTA, GEORGIA

I love *that I can wear jeans to work.*

My biggest on-the-job challenge is *getting clients to approve my best work.*

The advertising I am most like is *a print ad: simple, straight-forward, clever.*

My favorite advertisement, ever, is *anything by Nike.*

My most challenging, successful project was *encouraging people to conserve energy. We used an emotional incentive: Do it for those you love.*

If I weren't a Copywriter, I'd be *an English Teacher.*

○ ① 🎭 🌐 🔍 Use the library or an online search to report about one, two, or three of the most memorable *icons** of all time. Do you recognize any of them?

*An **icon** is a character that represents a product, service, or message.

⬆ ② 🎭 🔍 Walk, bike, or ride around town to find two, three, or four advertising icons. (Hint: Try looking on billboards or storefronts.)

⬆ ② 🎨 💡 Create an icon for your favorite restaurant. Is it a person or animal? Is there a costume? What colors? Use markers, crayons, and paper or a computer program to show what your icon looks like.

WHY DOES COPYWRITER DAVID THINK HIS CAREER IS AWESOME?

"I get to do something different every day, in a fun, exciting environment. And did I mention I get to wear jeans and a T-shirt to work?!"

- ③ 🎭 🌐 🔍 Visit an advertising-specific museum in your area, or a museum with special exhibits dedicated to advertising legends and/or icons. Once there, look for one, two, or three facts about advertising you didn't know before, then report about them when you get home.

- ③ abc ☼ 💬 Shadow a Copywriter. (Look in the phone book or online for an advertising agency in your area.) Mail or email a thank-you note afterward.

Typically, ads are developed by a team of one Art Director and one Copywriter. Art Directors are skilled at the visual aspects of advertising: photography, graphics, and layout (placement of the text, graphics, and photographs on a page). Copywriters handle the language: scripts and copy (the words in an ad).

Develop Strategies

- ① 💡 Find a sales opportunity. (Did Mom just bake the most mouth-watering lemon pie?) Create a list of two, three, or four reasons why your product will sell. (Maybe all the other bake sale pies are usually pumpkin or cherry?)

  ⬆ ① 💡 Identify one, two, or three challenges for your product. (Unlike cookies, a slice of pie requires a fork and plate.)

  ⬆ ① 💡 Name your target audience. (Who is most likely to buy Mom's pie? Kids who love the flavor lemon? Moms with a sweet tooth? Teachers who need a pick-me-up?) Copywriters define their target audience to help them create more personal advertising. The more personal the advertising, the more likely the target audience will listen to the message!

Create Concepts

- ① 💡 abc Write an outdoor ad. Try a billboard for your most favorite fruit or vegetable. Can you deliver your message in eight words or less? Six words or less?

(↑)(1)(✎)(💡) Write your message on a big piece of paper, then flash it to Mom or Dad—only allow him three seconds to read your message. Did he understand what you were trying to sell?

○ (2)(✎)(💡)(ᵃᵇ𝒸) Write a *print ad** for your most favorite toy. (You can design your ad on a plain piece of paper using crayons, markers, stickers, and cutouts from magazines. Or use the computer and downloadable clip art.) Start by identifying the absolute coolest thing about your toy. Write (or type) that at the top—that's your headline. Then add copy and a *visual***. Finally, post your ad where your family can see it.

○ (2)(💡)(ᵃᵇ𝒸) Write a TV *spot*** about your most favorite outdoor product. For inspiration, check out the sample TV script on page 350.

(↑)(1)(⏱) Read your spot out loud, acting out the action parts, too. Use a stopwatch or the clock on your computer to time it—is your spot at thirty seconds (the most common length of TV commercials)?

(↑)(3)(💡)(☼)(💬) Ask Mom or Dad to use a video or digital camera to film your spot, using friends or siblings as Actors, and dress-up clothes for costumes. (Why can't *you* film it? Because a Copywriter's job during filming is

Copywriter David earned a bachelor of arts degree in communications from the University of California at Santa Barbara, and also has a master's degree in journalism. He wrote for a daily newspaper in Colorado before switching to advertising. He's been a Copywriter for seventeen years, and has worked on projects for McDonald's, the DC United soccer team, and the Prince William Cannons minor league baseball team.

Print ads are found in newspapers and magazines.

Visuals refer to photographs or illustrations.

Spot is another way to say "ad" in radio or TV.

to make sure the Actors say all their lines according to the script, or to make on-the-spot judgments if a new line sounds better—or funnier!)

○ ② 💡 ⒜ Write a radio spot for your most favorite place to visit. Music and sound effects put your audience where you want them to be. (Screaming wind? That's a roller coaster! Rolling waves? The seashore! Lots of "shush-ing"? The library!) You'll find a sample script on page 351.

⬆ ① ⒜ 🕐 Read your spot out loud, using a stopwatch or the clock on your computer to time it. Add or subtract language to it, until it's at sixty seconds. Then edit it down to thirty seconds— tell the same story in half the time!

DID YOU KNOW?

Copywriters need to know the who's who and what's what of popular culture. Which means watching TV, going to the movies, and reading magazines are all part of the job!

⬆ ③ 💡 ☼ 💬 Record an Actor (Mom? Dad? Neighbor's dog walker?) reading your spot into a cell phone, camera, computer, or tape recorder. If you have audio programs on your computer, you may be able to add background music and sound effects. Just remember: a Copywriter's responsibility is to make sure the Actor reads all the lines scripted, not to be the one acting.

CAREER CROSSING

COPYWRITERS WORK WITH:

Account Executives

Art Directors

Media Buyers

Printers

Proofreaders

Costume Designer

It's the end-of-the-school-year play and you're a tomato. Not an exotic eggplant. Not a fun-to-say kumquat. But your standard, garden-variety tomato. Fine, you think, I'll spice things up with a neon-green stem and fancy drops of dew fashioned from leftover bubble wrap. Take a bow, Costume Designer—well done!

Jump In

○ ① 🎭 🌐 🔍 Use the library or an Internet search to report about the history of costume design. (At one time, Costume Designers had to make male performers look female!)

○ ① 🔍 Report about the costume designer for your favorite *show** (you'll find her name listed in a *playbill***, as a *closing credit****, or by an online search). Has she worked on any other shows? Won any awards for her work? Have any upcoming projects?

○ ③ 💡 🎭 🎬 🔍 Rent or buy a movie someone from an older generation enjoyed years ago that has since been remade (like *Father of the Bride* or *Charlie and the Chocolate Factory*). Watch both movies (or,

COSTUME DESIGNERS:

- Draw costume ideas
- Shop for clothes
- Sew (or oversee the sewing of) special outfits
- Fit Actors in their clothing
- Attend rehearsals to make sure costumes look right

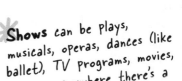

✳ **Shows** can be plays, musicals, operas, dances (like ballet), TV programs, movies, circuses—anywhere there's a performer and an audience.

✳ **Playbills** are theater programs listing details about the show.

✳ **Closing credits** refer to on-screen text that lists who was involved in the show's production.

SAYS MAGGIE WHITAKER, COSTUME DESIGN ASSISTANT, BERKELEY REPERTORY THEATRE IN BERKELEY, CALIFORNIA

I love *collaborating with such a diverse group of people.*

My biggest on-the-job challenge is *trying not to spend too much time driving around, hunting for that perfect piece of clothing.*

My favorite plays to costume are *new works, where my design helps the script evolve.*

The most embarrassing thing that happened to my design on stage *caused one of my actors to literally lose his pants—the back seam split!*

My largest budget? *$5,000.* Smallest? *$200.*

If I weren't a Costume Designer, I'd be *completely at a loss.*

at least, part of both movies) together. Compare the costumes. What is the same? What did the new Costume Designer change? And which do you think better fits each character?

○ ③ (abc) (☼) (💬) Shadow a Costume Designer. (Try calling a local theater to find one.) After spending time together, mail or email a thank-you note.

Come Up with Ideas

○ ① (🖐) (💡) Draw and cut out paper doll figures of one, two, or three characters from your favorite play, TV show, or movie. Then glue on scrap pieces

WHY DOES COSTUME DESIGNER MAGGIE THINK HER CAREER IS AWESOME?

"I get to work with the most interesting people, sometimes rock stars! I get to see my ideas come to life through collaboration with great people. I rarely handle the same problem twice. And it gives me a reason to buy books and fancy magazines!"

of fabric, yarn, pipe cleaners, broken bits of chain—whatever you have on hand—to dress your paper dolls in their new "costumes."

○ ② 💡 🔍 Look through books, websites, magazines, catalogues—anything that may inspire a new design for your favorite character's clothes. (Always thought Nemo could use a swimsuit? Hunt for summer fashion from the year the movie was set.) Photocopy or print out all the images you find and put them in a [CHARACTER'S NAME]'s Costume Folder.

⬆ ② 🎭 💡 Create a *character collage**, using your photocopies or printouts. Tape or glue your favorite looks to a piece of paper—then present your collage to your Director (Mom? Dad?). Together, narrow down what's most important for your character's overall look and *transformations***.

○ ③ 🎭 📖 🔍 Pick a *play*** or *screenplay**** and read it. (Your local Librarian will be happy to help find a perfect one for you.) List changes in

Costume Designer Maggie has been making performers look fabulous for twelve years. She has a master's degree in costume design from the University of California, San Diego, and had her designs presented at the 2007 Prague Quadrennial in the Czech Republic. She was also the Assistant Costume Designer for rock band Green Day's live performance at the 2010 Grammy Awards.

*A character collage artfully displays a character's personality.

*Transformations are when a character changes costume.

*Plays are stories written to be performed live.

*Screenplays are stories written specifically for film.

time, location, weather, and direct references to clothes—clues to the play's overall look and atmosphere. If you own the script, or have it photocopied, you can mark what you find with a highlighter and pen.

Sketch Ideas

○ ① 🎨 💡 Create a pencil sketch (colored pencils work great) of one, two, or three new costumes for your favorite character. Include accessories like belts and hats.

⬆ ② 🎨 Cut out pictures of your character's face to glue in place of her hand-drawn faces. Yes, real Costume Designers do this, too.

Manage Budgets

○ ② 🧮 💲 🔍 Determine the cost to create a favorite character's outfit, using a picture of your character in costume for reference. List every piece you see, including accessories. Then visit a department store or online stores to match a price with each item.

⬆ ② 🧮 💲 🔍 Re-create the same outfit, cutting your original costs in half. Look for coupons, sales, or clearance items that may not be an exact match, but look awfully close.

⬆ ① 💡 ♻ Re-create the same outfit, suggesting existing items that could be repurposed (such as using an old hoop earring as a bracelet). This is great for a small costuming budget *and* the environment.

Prepare for Production

○ ① 💡 🔍 Prepare a *pieces list** for your favorite character (a work sheet is on page 352; a downloadable version is at EarnMyKeep.com). Watch her show (or read the script). Note every time your character appears and the clothes worn.

*A **pieces list** refers to the individual pieces of an actor's costume.

○ ① 💡 ☼ 🔍 List your production team (Set Designer, Lighting Designer, Sound Designer, Choreographer, Director) and why it's important for a Costume Designer (YOU!) to tell each member about his plans. (You may need to do some library or online research to find out.)

○ ② 🌀 💡 🔍 Use only your memory to make a list of what your favorite cartoon character wears. Then dress up your Actor (Mom? Dad? unsuspecting Baby Bro?) using what you can find or make *in-house**. Now find a picture of your character—did you get everything? Even the accessories? If not, find what you need to complete the look.

> ❋ **In-house** refers to items already on hand.

SO YOU WANT TO...STAGE YOUR OWN COSTUME REHEARSAL

○ ③ 🌀 💡 ☀ 🙂 Rehearsals are your chance to find out what does (and doesn't!) work in front of a real audience.

DID YOU KNOW?

Everywhere a Costume Designer goes is an opportunity to be inspired—noticing the way clothes move and the way they make people feel are details that just may show up onstage!

1. Create costumes for a play set to a nursery rhyme ("The Cow Jumped Over the Moon"?).

2. Dress one, two, or three Actors (Mom? Dad? Cousins?) for their parts—this is called *fitting*. Do the costumes fit comfortably? Are the Actors happy with them? Make adjustments as necessary.

3. Move your Actors to the stage—you sit where the audience would, taking notes as you watch the costumes in action. (Do your cow's udders keep her from clearing the "moon" [the bathroom stepstool]? Is your dish's cardboard plate too wide to fit through the doorway as she tries to run away with the spoon?)

4. Make quick changes to your costumes, as needed. (Tie up your cow's udders. Use a pair of scissors to make your dish's plate smaller.)

CAREER CROSSING

COSTUME DESIGNERS WORK WITH:

Assistant Designers

Craftspeople

Drapers

Stitchers

Tailors

Your room is the BEST (even if Mom thinks it's too messy). Your posters, your pictures, your books, your games—all together they're a collection that tells visitors a story about you. Curators work the same way, gathering and displaying collections to tell stories about history, art, culture, sports, music, animals—anything you can dream up!

curators:

- Collect museum artifacts by contacting lenders and donors
- Research the history of museum artifacts
- Create exhibits

Jump In

- ③ 💡 🎭 🌐 🔍 Visit a museum—any museum. Check out the labels next to each item, the number of items, and if the *donor's** name is listed. Report about what you think the Curator wanted you to learn from one, two, or three *exhibits*** you see.

  Even zoos, aquariums, and botanical gardens are museums.

  - ⬆ ① 🔤 ☀ Write a letter or email to the museum's Curator, sharing what you liked about her exhibits. (For the museum's address, check a phone book or online.)

  *Donors give or lend something they own.

- ③ ☀ 💬 🐦 Volunteer at a local museum by folding flyers and stuffing envelopes (or helping out with another age-appropriate task).

  **Exhibits are displays for public view.

SAYS MEREDITH E. RUTLEDGE, ASSISTANT CURATOR, ROCK AND ROLL HALL OF FAME AND MUSEUM IN CLEVELAND, OHIO

I love _collections that involve solving a mystery._

My biggest on-the-job challenge is _trying to get an artifact from someone who doesn't want to give it up!_

My most interesting donor is _John Lennon's family._

I'm most proud to have completed an exhibit on _the folk artist, Lead Belly._

My fantasy *Night at the Museum* would be _at "my" museum, with my heroes coming to life for the biggest all-star jam ever._

If I weren't a Curator, I'd be _researching rock stars. It's just what I do!_

Research Artifacts

○ ① 💡🎭💡🔍 Solve the mystery of an item's *provenance**. Ask Mom or Dad

> *Provenance* refers to an artifact's origin.

to give you an item with an imaginary history, like a bandana (one of the original American flags?), the plastic thingy that keeps a bread bag closed (Elvis Presley's guitar pick?), or a video arcade token (a Roman gold piece?). Use the library or the Internet to report about where your item came from, how old it is, and one, two, or three interesting facts about it.

○ ② 💡🔍 Combine two seemingly unrelated *collections*** (like baseball and music) to display for a day. Search for

> *A collection* is three or more like things, grouped together.

commonality—say, display a collection of songs (printed-out lyrics) about base-ball (like "Take Me Out to the Ball game"). Making these kinds of connections helps Curators create exhibits that tell more interesting, well-rounded stories.

Collect & Maintain Artifacts

○ ① ⊛ ⊙ Create a collection of your favorite things (board games? stickers? soccer posters?), using only items from home. Display it for a day in a highly visible (but not likely to be disturbed) spot (your bedroom dresser? the not-used-so-often dining room table?).

Your collection could include sports memorabilia (like trading cards), art supplies (like colored pencils), books, stuffed animals, dolls, action figures—even hats or fuzzy slippers!

⊙ ① ⊙ Fill a gap in your collection—do you have every classic board game but one? Borrow one from a friend, or buy secondhand.

Sometimes it takes Curators years before they can convince someone to donate or lend an artifact.

○ ① ⊙ ⓐⓑⓒ ☼ Convince a donor (Mom? Dad?) to lend you an item (Mom's prettiest perfume bottle? Dad's backboard-breaking basketball?) you really want to display in your "bedroom museum." Deliver two, three, or four reasons for why the item should be loaned. Also state what you intend to do with it and when you will return it. (Being polite and convincing is what's important here. Mom or Dad may not think lending the item is in your best interests, and that's OK.)

○ ② ⊙ ▦ ⊙ Catalogue a collection of ten books, DVDs, or CDs. On paper (or the computer), list each artifact's name, age, measurements, and place of purchase.

Curator Meredith graduated from Sarah Lawrence College with a degree in cultural anthropology and theater. In high school, she worked as a museum "reenactor," demonstrating eighteenth century pottery techniques to school groups. She's also worked at a record label, for a record store, and has even been responsible for keeping track of all business and production-related research for Children's Television Workshop (the folks who produce *Sesame Street*).

(↑)(1)(☼)(⏱) Loan out one of your artifacts, noting to whom it was loaned. After two, three, or four days, politely request the item's return.

Create Exhibits

○ (1)(💡)(🌐) Design the Museum of [YOUR NAME HERE] by listing five, seven, or ten exhibits in it, such as displays of your baby things, photos of places you've visited, and/or awards you've earned.

(↑)(2)(🧭) Create a guide map for your museum, using markers, crayons, and paper or a computer program. Include where visitors will find each exhibit—you can even place the exhibits in the order you want them viewed.

○ (3)(🧭)(💡)(🌐)(☼) Use labels to turn a room in your home into a museum of THE BEST THINGS EVER! Try the family room: think that lamp looks like an Egyptian mummy? The couch like a stegosaurus? The throw rug like a magic carpet? Using sticky notes, or paper and tape, hang labels next to these items, stating what each is and where it's from. Then invite visitors (Mom, Dad, the neighbor's uncle) to move through your museum, learning as they go.

(↑)(1)(💡) Give each of your labels more detail (such as an interesting fact about stegosauruses your visitors may not know).

WHY DOES CURATOR MEREDITH THINK HER CAREER IS AWESOME?

"I get paid to research and follow the careers of Musicians—something I'd be doing even if it wasn't my job. I never imagined that what I loved to do as a kid would one day become my career!"

DID YOU KNOW?

Some Curators gather accurate information for their exhibits by spending time with the family, friends, and descendants of the world's most celebrated people!

(⬆)(1)(⚓)(💡) Add props to your artifacts to make them even more believable. Could the Egyptian mummy-lamp use a wrapping of toilet paper? Could the magic carpet use a sprinkling of (vacuum-able) glitter?

Raise Funds

○ (3)(💡)(abc)(☼)($) Raise funds to add a new artifact to a collection of your favorite things. (This is above-and-beyond your Earn My Keep allowance.) Sell cookies. Open a lemonade stand. Write a persuasive letter to Grandma (include three great reasons of why she should consider donating money to your collection). Make sure to thank everyone who contributes. Once you've raised the funds, purchase your new artifact.

(⬆)(1)(💬) Introduce the public (your family and/or friends) to your collection's new addition, stating why it's important and what visitors will enjoy most about it.

SO YOU WANT TO...EXHIBIT A LITTLE FAMILY HISTORY

○ (3)(⚓)(💡)(🌐)(🎨)(abc)(☼)(💬)(🔍) Design an exhibition from start to finish that will make someone in your life feel fantastic.

1. Select your exhibit's subject: someone from an older generation.

2. Research your subject's history (ask five or six questions, such as "When were you born?" "Where were you born?" and "How old were you when you first rode a bike?"). Write the answers to each question on individual pieces of paper.

3. Find three or four pictures of your subject. Ask your subject to help you label the pictures on sticky notes (one note per picture). Include: when the picture was taken, where it was taken, and what was happening.

4. Ask your subject for items that may help tell his story in a meaningful way. (So if Grandpa once won a golf tournament, ask, politely, if you can display one of his golf balls.) Write labels for these items as well.

5. Display the interview answers, pictures, and artifacts (and your labels) in a clean place, such as on an empty desk or folding table.

6. Invite visitors to learn something new by visiting your exhibit!

CAREER CROSSING

CURATORS WORK WITH:

Delivery Personnel

Exhibit Builders

Marketers

Newspaper Editors

Registrars

Dietitian

You know too much candy makes you feel sick. Oranges make you feel energized. Turkey makes you feel sleepy, and cold juice, totally refreshed. Knowing what keeps your body going (and what doesn't!) makes you a good Dietitian. Sharing the info with everyone you love makes you a great one!

Jump In

DIETITIANS:

- Evaluate how people eat
- Teach people how to plan healthy meals
- Monitor the foods people choose, for the healthiest result

○ ① Visit the library or the Web to report about the history of the Food Pyramid. How has it changed to match our nation's health, over time?

① Use markers, crayons, and paper to draw your own Food Pyramid. When you're done, name a favorite food that falls into each of the food groups.

○ ② Take a tour of the grocery store—as a Dietitian. Notice how all the fresh food (fruit, veggies, meat, and dairy) is around the outside, and the processed foods are displayed on the inside. Then go down the aisles, identifying two, three, or four healthier choices you find there. A multigrain snack bar? A low-sugar juice? Low-sodium soup?

○ ③ Shadow a Dietitian—maybe she's making a presentation at a local school, or working on adapting a meal plan for one of her patients! Mail or email a thank-you note soon afterward.

says SHELLEY SCHWARTZ, RD, owner,
EXERCISE NUTRITIONAL HEALTH! in ORLAND PARK, ILLINOIS

I love _helping people feel good with food!_

My biggest on-the-job challenge is _calorie-calculating computer software that doesn't work right._

I think the Food Pyramid is _a wonderful at-a-glance tool for healthy eating._

My most successful client once told me _she couldn't have done it without me._

The healthiest food on the planet is _different for everybody._

If I weren't a Dietitian I'd be _I'm not sure—I really love what I do!_

Evaluate Patients

o ① 🔍 ⚗ Use the library or an Internet search to report about the building blocks of food: carbohydrates, proteins, and fats. What are they? What do they do? And how many calories does each have?

⬆ ① 🧮 ⚗ Calculate how many calories a kid your age needs. What about two years from now? (This information is also at the library or online.)

⬆ ② 🔬 🧮 💬 ⚗ Create a chart that lists the caloric needs for everyone who lives with you. Present it to your family over a healthy dinner.

Dietitian Shelley graduated from Indiana University, Bloomington, with a bachelor of science degree in applied health science. She has been working as a Registered Dietitian for thirteen years. To earn the "Registered" in her title, she completed a one-year internship at Indiana University Medical Center, which qualified her for the required exam.

○ ③🔍⏱ Keep [YOUR NAME]'s Food Journal for three, four, or five days. Be accurate and honest. Note when you eat, what you eat, and how much you eat. Include condiments like ketchup and mustard, and what you drink, too.

⬆②💡🔍 Analyze your reporting. Do you find you're hungriest in the morning? After school? Dietitians help people realize that how much they really eat is typically more than (and not as healthy as) what they think they eat. Use a cookbook, the library, or Internet to find one, two, or three healthy foods that could replace unhealthy choices.

> **WHY DOES DIETITIAN SHELLEY THINK HER CAREER IS AWESOME?**
>
> "When I help people eat well, I'm helping them feel better and have more energy!"

Educate Patients

○ ①🔍⏱ List one, two, or three things that would happen if your favorite healthy food was omitted from your diet (oh, no!). What vitamins and minerals do you get from, say, avocados, and how do they keep you healthy?

⬆①💡🔍 Identify a healthy replacement food for one, two, or three of the following: vegetarians (none of whom eat meat); people with allergies (pick: egg, peanut, or milk); people who are gluten-intolerant (they can't eat wheat).

○ ①😎🔍🎭 Use the library or an Internet search to learn about seasonal foods—report on what makes them an important part of a healthy diet. Then identify which seasonal foods are available in your region, right now.

Some Dietitians (for instance, Hospital Dietitians) create meal plans that affect hundreds of people!

⬆①😎🔍🎭 Eat a different seasonal food every day for three, four, or five days. You'll find these fruits and veggies at a farmer's market or your grocery's store "local produce" section.

o (2) (abc) (Q) (A) Ask Mom or Dad (your patient) to make a list of three, four, or five of his favorite foods. Use a library or online search to report about these foods: are they whole foods from a particular country? Processed foods from an American manufacturer? How many calories are in one serving? Do they offer any nutritional benefits like vitamins, minerals, or antioxidants? Discuss your findings with your patient.

o (3) (💡) (abc) (☀) (⏱) Help promote healthier snacks in school. If your school has a junk food or soda vending machine, write a letter to your principal explaining why these foods are poor choices for children (include at least two good reasons). Then offer an alternative you and your friends would enjoy.

Plan Nutritious Meals

o (1) (💡) Eat a rainbow (red, orange, yellow, green, blue, and purple) of fruits and/or veggies every day for one, two, or three days.

o (2) (💡) (Q) Develop two, three, or four snacks that incorporate at least three food groups from the Food Pyramid, like Ants on a Log (celery filled with a mix of cream cheese and/or peanut butter, topped with raisins) or a yogurt parfait (low-fat yogurt layered with fruit and granola).

DID YOU KNOW?

Dietitians know how to use food as medicine! They teach us how the right foods can eliminate the need for medications, like those for high blood pressure and diabetes.

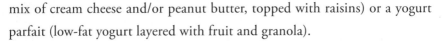

(⬆) (1) (☀) Make one of your snacks and share it with family and/or friends.

o (2) (💡) (👵) (Q) Give someone from an older generation's favorite recipe a makeover. Swap out: regular pasta for whole grain pasta; regular dairy products for low-fat or fat-free versions; regular eggs for egg whites or an egg substitute; or oil for applesauce (if baking).

(↑)(2)(🍒) Make the dish. If you're able, share the making with the recipe's owner. The new version doesn't have to taste exactly like the original to still be delicious.

○ (2)(💡)(🔍) Use the Food Pyramid (online or in a library book) to create a healthy, one-day personalized meal plan for Mom or Dad (your patient) to follow. Try to fill it with foods already in your kitchen.

(↑)(1)(☼)(🔍) Review the experience with your patient the next day—did he have trouble sticking to it? Was he hungry or satisfied? Does he feel better because of it?

○ (3)(💡)(⚗) Develop a three-, four-, or five-evening dinner plan for your family. Make sure each meal includes: a *protein**, a *starch***, and a vegetable. (A healthy example is grilled chicken, sweet potatoes, and broccoli sprinkled with low-fat cheese.) Then put your plan into action—you can even include fresh fruit with a drizzle of honey for dessert!

Protein is in foods like fish, poultry, eggs, and yogurt.

Starchy foods (also called complex carbohydrates) include bread, pasta, and rice.

CAREER CROSSING

DIETITIANS WORK WITH:

Chiropractors

Doctors

Nurses

Personal Trainers

Physical Therapists

Diplomat

S o it's quite a trip to visit your cousin. She lives pretty far away. And as she shows you the sights, you can't help but share how it compares to your hometown. She's fascinated by your stories and descriptions—as if you were a real Diplomat, introducing your culture to your new host city!

Jump In

○ ① 💡 ⏱ Imagine what it would be like to be sent to live and work in a foreign country—with two days' notice! List what you would pack, rescheduling you'd have to do (piano practices? birthday parties?), and how you'd prepare your home (stop the mail?). What would make this kind of adventure exciting?

○ ① 🔍 Use the library or an Internet search to list one, two, or three facts about embassies and consulates.

⬆ ③ 🎭 🔍 Visit an embassy or consulate that's near where you live or vacation. Name one, two, or three ways the embassy building represents its home country.

○ ② 🔤 💬 Learn five words in a foreign language. Ask a friend, a neighbor, a teacher—anyone you know who speaks that language fluently. Diplomats often receive training to learn more than their *native tongue**.

DIPLOMATS:

- Tell the rest of the world about the United States of America
- Work in embassies in foreign countries
- Promote growth of American businesses in other countries
- Give people in other countries visas to visit the United States
- Help Americans when they have problems while traveling overseas

Native tongue means the language someone learns as a child.

SAYS MARIA HIGGINS, DIPLOMAT,
U.S. EMBASSY IN BOGOTA, COLOMBIA

I love _meeting people who are so different from my friends at home._

My biggest on-the-job challenge is _adapting to different cultures._

I know _two_ languages fluently: _Spanish and Portuguese. I also speak a little Shona (Zimbabwe tribal language)._

Thanks to my career, my passport has _more stamps than I can count._

The best foreign food I've ever eaten on the job is _tacos al pastor in Mexico._

If I weren't a Diplomat, I'd be _a Lawyer._

○ ② 😊 👥 🔍 Ask someone from an older generation if she has ever lived in a foreign country. If so, talk about it. Can she tell you something about the country few others would know? If she never lived abroad, or cannot recall a fun detail, do some research about a country of choice, together.

○ ③ 🔤 ☀ 💬 Shadow a Diplomat. (Some live on university campuses throughout the United States. Try calling a local school, or clicking the "Contact Us" page at www.careers.state.gov.) Mail or email a thank-you note after your meeting.

Another great resource for Diplomat-related info and activities is www.future.state.gov.

Apply Public Diplomacy

○ ① 💡 🔤 ☀ 💬 🤝 Apply your diplomacy skills. The next time you see two people arguing (like siblings or friends), suggest a more peaceful

WHY DOES DIPLOMAT MARIA THINK HER CAREER IS AWESOME?

"I get to live and work in exotic places, learn to speak different languages, and make friends with people from other cultures!"

way to solve their differences. Try to get each person to see the other's point of view.

- ① 💡 🎭 ☀ Create a list of two, three, or four of your family's foreign policies—the way your family interacts with others outside of your home. Do you bring a gift when you stay overnight at your cousins'? Say "please" and "thank you" to the waiter at your favorite restaurant?

  ⬆ ③ 💡 🎭 🔍 Use the library or an Internet search to report about one of America's foreign policies. Do you agree with it? If not, how would you change it?

  ⬆ ③ 🎭 🔤 ☀ 🖐 Explain that foreign policy to someone who does not know about it. Diplomats ensure America's policies are understood by others.

- ② 🎭 🌐 🔍 Research the culture of a foreign country (say, China). Make two lists: Same and Different. What parts of their culture are similar to ours (love of family)? What parts are different (how we greet each other)?

- ② 💡 🎭 🔍 🖐 Create a sister city of your hometown. Use the library or Internet to find a foreign city with roughly the same population, climate, and industries. List one, two, or three ways you and your sister city's Mayor could share ideas and experiences, such as, "Create an exchange program for teachers to trade places for a week," or "Host a soccer tournament where both cities compete."

- ③ 🐾 💡 🎭 🌐 🔤 💬 🔍 🖐 Introduce foreigners (Mom or Dad) to an American tradition (Thanksgiving? baseball? jazz music?) by hosting a

Diplomat Maria graduated with a bachelor of arts in international relations from the University of North Carolina, Chapel Hill, and has a master of business administration. She studied abroad in Valencia, Spain, for one year, and that's when she realized she loves living in foreign countries. As a Diplomat, she has lived and worked in Argentina, Colombia, Mexico, and Zimbabwe.

For example, one of Miami, Florida's sister cities is Palermo in Italy!

cultural program. First, research your subject: its history, its importance, how your family incorporates the tradition into your lives. Then gather any props you may need—posters, music, art. Finally, invite your guests and teach them about the tradition. (You may want to practice first.)

Promote Economic Development

○ ② 💡 🎭 🔍 📋 Connect an American company with a *developing country** that could use its services. For example, what kind of company could help a nation that's trying to build a water system?

⬆️ ② 💡 🔍 List three reasons why the country should hire the company to do the job. (You may need to do some library or online research.)

○ ② 🎭 🔍 Identify a good business opportunity for an American company in a foreign country. First, pick a country—say, Belgium. Learn about its culture in the library or online. Then name an American company that may flourish there. Bicycling is very popular in Belgium, so Schwinn (an American bike manufacturer) may succeed!

○ ② 💡 🔤 ☀️ Persuade your *host country*** (represented by Mom or Dad) to allow an American company (your choice) to do business there. List three, four, or five reasons why, say, Brazil should open its borders to Crayola.

⬆️ ② 💡 🔤 ☀️ 🔍 Provide counterarguments to your host country's reservations (have Mom or Dad tell you why they don't want Crayola doing

✱ A developing country refers to one that is low- to mid-level, economically.

DID YOU KNOW?

Diplomats get to travel to every part of the country where they serve. In many countries this means riding in helicopters, boats—even on horseback!

✱ Host country refers to the nation in which Diplomats (or their embassies) are located.

business there). You may need to do some library or Internet research before you can answer.

Serve Citizens

o ① 😊 🔍 Use the library or an Internet search to define two, three, or four different kinds of passports: tourist, service, diplomatic, or emergency.

Going out of the country? Apply for a real passport as a task.

⬆ ① 🔍 ✋ Define what a Diplomat can do to help a traveler who has lost his passport.

⬆ ① 😊 ▦ 🔍 Ask to see Mom's, Dad's, or another adult's passport. Count the stamps and list where they're from.

⬆ ② 🎨 💡 😊 Use the passport for inspiration to create your own with paper, markers, and crayons—then "stamp" it from countries you hope to visit.

CAREER CROSSING

DIPLOMATS WORK WITH:

Foreign Government Officials

International Organization Representatives

(like Red Cross and UN)

Journalists*

Members of Congress

Translators*

Disc Jockey

G etting ready for school? You've got a song for that. Taking a big test? You've got a song for that. Hanging out with your favorite friends? Oh, you've got a great song for that. The fact is, you always know the perfect tune to get everyone movin' and groovin'. So press play to start the sway, DJ!

Jump In

○ ① 😃 🌐 🔍 Visit the library or the Internet to uncover why *Disc Jockey** used to be spelled Disk Jockey.

○ ① 💡 😃 🌐 🔍 Listen to the five most popular songs of the year you were born (try looking for them at the library or online). Then listen to the five most popular songs of last week. List three ways they're alike, and three ways they're different.

○ ① 😃 🔍 Get to know a new musical *genre***. Do you usually listen to pop? Listen to one, two, or three jazz tunes. If you're a fan of reggae, try one, two, or three classic rock jams. Remember, Disc Jockeys play music their listeners enjoy, which may be different from what they themselves enjoy.

⬆ ② 😃 🔍 Find one, two, or three songs that combine seemingly un-related genres. For example, some

Disc Jockeys are also called DJs or deejays.

DISC JOCKEYS:

· Play music on the radio, at events, or in dance clubs
· Create special mixes of songs called "remixes"
· Interview newsworthy people on the air (Radio DJs)
· Plan and direct the schedules of special events (Mobile DJs)

Genre refers to a style of music (like rock, country, or classical).

SAYS MARC SUMMERSETT, DIRECTOR OF ENTERTAINMENT, CE ENTERTAINMENT IN TUCSON, ARIZONA

I love _to give my clients the best night of their lives._

My biggest on-the-job challenge is _packing up the equipment after an exhausting day._

The song that always gets a crowd going is _different for every crowd!_

My all-time favorite event was _a wedding. I mixed a song with a message I recorded from the bride's mother, who was in the hospital—a deeply rewarding gift._

My heaviest piece of equipment weighs _more than one hundred pounds._

If I weren't a Disc Jockey, I'd be _a Movie Critic._

songs blend hip hop and rock 'n' roll. Country crossovers are blends of country and pop.

○ (1) (💡) Tell a story by singing or playing three, four, or five tunes. Is it a story about friendship? Love? Travel? So, say, your story could be: "Rain, Rain Go Away," then "The Itsy Bitsy Spider," then "Here Comes the Sun."

(⬆) (1) (💡) (🔍) Play your song "story" for someone (Mom? Dad? the Crossing Guard?), without telling her about your tale. Can she figure it out based on the songs you play and the order you play them?

○ (2) (🧮) (🔍) Use a clock or a stopwatch to find three songs that have the same beat per minute (BPM). To find a song's BPM, listen for its drumbeat. Then count the number of beats in fifteen seconds. Multiply that number by four to determine how many beats there are per minute.

(⬆) (1) (💡) (🧮) (🔍) Play your three songs, but add a new song in the middle— one that has a different BPM. DJs are skilled at mixing different beats in ways that listeners like.

○ ② 💡 🔍 Ask three people to list their five favorite songs. From those songs, pick the five you think most complement each other (to listen to the songs, try the library or an Internet search). Did you pick the five with the same beat? The same message? The same artist? Or another reason altogether?

○ ③ ⓐⓑⓒ ☼ 💬 Shadow a DJ. You'll have the best luck with a Mobile or Radio DJ (*Club DJs** work long after you've gone to bed). Either way, mail or email a thank-you note afterward.

Club DJs play music at dance clubs.

○ ③ 😀 🌐 🎧 🔍 Play DJ for someone from an older generation. Research what kind of music was popular when he was a kid (yes, you can ask him), use the Internet or library to find a few of those songs, then invite him over to enjoy. Have fun discussing the memories they stir up.

Disc Jockey Marc graduated from Ferris State University in Michigan with an associate's degree in applied arts—journalism. He's owned and operated CE Entertainment, LLC, for ten years, and is also the president of the Southern Arizona American DJ Association. For his first job as a Disc Jockey, he used a home CD changer. But even without the fancy DJ equipment, his clients said it was the best wedding they had ever attended!

○ ③ ☼ 💬 🔍 🕐 🎧 Invite your friends and/or family to a DJ [YOUR NAME HERE] Dance Hour (or half-hour, or quarter-hour) in support of a social or environmental issue that's important to you. Tell guests their entry fee (50¢?) will be donated to your cause. At the party, talk about your cause, or pass out flyers. But mostly, play music that keeps your event lively. Be sure to thank your guests. And as soon as you're able, donate your proceeds.

DJ on the Air (Radio DJ)

○ ① 💡 Create a daily playlist. First pick your favorite day of the week, then select three, four, or five songs that make great background music for that day's events. Love Fridays? Name your favorite get-up-and-go song for the morning. A slow song for the ride to school. Rock 'n' roll for the ride home. And a lullaby for bedtime.

○ ① 💡 ☀ 💬 Interact with a "listener." Sit opposite Mom or Dad, with your backs to each other (so you can't see each other's faces). Have her pretend to "call in" to ask you a question ("Can you play my favorite song?" or "What did you think of that game last night?"). Radio DJs talk with listeners on-air all the time. Be polite, friendly, and helpful.

○ ② 💡 🔍 Listen to the DJs on your favorite radio station in the morning, afternoon, and right before bed. List the different DJs' names and personalities (funny? friendly? serious about music?). Do their personalities match up with their time *on the air**? (So is the lively guy on air in the morning, when people need a pick-me-up?)

On the air refers to live broadcasts transmitting across airwaves.

DJ at Events (Mobile DJ)

○ ① 🔍 Use the library or the Internet to define a Mobile DJ's most important tools: turntables, mixers, records, CDs, and MP3 files.

○ ③ 💡 ☀ 💬 🕐 Be a Master of Ceremonies (MC) for dinner. First plan the sequence of events. (Does everyone take a seat? Do you eat a salad first? Dance after dinner, but before dessert?) Next, prepare your music (use an iPod,

DID YOU KNOW?

Mobile Disc Jockeys can devote up to eighty hours of preparation for one four-hour event. It's all for the love of music!

computer download, or CD). Then invite your family to an evening of dinner and dancing, politely directing them to do what you've planned.

○ ③ 💡 ☼ 💬 🔍 🕐 DJ an event (Mom or Dad's choice). Your tasks are to determine/gather the five songs that will best suit their needs, check out the venue* a day in advance, set up your equipment (iPod, computer, CD player) at least an hour before the event's starting time, MC the event (see the task above for what MCs do), and play music to keep the party going!

*A **venue** is where an event takes place.

CAREER CROSSING

MOBILE DISC JOCKEYS WORK WITH:

Catering Directors

Event Planners*

Photographers*

Talent Agents

Videographers

Entomologist

*L*emonade, flip-flops, and running through sprinklers? No, the best part of summer comes out at night, when Mother Nature gives little Entomologists a gift: a magical light show of fireflies. You gently catch one in your hands, study the flickering on and off, and then release the firefly back into the air to brighten the night sky once again.

Jump In

○ ① 🔍 🧪 Identify one, two, or three surfaces in your favorite room (like your wooden desk and cotton blanket). Use the library or an Internet search to report about one, two, or three insects that may call those surfaces home. Now you know why it's important to keep things clean!

○ ② 🔍 🧪 🐾 Report about the honeybee crisis—information can be found in the library or on the Internet. Also list one, two, or three ways Entomologists play a big part in saving the bees.

⬆ ① 🔍 🧪 Visit the library or the Internet to list one, two, or three other products we get with help from insects (other than honey!).

○ ③ 🔍 🧪 Visit a local insect fair, insect museum, or insect zoo (more general museums and zoos may also have insect exhibits). Once there, find and list one, two, or three insects you won't find in your own backyard. Also list one, two, or three insects you will.

ENTOMOLOGISTS:

- Study insect biology (like where insects live and what they eat)
- Perform field and laboratory trials to determine insect traits or pest management techniques
- Teach the public about insects

All bugs are insects, but not all insects are bugs. "Bug" actually refers to a suborder of forty thousand species of the millions of types of insects!

SAYS WIZZIE BROWN, EXTENSION PROGRAM SPECIALIST-INTEGRATED PEST MANAGEMENT, TEXAS AGRILIFE EXTENSION SERVICE IN AUSTIN, TEXAS

I love _that there's always something new to learn about insects._

My biggest on-the-job challenge is _working while getting stung by fire ants!_

The most exciting place I've ever found an insect is _under cow patties—the cutest little dung beetles._

My family reminds me of _leaf cutter ants because we all eat food grown in our garden._

The coolest thing insects do is _dry out during drought, then rehydrate when it rains._

If I weren't an Entomologist, I'd be a _Professional Organizer._

○ ③ⓐⓑⓒ☀☺ Shadow an Entomologist. To find one, call a local university's entomology department, a museum, zoo, or botanical garden—even a local beekeeper. After your time together, mail or email a thank-you note.

○ ③💡🐛🔍☺ Create an insect-friendly garden with someone from an older generation. Plant a few native plants with a variety of colors and blooming periods, add a shallow dish of water with sand or stones, and scatter shelter areas of leaf litter.

Study Insect Biology

○ ①🔍⚗ Use the library or an Internet search to list two, three, or four characteristics every insect has in common. (Size, shape, behavior, and habitat are not any of them.)

WHY DOES ENTOMOLOGIST WIZZIE THINK HER JOB IS AWESOME?

"I get paid for doing something I love to do—play with bugs!"

(⇧)(1)(🔍)(🧪) List the world's strongest, oldest, and most dangerous insects.

○ (1)(🔍)(🧪) Use the library or an online search to define "arthropod," "vertebrate," "invertebrate," "endoskeleton," and "exoskeleton."

(⇧)(2)(🎨)(💡)(🧪) Draw a picture of what a beetle would look like with an endoskeleton. Then draw a picture of what YOU would look like with an exoskeleton.

*One out of every four animals on Earth is a type of **beetle**!*

○ (1)(🔍)(🧪) Use the library or an Internet search to list two, three, or four details about your favorite insect: its common name, scientific name, *habitat**, and diet.

(⇧)(1)(🔍)(🧪) Report one, two, or three interesting facts about your favorite insect. For example, the Egyptians worshiped the scarab beetle (which you may know as the dung beetle!).

***Habitat** is the environment in which the insect usually lives.*

(⇧)(2)(🎨)(💡)(🔍)(🧪) Create your favorite insect using markers, crayons, construction paper, recycled cereal boxes, glue, glitter—whatever's on hand. Check in a library book or online to find an accurate picture to copy.

Study Insect Behavior

○ (1)(🔍)(🧪)(🐞) Catch one firefly in a clean glass jar with a lid (with holes punched in it). Watch and try to identify the firefly's flash pattern. IMPORTANT: After a few minutes or so, release the firefly.

If your firefly stops flashing, you may need to collect a second one—fireflies flash in response to other flashes!

(⇧)(1)(🔍)(🧪)(🐞) Conduct the same research with a second firefly. Then compare the two insects' flash patterns—no two are alike!

(⇧)(1)(🔍)(🧪) Use the library or an online search to report about what makes fireflies glow.

○ (1)(🔍)(🧪) Visit the library or the Internet to define an insect's life stages: egg, larva or nymph, pupa, and adult.

⬆️ ② 🔍 ⚗️ 🌱 Cut a small piece of fruit and place it in a jar without a lid (at first). Once the fruit has attracted fruit flies, place the lid on the jar (poke holes in the lid and place a fine mesh covering between the jar and lid so the insects don't fly out through the holes). Watch as the fruit flies lay eggs, the eggs hatch, and tiny maggots devour their breakfast—all within two or three days! IMPORTANT: Release your maggots into the garden when they're done eating.

The maggots help the fruit decompose (or rot) by eating it

○ ② 🔍 ⚗️ 🌱 Find an old piece of tree bark, or a fallen log, on the ground. Lift it up and report about what you see. Can you count the insects there? Are there different kinds, or are they all the same? What did they do when you lifted the bark or log? IMPORTANT: Be gentle! Be kind! Respect our insect friends!

DID YOU KNOW?

Entomologists keep live insect friends close at hand so they're always ready to share some real-life entomology know-how.

⬆️ ② 🎨 🔍 ⚗️ Draw a picture of one of the insects you see (you'll have to bring a notepad and crayons, colored pencils, or markers with you to the field). At home, use a library book or the Internet to identify what *specimen** you found (you may know right away it's a beetle, but what *kind* of beetle?).

*A **specimen** is an individual insect.*

⬆️ ① 🔍 ⚗️ Use the library or an Internet search to define "scavengers" and "decomposers."

○ ② 🔍 ⚗️ Grab a flashlight and report about what kinds of insects you find after dark. (First look in a library book or on-line to identify which nocturnal *species*** are native to your area.)

***Species** are groups of living things similar to each other in every way.*

○ ③⊛⊛⊛⊛⊛ Build your own Berlese funnel—it's a great way to observe the wonderful creatures that call Earth's soil home. You'll find tons of easy instructions online (or try a library book). Make sure to use directions that allow you to release your captured bugs (versus save your captured bugs), and keep your lamp at a safe distance from your damp leaves.

Entomologist Wizzie graduated from Ohio State University with a bachelor of science degree in entomology, and from Texas A&M University with a master of science degree in entomology. She's been working with insects for more than sixteen years, doing such things as raising them, studying their biology, and teaching others what she's learned.

CAREER CROSSING

ENTOMOLOGISTS WORK WITH:

Communications Specialists

Farmers

Horticulturists*

Pest Management Professionals

Research Scientists

Environmental Planner

Y ou really, really, *really* wanted to build a tree fort in the really, really, *really* tall tree in your back yard. Dad even said it was OK. But then you both noticed a bird's nest, high in the branches. So the Environmental Planner in you picked a different tree—which made those baby birds really, really, *really* happy.

Jump In

o ① 🎭 🌐 🔍 Use the library or an Internet search to learn about the United States Environmental Protection Agency (EPA). List when it was founded, what its mission is, and one, two, or three of the issues it's working on. (P.S. The EPA is a fantastic resource for environmentally friendly activities.)

o ② 🖐 💡 🔍 🧪 Define the word "habitat," using a dictionary, library book, or online search. Then draw or create your favorite wild animal's habitat on paper with markers and crayons, or get crafty with an empty shoebox.

  🔝 ① 💡 🗨 Name a human project that could affect your animal friend (does he love marshy waters that would dry up if a dam was built?).

o ③ 🔤 ☀ 🗨 Shadow a local Environmental Planner—use the yellow pages or an Internet search to find one in your area. Mail or email a thank-you note afterward.

ENVIRONMENTAL PLANNERS:

- Assess the potential impact of human construction on the environment
- Advise government officials on how to protect natural resources while building and improving parks, roads, airports, dams, and buildings
- Encourage the public to look for alternatives that avoid or lessen environmental impacts.

SAYS CAROL SNEAD, ENVIRONMENTAL PLANNER,
HDR IN PORTLAND, OREGON

I love _uncovering a site's environmental issues._

My biggest on-the-job challenge is _helping people with different points of view agree on how a project should move forward._

The first time I convinced a company to change its plans, _we avoided harming a pristine wetland habitat._

My favorite green building technology is _green roofs—they capture rainwater to irrigate rooftop gardens!_

The easiest construction to make environmentally friendly is _parking lots._

If I weren't an Environmental Planner, I'd be a _Mystery Writer._

Assess Impacts

○ ① 💡 🔍 🐾 Take a tour of your home. As you walk through each room, note where your family could be more environmentally friendly (open the drapes to use more natural light? set out a recycling bin? install energy-efficient light bulbs?). Then put one, two, or three of your ideas into action.

○ ① 🔢 🔍 🐾 Place an empty container or drinking glass under a dripping faucet (it's OK to ask Mom or Dad to make the faucet drip, if you don't have one that leaks). Leave the faucet dripping for one hour, then use a ruler to measure how much water was wasted from those few little drips. (When you're done, use what you've collected to water a plant or fill the dog's water bowl—don't waste it!)

If you do have a faucet that leaks, get it fixed!!

⬆️ ① 🔢 🐾 Calculate how much water that leaky faucet would waste over one day. One week? One month? One year?

○ ① 💡 🔍 ⚗️ 🌍 Find some back-yard friends (like roly-poly bugs under a rock). Watch them for a bit (once they forget you're there and go back to their roly-poly business). In a minute or so, add a man-made item to their environment (a metal spoon? toy train?). Report on what happens. Do they scurry away? Try to move it? Ignore it? How would they get to food that's now trapped under the object? What would happen if the object is on top of where they sleep? IMPORTANT: Observe, don't disturb—no creature-squishing allowed! And remember to pick up your object when you're done.

> *Environmental Planner Carol* earned her master of science degree in geology from Rutgers University. Her first job twenty years ago was working with the public and government agencies to determine how a new highway would impact the environment. This got her thinking beyond rocks, and launched her into the world of environmental planning.

○ ② 🌐 🐞 🔍 🌍 Ask someone from an older generation about a construction project that happened in her hometown when she was little. Together, research the impact that project has had on the environment since. A Librarian may have access to historic aerial photographs. If not, try asking at a local historical society.

○ ② 💡 🔍 ⚗️ 🌍 Before dinner, turn a radio, iPod, or digital TV service to music your family enjoys, at a comfortable listening level. Halfway through dinner, turn the music louder for five minutes. Later, report about what occurred as a result of the noise (Dad had to yell to get the ketchup passed to him?). Then list one, two, or three possible long-term effects of this kind of noise pollution (Dad gets a sore throat?). Lastly, assuming the volume level can never be lowered, offer a solution (or two) that would reduce its

> WHY DOES ENVIRONMENTAL PLANNER CAROL THINK HER CAREER IS AWESOME?
>
> "I get people to consider what would be best for the environment when deciding what they want to do!"

impact on your family (put a pillow over the music source to make it softer?). Environmental Planners look for alternatives to lessen all sorts of impacts of developmental projects. Sound barriers, such as noise walls along a highway, are a great example.

⬆ ① 🔤 🐾 Post a report (handwritten or typed) in a visible place (the fridge door?) for public review.

Make Recommendations

○ ① 🔍 🐾 Use a library or Internet search to report about environmental sustainability (it sounds fancy, but it's really an amazing thing).

⬆ ② 💡 🔍 🐾 Walk, bike, or drive around town. List one, two, or three local examples of environmental sustainability.

⬆ ② 🎨 💡 🐾 Create an entirely sustainable community using markers, crayons, and paper. Draw *green buildings** and lots of bike paths. Think about where your community will get its water, energy, and food.

*✳ **Green buildings** conserve energy and water, reduce waste, and are built with sustainable materials.

○ ② 🔍 🐾 Start a [YOUR NAME HERE]'s Environmental Planning News and Trends folder. Cut out (and read) one, two, or three newspaper articles (or print out online articles) that cover environmental planning issues—a new building or bridge, or perhaps an existing structure that's causing environmental problems.

⬆ ③ 💡 ☀ 💬 Lead a discussion about one of the articles with your family. Assign one person (or team) to represent the *project proponent***.

*✳ **Project proponent** refers to the organization wanting to do the work.

Assign another person (or team) to represent the environmental interests. Give your participants time to read the article. Then allow each side to speak for one or two minutes, expressing their points of view on the project—for instance, why a new building should (or should not) be built. Ask them questions. Consider their answers. Then offer your Environmental Planner solution!

o ② Solve a developmental challenge: more people are moving to your town, which means more cars and the need for more roads. But more cars increases air pollution and new roads destroy more of the environment. Use markers, crayons, and paper or a computer program to create a brand-new way to move people around town.

① Identify the environmental impacts of developing your new solution. (So let's say you create a vehicle that doesn't need gas or roads. What resource would power it, and what would happen to the environment if you suddenly needed tons of that resource to run your vehicle?)

CAREER CROSSING

ENVIRONMENTAL PLANNERS WORK WITH:

Architects

Biologists

Transportation Engineers*

Urban Planners*

Water Quality Scientists

When do your Event Planner skills kick into high gear? Every year, about a month before your birthday celebration, when you list which friends you want with you, what you should do, where you should go, and (of course) what type of cake you'll be eating. All the details for THE BEST BIRTHDAY PARTY EVER—at least until next year!

Jump In

o ② ⊛ ⊛ Print out or draw pictures of one, two, or three events your family has planned (your first birthday party? your goldfish's first birthday party?). Then staple them together to create a portfolio (a book of your "work"). Event Planners use portfolios like these to show potential clients their experience and style.

o ② ⊛ ⊛ ⊛ Ask someone from an older generation: "Who held the Event Planner role at your wedding?" (It was most likely her!) Together, report about when and where it was, who was invited, what the bride and groom wore, and (if there was a reception) what song(s) got everyone dancing.

o ③ ⊛ ⊛ ⊛ Shadow an Event Planner. She may even take you on-site to meet with one of her clients! Afterward, mail or email a thank-you note.

EVENT PLANNERS:

- Plan events like parties, weddings, conferences, and new product launches
- Coordinate logistics (like location and entertainment)
- Oversee the work of vendors like Photographers, Caterers, and Musicians
- Develop party themes, including invitations
- Help during set-up, and stay until after the last guest leaves!

SAYS LIZ SECCURO, OWNER/CREATIVE DIRECTOR,
DOLCE PARTIES IN GREENWICH, CONNECTICUT

I love that moment when my clients relax and smile while greeting their guests.

My biggest on-the-job challenge is clients who change entire color schemes, menus, or themes three days prior to their parties!

The most memorable event I ever planned included a six-foot birthday cake and Beyoncé as entertainment.

I once saved the day by helping the caterers whip up more food for thirty unexpected guests.

The funniest thing I saw at one of my events was the groom ripping his pants trying to break-dance.

If I weren't an Event Planner, I'd be lost.

Coordinate Logistics

o (1)(💡) List two, three, or four location suggestions for [YOUR LAST NAME HERE] Game Night. Identify what makes each an ideal spot for the event.

(⬆)(1)(💡)(🔍) Visit one of your locations. Does it meet your expectations? Does it pose challenges? (For example, is the basement play room too far from the kitchen for snacks?) Can the challenge be addressed to make the spot more ideal?

Event Planner Liz graduated with a bachelor of arts degree in English literature from the University of Virginia. She's been in the event planning business for twenty years. During her first party-planning job, she was paid no money for three months until she proved she could do the work. It was a risk she's glad she took!

○ ① 💡 🖩 Create a guest list for a pretend party for sixteen, twenty-four, or thirty-two people (include friends, family, local heroes, book characters, even movie or sports celebrities). Then create a seating chart, with tables that fit eight people each. Group people by those who'd most enjoy each other's company.

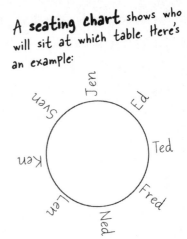

A **seating chart** shows who will sit at which table. Here's an example:

○ ① 💡 Create a menu for a tea party or backyard BBQ, listing the types of food appropriate for your event. Remember the drinks, too!

⬆① ② 🖩 $ Calculate how much your menu will cost for ten guests. First determine how much food you'll need, then find prices in the grocery store or online.

⬆① ② 🖩 $ Recalculate how much your menu will cost for fifteen people— this will require determining your price per person.

○ ② ☼ 🔍 Organize a dessert tasting (Event Planners love helping brides do this). Prepare two different healthy desserts (angel food cake with strawberries and low-fat whipped topping? bananas dipped in a bit of melted dark chocolate?). Then ask your bride (Mom? Big Sis? Dad in a wig?) to taste each and select a favorite. Serve the winner after a healthy dinner that night.

○ ② 🎨 💡 List one, two, or three *themes** for a birthday party, then use markers, crayons, and paper to design a table centerpiece that showcases one of your themes. So, a beach-themed party may have buckets filled with sand and seashells.

✳ A **theme** is what your event is all about, like a place, book, decade, or country.

⬆① ① 💡 🖩 $ Calculate the price to do your centerpiece in real life. For example, how much for a bucket? Sand? Seashells? Now imagine you have seven tables for people to sit at—calculate the cost of all seven centerpieces together. Can you save money, by, say, using sand from your sandbox?

⬆ ② 🎨 💡 Use items you find around your home to make your centerpiece—then display it on the kitchen table.

WHY DOES EVENT PLANNER LIZ THINK HER CAREER IS AWESOME?

"I get to help people celebrate the happiest moments in their lives!"

⬆ ② 🎨 💡 Make one, two, or three *favors** to go with the theme, using items you have on hand.

○ ② 🎨 💡 🔤 Design and create an invitation for a party celebrating an anniversary special to your family (when you moved into your home? adopted your family pet? finally cleaned out the garage?). Include the purpose of the event, who's hosting, where and when it will be, and how people can *RSVP***.

*Favors** are gifts hosts give out to their guests, like magnets, friendship bracelets, and Matchbox cars.

*RSVP** is French for *répondez s'il vous plaît*. It means, "Please respond."

⬆ ③ ☀ 💬 Host your party at dinner. Help prepare a favorite family meal and encourage everyone to share one happy memory about the anniversary.

Implement Plans

○ ② 💡 ☀ 🔍 ⏰ Arrange a [YOUR LAST NAME HERE] Movie Madness Night. Organize the time, date, snacks, and, yes, the movie (rented from the video store or borrowed from the library). Make sure to check your equipment before the evening: is your VCR or DVD player working properly? If not, get it fixed prior to your event.

○ ③ 🎨 💡 ☀ 🔍 🧪 🕐 ⏰ Host a *Be Nice to Nature at Night!* event. Pass out flyers with information about regional nocturnal animals and ways to keep them safe. Hand out flashlights for a nighttime neighborhood (or backyard) walk, and repurposed shopping bags for water and healthy snacks.

o ③ 💡 🌞 $ ⏱ Invite your family to a [YOUR FAVORITE SPORTS TEAM HERE] Day. Use your budget to go all-out, with tickets to a game, a plan to eat at a local eatery, and/or a tour of the stadium, field, or arena. Or host at home, with team-themed snacks and the game on TV. Most important in this task? Refreshments! Whether out or at home, make sure everyone's happy and fed.

DID YOU KNOW?

Event Planners drink lots of water and get lots of sleep (when they're not working). Why? They need to stay healthy to be at the events they plan!

SO YOU WANT TO...PLAN A SLUMBER PARTY

o ③ 🚲 💡 (abc) 🌞 🗓 $ 💬 🔍 ⏱ When's a good time to plan a sleepover? Any time!

1. Identify your slumber party's date, start time, budget, and theme (cooking? movies? summer in winter? winter in summer?).

2. Create a guest list, and invite your guests (make themed invitations, call, or invite them while at school).

3. Prepare and/or "hire" your entertainment (Mom's karaoke machine? Dad as Magician? dance music on your iPod? an All-Star Contest of who can hit a baseball farther or shoot more hoops?).

4. Establish your menu (including breakfast) and create a schedule of events (arrival time, meal time(s), entertainment time, etc.).

5. OPTIONAL: "Hire" a Photographer (ask Big Bro very, very nicely).

6. One day before your event, buy the food, confirm your entertainment, and make sure you know where your sleeping bag is!

7. The day of the event, prepare your food and clean your venue (your home).

8. At event time, welcome your guests with a big smile. Then use your Event Planner skills to keep your evening/morning running smoothly.

9. And most of all: enjoy!

CAREER CROSSING

EVENT PLANNERS WORK WITH:

Caterers

Entertainment Booking Agencies

Floral Designers

Photographers*

Stationery Designers

Geneticist

Just over the pond at the petting zoo was the most adorable sight: one… two…three…four ducklings, all in a row, walking right behind their mom. And as they waddled by you noticed something: Mom was pure white, but her offspring were grey. Your inner Geneticist was puzzled, until you saw Dad, and his grey body, waddle into sight, too!

Jump In

- ② Visit the library or a website to report about ecosystems (what are they? why are the interactions among the plants and animals important?). Then grab an empty shoebox to create your own replica of your choice of ecosystem (coral reef? meadow? rainforest?) using natural items you find in and around your home. (Rocks with holes? Ocean corals! Bits of grass? Mossy rainforest floor!) Try twigs, soil, even dead leaves.

GENETICISTS:

- Collect DNA from people, plants, and wildlife
- Analyze DNA in laboratories
- Uncover the best ways to protect the health and future of living things

- ③ Shadow a Geneticist. To find one, try calling the biology, ecology, or genetics department at a local university (or searching on the school's website). After your time together, mail or email a thank-you note—maybe even including a drawing of what you learned.

Study Genes

- ① Use the library or an online search to report about genes and genetic diversity.

Goldfish have more genes than humans!

SAYS FAITH M. WALKER, PHD,
DEPARTMENT OF BIOLOGICAL SCIENCES,
NORTHERN ARIZONA UNIVERSITY IN FLAGSTAFF, ARIZONA

I love _fieldwork, since I get to be in beautiful places._

My biggest on-the-job challenge is _keeping tarantulas out of my shoes when I spend the night at my overseas field sites._

I once followed a _father emu and his babies for miles in the remote Australian bush._

My favorite way to collect DNA samples is _from hair and feces (yes, poop!)._

The absolute coolest fact about genes is _they can tell stories._

If I weren't an Geneticist I'd be _a Paleontologist._

(↑)(2)(🔍)(⚗)(⏱) Visit the library or the Internet to list one, two, or three ways global warming affects plants, and how a plant's genes could change to help it adapt and survive.

(↑)(2)(🎨)(💡)(⚗) Use construction paper, markers, felt, yarn—whatever you can find—to bring your adapted species to "life."

○ (1)(💡)(🔍)(⚗) Taste the benefits of genetic diversity: buy three or four different kinds of apples (Gala? Golden Delicious? Granny Smith? Macintosh?), oranges (orange? tangerine? clementine?), or grapes (green? red? black?). Put on a blindfold, then taste each individually. Report about the differences between the varieties.

Geneticist Faith graduated with a bachelor's degree in biology from Northern Arizona University and a PhD in conservation genetics from Monash University in Victoria, Australia. She's studied animals all over the world, including De Brazza's monkeys in Africa, southern hairy-nosed wombats in Australia, and beavers in North America.

- ② 🧪 💡 🗒 🔍 ⚗ Find an insect or spider on a plant in your yard, a vegetable garden, or a nearby park. Draw or photograph your insect or spider, the plant's leaf, and the plant's stem. Also measure the plant's height. Afterward, use a library book or Internet search to uncover which features make that plant attractive to that insect or spider. (Was it an aphid that likes the sweet sap inside that tulip's stem? The aphid's love of that taste is genetic.)

- ② 💡 🔍 ⚗ Spend an evening outdoors, looking for one, two, or three animal parents and their young—insects count, too. (You may want to research beforehand, so you know which *nocturnal** animals live in your area.) List why you think each group of parent and offspring is related (look the same? sound the same?).

Nocturnal animals sleep during the day and are active at night.

- ③ 💡 🔍 ⚗ Visit a farm or petting zoo (call first to make sure at least one of the animals has babies you can observe). List one, two, or three similarities between the parent and offspring.

WHY DOES GENETICIST FAITH THINK HER CAREER IS AWESOME?

"I get to uncover secrets about animals and the web of life!"

Collect & Analyze DNA

- ① 💡 ⚗ 🐾 Describe how you could collect *DNA*** from one, two, or three animals in your yard or nearby

DNA is where organisms store information about themselves: what they look like, eat—everything!

park—without catching the animal. (For instance, snail DNA could be extracted from snail slime trails. What about birds? or snakes?) Many Geneticists work this way, collecting DNA in manners that do not disturb their subjects or their habitats.

- ⬆ ② 💡 🔍 ⚗ 🐾 Do it! (You may want to wear gloves and bring small jars or envelopes to collect your samples.) Then tape your samples to a piece of paper, labeling the animals from which they came.

○ ② ⚗ 💡 🔍 ⚗ Brush a dog with a grooming brush. Take a close look at the hair you collect—can you see a small, ball-like bit at one end of any of the hair strands? That's the follicle,

Beavers have tiny hair follicles. Wombats have big, fat ones. The bigger the follicle, the more DNA.

and it's where the DNA is stored. Tape the hair to a piece of paper and draw what you think dog DNA looks like.

○ ② ⚗ ⚗ Collect an animal footprint (Wildlife Geneticists get to look for all kinds of animal signs!). Look in your yard or a nearby park for animal tracks in muddy places. Pour plaster of Paris (you can get it at a craft or hardware store) into the track and leave to harden (follow the directions carefully and safely). When it's solid, use a spoon to help pull out your new footprint cast.

DID YOU KNOW?

Geneticists can help save endangered animals— studying animals' genes can reveal the best way to promote their survival.

Research DNA

○ ② ⚗ 💡 🔍 ⚗ Make a replica DNA molecule. First, look up samples in a library book or online. Then use yarn, glue, and paper for a 2-D version, or pipe cleaners for a 3-D version.

○ ③ 🔍 ⚗ Visit a local rose garden (they're often at botanical gardens or conservatories). Report about the number of varieties you see. Then choose two, three, or four for closer study, reporting about each specimen's color, number of blooms, and scent.

○ ③ ⚗ 🔍 ⚗ ⏱ Identify an outdoor flower, plant, fruit, or vegetable that grows in your yard or nearby park and in a yard or park located near the home of someone from an older generation (you can determine your common species over the phone). For three, four, or five days, you BOTH keep a log of the plant's activity at the same time(s), maybe 7:30 a.m., 3:00 p.m., and 7:30 p.m. Note how many insects are on the plant's leaves, how tall the plant is, how many leaves it has, and how long the leaves are. After your days are up, compare notes. How do your results vary because more than one Scientist conducted the research? How do the different locations affect the insect community in which the plant lives? And do you think genetics is responsible for any of the differences?

SO YOU WANT TO...LEARN ABOUT HUMAN GENES

o ②🖲🔍⚗️ Every living thing has DNA. So while some Geneticists study plants or wildlife, others study how genes and heredity work, human-style. You can too.

1. Make the batter for (1) chocolate-chip cookies and (2) M&M cookies.

2. Separate each batter in half. Bake one half of each batter as is. Mix the other halves together (to make chocolate-chip-M&M cookies), then bake those too.

IMPORTANT

Stay safe! Never use a stove, oven, or other kitchen appliance without an adult's supervision.

3. Examine four of your "mixed" cookies (wait until they're cool enough to touch!), and report about what you see. Do some have more chocolate chips than M&Ms? Do others have more M&Ms than chocolate chips?

4. Discuss the lesson learned: if Mom's genes are represented by the chocolate-chip cookies, and Dad's genes are represented by the M&M cookies, you're the tasty chocolate-chip-M&M cookie result! BUT despite having the same "parents," not every cookie has the exact same number of chocolate chips or M&Ms (just like how you are different from your siblings).

5. Dunk your cookie subjects in milk. Yum!

CAREER CROSSING

GENETICISTS WORK WITH:

Biologists

Botanists

Entomologists*

Ornithologists

Statisticians

I t's the one you spend all summer searching for—that perfect rock, round and smooth. Worn away by millions of years of rain and wind, you'll keep that rock in your pocket as a reminder of what all Geologists know: the best things in the world are found in the Earth!

Jump In

○ ① 🎭 🔍 ⚗️ Identify your state's mineral or rock (many states have them), then use a library book or online site to report why it's important to your state. If your state has not named an official mineral or rock, list one, two, or three reasons your favorite mineral or rock is a great candidate for the position.

○ ② 🎭 🎨 🔍 ⚗️ Visit the library or the Internet to research the *birthstone** of someone from an older generation and where it may be found. Create a report, complete with a colored-in drawing or printed-out photo of the stone, and present it to him.

* A **birthstone** is a stone that symbolizes a person's birth month.

○ ③ 🔤 ☀️ 💬 Shadow a Geologist. Whether she shows you around the laboratory or brings you on-site in the field, mail or email a thank-you note after your time together.

GEOLOGISTS:

- Study the Earth and objects in the solar system
- Work with rocks and minerals, soils, the atmosphere, deep earth, volcanoes, and glaciers
- Uncover how the Earth helps to support and provide for human activities

SAYS KARIN OLSON HOAL, RESEARCH PROFESSOR, DIRECTOR OF THE ADVANCED MINERALOGY RESEARCH CENTER, COLORADO SCHOOL OF MINES IN GOLDEN, COLORADO

I love _the travel, the people, and the work outside in extreme conditions._

My biggest on-the-job challenge is _(when I'm in the field) the bugs!_

The most amazing discovery I ever made _was a diamond in the Kalahari Desert._

The first time I saw a meteorite, I _was amazed that a rock from outer space was in my hand._

Crystals are most vibrant when _seen growing naturally, with other minerals, in the rough._

If I weren't a Geologist, I'd be _a Musician._

Study Earth's Materials

○ ① 🔍 ⚗️ Visit the library or the Internet to report about each of the Earth's four layers: crust, mantle, outer core, and inner core.

⬆️ ① ⚗️ Eat the Earth! Start with an apple. Its core is like the Earth's core, the flesh like the mantle, and the skin like the crust. Dip your Earth in caramel (oceans) and roll in crushed nuts or sprinkles (land or continents). If you'd like, make an extra to share.

Geologist Karin studied geology at St. Lawrence University in New York, McGill University in Montreal, and the University of Massachusetts. She worked at the University of Cape Town in South Africa, the New York Geological Survey, and in mining and research companies, before settling into her current position at Colorado School of Mines.

(⬆)(1)(⚗) Eat the Earth, version two. Hard boil an egg. When it's cooled, slice it down the middle. The yolk is the core, the white is the mantle, and the shell is the crust—look at how thin the crust is compared with the other layers.

o (1)(🔍)(⚗)(👐) Visit the library or Web to define "carbon footprint." Next, calculate your family's carbon footprint (you can find easy-to-use calculators online). Lastly, make one, two, or three household changes to lessen your family's environmental impact.

o (2)(🎨)(💡)(🔍)(⚗) Find examples of igneous rock, sedimentary rock, and metamorphic rock (use a library book or online search for definitions). If you can't find real-world examples in your neck of the woods, make some. Use construction paper, tissue paper, markers, felt—whatever you have on hand to create your "rocks."

> WHY DOES GEOLOGIST KARIN THINK HER CAREER IS AWESOME?
>
> "It's given me an exciting life, with travel to exotic places and the chance to meet some really wonderful people from around the world!"

o (2)(💡)(⚗)(👐) "Bake" a mud pie. Build it layer by layer, starting with some thick mud. Layer on some gravel. More mud. Sand. More mud. Dirt. More mud. Then use a wide straw to drill into it—what does your straw pull out? And what are you going to do with the earth in the straw? Geologists have to consider these details before mining for rocks!

o (2)(🔍)(⚗) Use the library or the Internet to define "quarry." Then visit one near you—it's pretty cool to see the different layers of rock, revealed.

o (2)(🔍)(⚗) Fill empty jars with samples of earth from two, three, or four different areas in your neighborhood. Describe the different colors of soil and/or types of rocks—different places have different minerals.

(⬆)(1)(🧩)(🔍)(⚗) Ask someone from an older generation who lives in a different neighborhood (or even state) to add a sample from her yard, or near her home, to your collection. If she's mailing her sample, make sure she puts it in a sealable bag.

⬆️ ① 🐾 Use the rocks to liven up a garden path.

○ ② 🔍 🧪 Collect a sample of your home's tap water in a clean jar (wash and dry one from a recycle bin) and bring it to your local municipal center to be tested for minerals. Or ask your local water supplier for a copy of your area's local water report—it may reveal the minerals and chemicals in it.

○ ② 💡 🔤 🔍 🧪 Create a poem, song, or story about one, two, or three of the elements most abundant in Earth's crust: oxygen, silicon, aluminum, iron, calcium, sodium. (Use the library or the Web to learn about each element first.) Why not write or sing about *every* element in Earth's crust? There are ninety in total!

○ ② 🔍 🧪 Grow your own crystals. Search in the library or online for how to try this at home (or pick up a kit at a craft store). Just note: all of them use salt.

⬆️ ② 🔍 🧪 Grow your own crystals again, but with a different kind of salt. (Used table salt last time? Try sea salt or Epsom salt.) Report about the differences in your crystals.

Study Earth's Processes

○ ① 🔍 🧪 Use the library or websites to report about two, three, or four of the following: earthquakes, landslides, soil erosion, volcanoes, glaciers. Also list why their study is important to Geologists.

○ ① 🔍 🧪 Report about the four types of volcano landforms: lava flows, volcanic peaks, calderas, and volcanic necks.

⬆️ ① 🎨 🖍️ Use markers, crayons, and paper to draw your favorite of the four types.

DID YOU KNOW?

Geologists can study everything in the universe—even people. We're made up of the same tiny bits that formed the Earth, came up through volcanoes, and are in the plants we eat!

(↑) (2) (🪨) (💡) (🧪) Create a 3-D version of your favorite type, using hints from a library book or Internet search.

○ (1) (🌐) (🔍) (🧪) Use the library or an Internet search to report about how diamonds come from really old volcanoes. Then research if any volcanoes have ever existed near where you live—if so, there could be diamonds in the area.

Study Earth's History

○ (2) (💡) (🌐) (🔍) (🧪) Find an "ancient rock" in your yard or a nearby park.

*Terrain refers to a ground's characteristics (like rocky, muddy, or grassy).

Take note of its surroundings—near a waterfall? Buried in a vegetable garden? Then use the library or the Internet to report about your region's *terrain* * millions of years ago. Can you determine what it looked like, and how it may have changed over the years to look like it does now?

○ (2) (💡) (🧪) Ask Mom or Dad to plant "microbes" or "bacteria" (honey? white craft glue? blueberry jam?) on a "Martian meteorite" they "found." Your job is to identify each substance on it using clues you can see, smell, and touch—multicolored? fruity? sticky? Once you've named all the substances, report about the life that exists on Mars (Martians survive on a mixture of honey and blueberry jam, and have boogers that resemble white craft glue!).

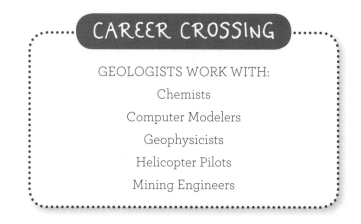

CAREER CROSSING

GEOLOGISTS WORK WITH:

Chemists

Computer Modelers

Geophysicists

Helicopter Pilots

Mining Engineers

Guest Relations Manager

Someone's coming to visit! You wash the sheets for the bed, make space for clothes in the closet, prepare a special meal, maybe set out flowers—even the tiniest touches can make a guest feel welcome. And if you enjoy being a Guest Relations Manager at home, imagine doing it for hundreds of guests, every day!

Jump In

- ① 🌐 🍒 🔍 Ask someone from an older generation to relive a favorite hotel experience—how old was she? Where did she stay? Who was she with?

- ③ 🔍 Visit a local hotel. Bring a little snack and spend some time sitting in the lobby—report on what you see as guests come and go. Do they check in at the front desk? Grab food from the vending machine? Ask the *Concierge** for assistance? Guest Relations Managers are very aware of their guests' comings and goings.

- ③ 🔤 ☼ 🗨 Shadow a Guest Relations Manager. Make sure to *dress professionally*** and use good manners—you are representing his hotel! Mail or email a thank-you note after your time together.

GUEST RELATIONS MANAGERS:

- Take care of hotel guests
- Manage hotel staff
- Create loyalty programs to promote repeat business
- Provide VIP tours of the property

*The **Concierge** helps guests with things like sightseeing tours and dinner reservations.

Dressing professionally means nice pants or a dress. No t-shirts, shorts, or flip-flops.

says Jeffrey L. Mayer, Guest Relations Manager, The Hotel Hershey, Hershey Entertainment and Resorts in Hershey, Pennsylvania

I love _when a guest's happy face says our team has gone above and beyond._

My biggest on-the-job challenge is _working with a guest who did not enjoy the experience._

The most bizarre request I've granted is _putting a bedrail down the middle of a king-sized bed to separate a couple._

My most favorite guests ever _celebrated their 100th visit during Hershey Park's 100th anniversary._

On my pillow I like _a fresh scent._

If I weren't a Guest Relations Manager, I'd be _golfing._

Take Care of Guests

o ① 💡☀ Ask Mom or Dad to act as a guest at your hotel—an unhappy one. (Most uncomfortable bed ever? Unstocked mini bar? No hot water in the shower?) Offer one, two, or three ways to handle his issue. Remember to be polite.

o ② 💡☀ Welcome Mom or Dad home from work, or a sibling home from school. Invite her in with a light snack and beverage. Offer to take her bags into her room. Suggest she relaxes for a moment before dinner is served.

WHY DOES GUEST RELATIONS MANAGER JEFFREY THINK HIS CAREER IS AWESOME?

"I get to meet new people all the time and build meaningful relationships. And when I learn each guest's preferences, I can deliver exceptional service!"

○ ② 💡 Create a hotel guest loyalty program (and not just for overnight guests). Encourage repeat visits with perks like first priority for sitting in the comfy chair, extra time with your newest toy, and/or the largest piece of dessert.

☝ ② 🤝 💡 Name your loyalty program anything you want (say, Hotel [YOUR LAST NAME HERE]'s Loyalty List Program?) and use crayons, markers, and construction paper to make loyalty cards—little cards with your program's perks written on them. Pass them out to guests to entice them to visit often.

> *Guest Relations Manager Jeffrey* started at The Hotel Hershey as a Bellman, and over the past twelve years, has been a Valet Attendant, Driver, Front Office Supervisor, and Assistant Front Office Manager before being promoted to Guest Relations Manager. Always excited to learn more about his industry, he's recently accepted the Assistant Food and Beverage Manager position. He has also earned several professional certifications from the American Hotel & Lodging Association.

○ ② 🤝 💡 ☀ Say good-bye to a guest with a departing gift. Print out a picture of you and your guest and frame it. Or make a card that describes one of your favorite memories of the time you spent together.

Oversee Staff

○ ① 💡 ☀ Monitor *staffing** levels to maximize service. Could Mom use an extra hand making dinner? Would Dad's yard work be done faster if you helped? Identify one, two, or three areas of improvement, then pitch in.

Staffing refers to a group of employees.

○ ① ☀ Establish a positive environment of respect and appreciation by recognizing outstanding performance two, three, or four times. Thank Dad (restaurant Chef) for a delicious meal. Applaud Mom for her quick *valet***

Valet is pronounced vaa-lay.

service (clean laundry). Commend your sister for her energizing recreation program (chasing her through the living room).

Manage Venues

o ① (💡)(☀)(🕐) Respond (politely) to one, two, or three issues in a timely manner. Perhaps Mom notices the lights were left on in the bathroom. Maybe Dad saw your skateboard at the foot of the stairs (so not safe!). Hear the issue, then act fast—Guest Relations Managers keep their venues in tip-top shape.

o ② (💡)(☀) Uphold the *diamond standard** for your room for three, four, or five days. Keep your bed made, your clothes off the floor, and your toys where they belong. Welcome guests into your room with a smile and offer an activity you are willing to share.

*The "diamond standard" means sparking clean and spotless—everything in its place.

(⬆)① (☀)(🕐) Expect a random room inspection to happen at any time.

o ② (💡)(🕐) Supervise product delivery. First make a list of items in need of re-stocking in one, two, or three rooms in your home. (Do the bedrooms need clean sheets? Do the bathrooms need fresh towels? Does the kitchen have food for dinner?) Schedule a delivery of these items; then check them off as they arrive.

DID YOU KNOW?

Guest Relations Managers build relationships with guests to learn about birthdays, anniversaries, special events—then they treat these guests to surprises like room upgrades!

o ② (💡) Perform an inspection of the entry to your home. Is it tidy? Organized? Welcoming? Make any corrections, then inspect this area every day for three, four, or five days.

- ② 🕐 Incorporate a green initiative for handling waste. Designate a trash can for cans and bottles, then deliver it to a local recycling collection site or (if your county participates) leave it on the curb for recycling day pick-up.

SO YOU WANT TO...MAKE A GUEST FEEL WELCOME

- ③ 🚫 💡 🔤 ☀ 😊 ⏰ Got a *VIP** coming to visit? Welcome them hotel-style!

  VIPs are Very Important People. These are often repeat or important guests.

  1. Call your guest a day in advance to ask if there's anything she'll need (her favorite cereal? the latest issue of her favorite magazine? an extra roll of toilet paper?).

  2. Place a handmade card on a dresser, letting your guest know you are available to answer any of her questions or offer suggestions for what to see while she's in town.

  3. Place a handmade card on her bed, advising your guest of your spa treatments (a loofah in the shower), continental breakfast (toast and juice), and turndown service (a wrapped mint or chocolate left on her pillow before bedtime).

  4. Be at the front door when your guest arrives, with a, "Hello! How was your trip?" And, of course, a big hug!

  5. Start your guest's morning with a memo about the day's weather (check the newspaper, a news station on TV, or the Internet) and interesting things going on about town.

  6. OPTIONAL: Provide a Feedback card on the day of your guest's departure (photocopy the one on page 353, download it at EarnMyKeep.com, or create your own). This is your guest's opportunity to let you know what she enjoyed during her stay.

  7. Wish your guest a happy, safe trip home!

CAREER CROSSING

GUEST RELATIONS MANAGERS WORK WITH:

Administrative Assistants

Front Office Managers

Guest Services Managers

Managers on Duty

Sales Representatives

Horticulturist

In the spring, you help plant flowers. In the summer, you help pull weeds. In the fall, it's all about raking leaves (or not, if you live down South). And in the winter, Mother Nature pretty much takes over and you get a well-deserved break from being a Horticulturist. For most of the year, it's a dirty job. But you sure love being the one to do it!

Jump In

○ ① 💡 Liven up your home with flowers. Whether you pick some from your garden outside, choose a bouquet from a local grocery store, or order some from a local florist or nursery, select flowers that complement a room of your choice by color or style or season.

⬆ ① ⏱ Document the *accession** of your new plants: write down the time they arrived and where you placed them in your home.

○ ① 🔍 🧪 Identify three types of plants in your yard (yes, grass counts). If you don't have a yard, visit a nearby park.

⬆ ② 🎨 💡 Label the three plants. You can use store-bought labels or make some by attaching a piece of card stock to tree sticks (laminate the card stock after writing the name of the plant, so the ink doesn't run in the rain). Or use a permanent marker or paint to mark the plants' names on smooth rocks.

HORTICULTURISTS:

- Grow plants, including edible fruits and veggies, and ornamental trees and shrubs
- Keep the plants under their care healthy
- Design gardens

* **Accession** refers to the records used to keep track of a garden's plants.

SAYS SCOTT BRAWNER, HORTICULTURIST, ALASKA BOTANICAL GARDEN IN ANCHORAGE, ALASKA

I love working in the soil, getting dirty, outside, every day.

My biggest on-the-job challenge is mosquitoes (though they do pollinate a few native orchids).

If I were a plant, I'd be a Sitka Spruce tree—they live for hundreds of years, providing food and homes for animals.

My favorite tool is my pruning shears.

The most unexpected pests to my garden are black bears—I once had to stop a cub that wanted to play with a school group!

If I weren't a Horticulturist, I'd be a Vegetable Farmer.

⬆①💡🌱 Beautify one of the plants—could it use some *pruning**? A bit more water to liven it up?

⬆①🔍⚗️ Visit the library or the Internet to report about one of the plants: is it an *annual***? A *perennial****? How big does it get? Does it prefer sun, shade, or both? Does it flower?

o ③🔍 Visit a local botanical garden—and don't let bad weather stop you (just make sure to dress appropriately). List one, two, or three flowers or plants you particularly like, and why.

o ③🔤☀️💬 Shadow a Horticulturist. To find one, try calling a nursery, botanical garden, or the horticulture or agriculture department at a local university. After your time together, mail or email a thank-you note.

* **Pruning** means to cut back a plant's or flower's extra growth.

** **Annuals** are plants and flowers that survive for only one year.

*** **Perennials** are plants and flowers that survive more than two years.

Study Plants

○ ① 🔍 ⚗️ Use the library or the Internet to list one, two, or three facts about photosynthesis—the way plants make food.

⬆️ ① ⚗️ Grab a leaf (only one!) from an outside tree. Check out the veins that run through it—they work just like the veins that run through your body.

⬆️ ② 💡 🔍 ⚗️ 🕐 For three days, keep one of your houseplants in a dark closet (remember to water it!). Then move the plant to a sunny window for three days. Report what differences you see. Why is it important for Horticulturists to think about sunlight when planning their gardens?

○ ① 💡 Define a brand-new kind of plant (like a raspberry bush with non-squishable raspberries?). Horticulturists who work in the field of *commercial agriculture** develop plants that produce more crops, are easier to *harvest***, or store better for longer than the originals.

⬆️ ① 💡 List a pest that could damage your new plant breed, and what you would you do to stop it. For example, non-squishable raspberries would

Horticulturist Scott graduated with a bachelor of science degree in horticulture from Northwest Missouri State University and a master of science degree in horticulture from the University of Missouri. Over the course of his career, he's done landscaping, conducted plant research, and worked in a botanical garden. But his love for plants began much earlier—when he tended to them on his childhood farm!

WHY DOES HORTICULTURIST SCOTT THINK HIS CAREER IS AWESOME?

"I get to work outside every day, helping to make the world a beautiful place!"

*Commercial agriculture refers to the production of crops intended for sale.

**In horticulture, harvest means to collect a plant's seed, leaves, or stem.

be attractive to squirrels, which hold their food in their hands. So maybe your new raspberries grow with a scent that's icky to squirrels, but undetectable by humans.

(↑)(2)(⚘)(💡) Make your plant using crayons, markers, construction paper, pipe cleaners, feathers—whatever you want!

Protect Plants

o (1)(🔍)(👓) Use the library or the Internet to list one, two, or three endangered plants in your area.

(↑)(2)(👓) Visit one. While Conservationists work hard to protect these *species**, this may be your opportunity to see this plant before it's extinct.

o (1)(🔍)(👓) Research the benefits of slow-release irrigation (like "drip irrigation"), and why Horticulturists would use it for their plants.

Species are groups of living things related to each other.

(↑)(2)(⚗)(👓) Create your own slow-release irrigation system for a plant in your home. Find an empty plastic water or juice bottle. Cut off the bottom, then push the bottle, mouth first, into your plant's soil. Fill the exposed end of the bottle with water. Your plant will soak up only what it needs, as it needs it.

DID YOU KNOW?

Some Horticulturists work with zoos—they're in charge of making sure the grass there is safe for the animals to eat!

o (1)(🔍)(⚗) Use a library or Internet search to list one, two, or three benefits of *native plants***.

Native plants occur, develop, or exist naturally in an area.

(↑)(3)(⚘)(🔍) Research native plants that grow in the area where someone from an older generation grew up. Ask if she remembers seeing these plants when she was a kid. If you live in or near the area, visit these plants together.

Maintain Facilities

○ ① 💡 Organize your horticulture tools. Do you have an area in your home where you store the tools you use to plant? If not, grab a box, tub, or bucket and put them all together, in one place.

⬆① 🔍 Take note if something is missing from your set, like a pair of cutters or gardening gloves. Report what you find to your Executive Director (Mom or Dad), and discuss if it's the right time to purchase new ones.

○ ① ☼ Create a safe working environment. Are your rakes off the floor? Are pruning scissors properly closed? Is fertilizer in sealed bags away from pets and children?

CAREER CROSSING

HORTICULTURISTS WORK WITH:

Arborists

Contractors*

Fish and Wildlife Experts

Irrigation Specialists

Landscapers

Human Resources Manager

ittle Sis learned yoga's Downward Dog pose—you offered a (very loud!) congrats. Dad had a not-so-great day at work—you gave a (very big!) hug. Mom turned another year older—you sang a (very off-key!) "Happy Birthday." If your family were a company, you'd be the perfect Human Resources Manager, taking great care of all your employees!

Jump In

○ ③ ⓐⓑⓒ ☼ ⌣ Shadow a Human Resources Manager. Almost every business has someone who represents human resources. After spending time together, mail or email a thank-you note.

✳ Recruitment ads are advertisements for open job positions.

Hire Employees

○ ① ⓥ ⓐⓑⓒ Create a *recruitment ad*✳ for a new hire for your family. List the kind of responsibilities this new employee would have (taking out the garbage? buying birthday presents for your friends' parties? making after-school snacks?). Also list how much the job pays and if your employee gets any paid vacation time.

⇧ ① ✎ ⟲ Report on why it's illegal for Human Resources Managers to dictate gender, race, or religious preference in their ads.

⇧ ① ⓐⓑⓒ ☼ Recruit! Ask Mom or Dad to interview for the position.

HUMAN RESOURCES MANAGERS:

- Assist employees with ID cards and payroll
- Ensure all employees come to work
- Hire and fire employees (hiring is more fun!)
- Counsel and discipline employees for misbehavior
- Plan employee events, like holiday parties

SAYS CHRISTINA LEATHERS,
COMPENSATION AND BENEFITS MANAGER,
MGM GRAND HOTEL AND CASINO IN LAS VEGAS, NEVADA

I love learning about the culture and language of employees from around the world.

My biggest on-the-job challenge is terminating an employee with whom I've developed a relationship.

My first hire was a Receptionist.

The most unusual request I ever granted was allowing an employee to pick up their end-of-the-year holiday gift in July!

My favorite team-building exercise is a potluck because everyone enjoys food.

If I weren't a Human Resources Manager, I'd be an Accountant.

Ask questions about her background (experience), qualifications (skills), and strengths (why she thinks she's good for the job).

○ ③ 💡 🔤 ☼ Train a new hire (Dad?). Create and deliver a presentation about being an "employee" of your family. First, talk about your family history: when you started (Mom and Dad's anniversary?) and where you're headquartered (your address). Next, introduce the team: Mom? (upper management), Big Sis? (middle management), Ike the Iguana? (staff). Then review the new hire's responsibilities (delivering phone messages? watering the garden?). Finally, welcome your new employee with a big hug.

Support Employees

○ ① 💡 ☼ Smile, smile, smile. Ask Mom or Dad to be a disgruntled employee. What is his complaint? (Too few vacation days? Inconsiderate supervisor? Didn't get the promotion he felt he deserved?) Be a good listener and offer a solution.

○ ② ☼ Keep a secret. Confidentiality builds trust between Human Resources Managers and the employees in their care. Ask Mom to tell you a secret she'd like you to keep from another member of the family. Can you keep it for one, two, or three days? What's important is that other family members not know there's a secret being kept. After the time limit, you're free to share the news.

○ ② 💡 ☼ Acknowledge family members' "jobs well done" for two, three, or four days in a row. Leave a "You're fabulous for finishing French!" note for Big Bro when he completes a particularly difficult assignment. Then let Little Sis know that her extra fifteen minutes of violin practice provided an extra fifteen minutes of listening enjoyment for the whole family.

○ ③ 💡 🐛 🔍 Create a wellness program to strengthen an employee (someone from an older generation) in three key areas: mind, body, and spirit. For example, use the library or an Internet search to create a booklist on subjects of interest to your employee—this strengthens the mind. Provide a recipe for a healthy dinner—this helps keep the body fit. And recommend a stress-relieving hobby, such as knitting or bird-watching—this helps the spirit relax and rejuvenate.

Human Resources Manager Christina has attended Washington State University, as well as several other schools, in pursuit of her bachelor of arts degree in business management (she's taken time off in-between to become a Mom). She's been a Human Resources Manager for five years and is also a member of the Society of Human Resources Management.

👆 ② 💡 🐛 🔤 Enroll your employee. Explain your wellness program and answer any questions she may have. Then fill out paperwork together to make it official. (A photocopy-able enrollment form is on page 354. You can also download it at EarnMyKeep.com.)

○ ③ 💡 😊 Offer an employee (Mom? Dad? Big Sis?) a symbol of your appreciation of his generosity (a hug? a night of "no whining" at bedtime? the last fruit pop?) for completing an act of social consciousness (such as volunteering at a local hospital, library, or nonprofit). Join your employee when he volunteers!

○ ③ 💡 ☀ Promote teamwork. Choose a family-sized job and help Mom or Dad dole out responsibilities. Be prepared to break up the work with pick-me-ups like fun music or a silly, stress-relieving game, like Tag or Duck, Duck, Goose. And congratulate everyone when the job is done, crediting your team members for the contributions they made.

Promote Productivity

○ ① 🔍 Research a new process that benefits your company (your "company" being your family). Use a parenting magazine or the Internet to find a new way to spark conversation at dinner. Or be less rushed on school mornings. Or pass time on long car drives (no more sibling squabbles!).

⬆ ② ☀ 🔍 Give the new process a try.

○ ② 💡 ☀ ⏱ Find two, three, or four ways to help your family members, even when it's not your job to do so. Big Sis is running late for school and doesn't have time to make her bed, but you have a few minutes to spare? Make it for her. Mom needs to get dinner on the table but remembered she has a PTA meeting? Serve everyone sandwiches. Human Resources Managers generously pick up the slack when needed, even when the task is not their responsibility.

DID YOU KNOW?

Human Resources Managers know more about the ins and outs of every area in their company than anyone else working there!

> WHY DOES HUMAN RESOURCES MANAGER CHRISTINA THINK HER JOB IS AWESOME?
>
> "I get the unique opportunity to interact with the majority of my employees on any given day!"

○ ③ 💡 ☼ 💬 Build key relationships with one, two, or three professionals around town. Human Resources Managers know being respectful and kind to professionals in all fields can benefit their company. For example, being nice to the waitress at your local restaurant, and asking very politely, may get your "company" (your family) an extra dessert, for free. (Try not to be discouraged if this doesn't work—Human Resources Managers are *professional**, regardless of outcome.)

*Acting **professionally** means no whining or crying. Remain courteous with a smile.

CAREER CROSSING

HUMAN RESOURCES MANAGERS WORK WITH:

Communications Writers

Employee Relations Specialists

Employee Services Representatives

Event Planners*

Receptionists

Ahh, the family room. You've got the couch and TV just where you like them—far enough apart for movies, close enough for video games. You've got that little side table in the right spot for drinks and snacks. And your rug of choice is perfectly soft for a sleepover. Now imagine using those Interior Designer skills on the rest of your home!

Jump In

○ ③ 💡 🔍 Visit a local showroom (try a furniture store or the furniture section of a department store)—as an Interior Designer. Report about the displays: is there common use of furniture groupings (sofas, chairs, rugs, and lamps)? Are colors used in unique ways? Which display do you like best?

○ ③ (abc) ☼ 💬 Shadow an Interior Designer. Try asking one who works for herself as a freelancer or is the owner of her own company. Mail or email a thank-you note afterward.

Interior Designers:

- Create floor plans for rooms (where the furniture will go)
- Choose fabrics (like bedding), colors (like for paint), and accessories (like lamps)
- Ensure rooms have form (a style that appeals to the room's owner) and function (a style that makes using the room easy and fun)

Plan Spaces

○ ① 💡 ▦ 🔍 Move every article of furniture in one room three inches. Think anyone will notice? Is the dining room table blocking the kitchen entrance? Or is your alarm clock now unreachable from your bed? Interior Designers know the right placement of furniture is everything for comfortable living.

says Tammy Westgerdes, owner, TJ West Designs, LLC, in Indianapolis, Indiana

I love *helping clients create environments that are beautiful and functional.*

My biggest on-the-job challenge is *all the paperwork, including all the receipts!*

The first room I designed *was my childhood bedroom (plum and navy paisley).*

My favorite piece of furniture is *my grandmother's sofa (since reupholstered).*

A well-decorated space brings *peace and harmony to a home.*

If I weren't an Interior Designer, I'd be *...I don't know—I can't imagine doing anything else!*

○ ① Start a file, folder, or envelope of pictures of furniture cut from home furnishing magazines—pieces of furniture that'd look great in a room in your home.

② Use information from magazines or the stores' websites to add up how much your new room costs. Then try to beat that budget by finding online sales, coupons, or even similar pieces of furniture that are less expensive.

○ ② Use graph paper to plan furniture placement for a room in your home. First look in home furnishing catalogues or websites to find furniture you like. (Doing a den? You'll need a couch, an end table, and an entertainment

WHY DOES INTERIOR DESIGNER TAMMY THINK HER CAREER IS AWESOME?

"Nothing is better than when clients tell me they can't wait to get home from vacation because they miss their homes!"

center.) Then, on your graph paper, mark the *perimeter** of the room—one box equals one foot (note closets, doors, and windows, too). Now draw where the furniture would go (use a pencil). If the pieces don't fit, "rearrange" (erase and re-draw) until they do.

(↑)(1)(🎨)(💡) Draw *furniture templates*** on heavy paper (like poster board or even con-struction paper), cut them out, and use them over and over until you get just the right lay-out. This is how real Interior Designers avoid all that drawing and erasing!

Perimeter is the measurement of the borders of an object (like a room!).

Furniture templates are the outline of the space furniture would take up (like a rectangle for a couch, or square for a chair).

Develop Designs

○ (1)(🎨)(💡)(🔍) Find a patterned fabric you like (is it on a sheet? a blanket? a curtain?). Then look in magazines for a couch, a chair, a rug,

Interior Designer Tammy graduated with a bachelor of science degree from Ball State University. She's owned her company for six years, and it all started when her first client (who had originally hired her for ideas on fabrics, flooring, and colors) asked her to redo the entire home (including custom-designed dog beds). The project was even photo-graphed for a magazine!

and a throw pillow—all in the same color family as your fabric. Cut out and glue (or tape) the pictures onto a piece of paper to create a room that coordi-nates with the patterned fabric you like.

○ (2)(🎨)(💡) Turn your bedroom into a theme restaurant. First, take note of what you've got (bed? dresser? desk?). Think about how they could be repur-posed. (Is it an under-the-sea seafood restaurant? Your bed could be a table shaped like a boat!) Then use construction paper, markers, tissue paper, yarn—whatever's on hand—to bring your restaurant to life on paper.

① ② ⚓ 💡 Try it for another room: turn your kitchen into an art studio, the garage into a concert arena, or a bathroom into an airport terminal!

○ ② ⚓ 💡 Pick a room in your home that could really use some design help, then draw an updated version. For example: Mom and Dad's bathroom is covered in outdated wallpaper. So you draw a picture of how the space could look with polka-dots painted on the walls.

○ ② ⚓ 💡 🎭 Use recycled materials to create more space in an area that needs it. Is the laundry room piled with a mess of dirty

Make sure the materials you use are totally clean, so you don't attract bugs.

and clean clothes, empty detergent bottles, and old wire hangers? Turn empty, clean cardboard boxes (like from a buy-in-bulk store) and tubs (like butter containers) into great places to store big and little items not in use. And/or use brown bags from the grocery store for extra hangers. You can even decorate your "new" storage containers with paint and markers.

○ ② ⚓ 💡 🎭 🌐 🎨 Ask someone from an older generation to describe her childhood bedroom. Does she remember what her bedspread looked like? What dolls she had? Did she share a room with a sibling? Use crayons, markers, maybe pieces of fabric and glue to re-create it for her on paper.

Implement Designs

○ ① ⚓ 💡 🎭 Repurpose a piece of furniture or accessory. Would that little side table no one notices in the back bedroom be a great place for keys and mail by the front door? Would the rug in the hallway jazz up the kitchen? Interior Designers help people use items they already have in new ways—this saves money and gives new life to things that may otherwise end up in landfills.

DID YOU KNOW?

Home designs need to be fresh and exciting for years (who buys a new sofa every month?!). Which means Interior Designers aren't afraid to stay ahead of trends!

○ ① ⊛ Use the library or an Internet search to report about ergonomic design. List one, two, or three of its benefits (who knew the right chair could make you feel better?).

⬆ ① ⊛ Incorporate one example of ergonomic design into your home.

○ ② ⊛ ⊛ Design a space for a pet (real or imaginary). First think about what your pet needs for a comfy and functional environment (could your parakeet use a swing as well as a more decorative cage liner?). Then check out what you've got at home, or stop by a local pet store, to gather what you need to create a warm, welcoming space any pet would be proud to call home.

○ ② ⊛ ⊛ Decorate a room in a dollhouse or action figure playhouse. Use toy furniture, make-your-own furniture, hand-made wall art, cotton ball pillows—whatever you want to give the room a new look.

○ ③ ⊛ ⊛ Redesign your bedroom. First (yes, it's true) you need to clean it up. Next pick your theme—go with something you already have a lot of, like sports memorabilia, dolls, or cars and trucks. Then decorate, using these items in places where visitors can easily see your interests. (Line the baseballs up on a windowsill? Cover one wall with posters of trucks?)

⬆ ③ ⊛ ⊛ ⊛ ⊛ Research a new style (like art deco, eclectic, or minimalist). Then design your room to reflect it.

○ ③ ⊛ ⊞ $ ⊛ ⊛ Add some spice to a room with a flea market or consignment shop find. Flea markets and consignment shops are great places for unique, inexpensive and/or secondhand goods. (Or try a nonprofit organization that sells used furniture, like Goodwill—the money you spend helps others.) Set a small budget (say, $5), and see what goodies you can bring home.

CAREER CROSSING

INTERIOR DESIGNERS WORK WITH:

Cabinet Makers

Flooring Representatives

Furniture Wholesalers

House Painters

Lighting Specialists

As soon as your teacher introduced the new kid in class, you wanted to make her feel welcome. You noticed her shirt featured your favorite team (she may like hockey!) and her backpack sported a guitar sticker (she may play music!). So you got right to making a new friend, who was happy to confirm your Investigator skills were spot-on!

INVESTIGATORS:

- Solve crimes by uncovering what criminals are doing
- Recover stolen items and return them to their rightful owners
- Find evidence to determine who's at fault in an accident
- Locate people who are lost or missing

Jump In

○ ① 🎭 🌐 🔍 Visit the library or the Internet to report about the Federal Bureau of Investigation (FBI). When did it start? What is its main purpose? How many people work for it?

⬆ ② 🎨 🌐 🔍 Make an FBI badge using construction paper, markers, tape (or glue), and a safety pin. Since 1908 there have been four official badges—look in a library book or online to copy your favorite.

○ ② 💡 📖 Read a book about a classic kid-sized Investigator: Nancy Drew, Encyclopedia Brown, or Scooby-Doo. List what skills the Investigator used (such as listening, deductive reasoning, patience, communication, self-defense), and the big break that helped solve the case.

⬆ ③ 💡 🔤 📖 Write the next installment in the series—what mystery does your Investigator solve next?

○ ③ 🔤 ☀ 💬 Shadow an Investigator. He may give you a tour of his office or show you the tools he uses to solve cases, like covert cameras or computer programs! After your time together, mail or email a thank-you note.

says al cavasin, great northern sentry company
in jackson, michigan

I love _helping people solve their own problems._

My biggest on-the-job challenge is _sitting in a cold vehicle for ten or twelve hours, just to capture fifteen seconds of video._

Solving a case _once took me seven years._

The most valuable skill an Investigator has is _an ability to listen and learn from other people._

I once went undercover as _a dishonest, wealthy businessman. I wore a $1,000 suit, fake tattoo, and fake earring attached with a magnet (no way I was piercing my ear!)._

If I weren't an Investigator, I'd be _a United States Senator._

Protect Citizens

- ① 💡 List one, two, or three ways to protect the following: a bike, the trunk of Mom's car, a pet, or your Earn My Keep earnings.

- ② 💡🔍 Set up the following security measure to protect your bedroom: tape one end of a 12″ piece of thread to the inside door molding next to your door handle. From the outside, close the door slowly, draping the other end of the thread over the doorknob on the inside of your bedroom. Later, when you come back to your room, open the door slowly (just a little bit). If you can't see the thread still going over the doorknob, someone's been in your room.

WHY DOES INVESTIGATOR AL THINK HIS CAREER IS AWESOME?

"I get to use skills I've developed over a lifetime to help people solve their security problems. I really enjoy what I do, and thoroughly love the people with whom I work!"

(↑)(2)(💡)(🔍) Fold a bookmark or business card gently in half so it's springy (don't make a hard crease). Close your bedroom door, putting the card between the doorjamb and the door, about 6″ off the floor. Later, when you come back to your room, look for the paper to fall when you open the door—if it's already on the floor, someone's beaten you to it!

(↑)(2)(💡)(🔍) Dust a tiny bit of baby powder on your doorknob. If someone opens the door, the powder will rub off onto her clothes and you'll be able to identify your culprit.

○ (2)(🐾) Designate yourself the [YOUR LAST NAME] Family Security Officer for three, four, or five days. Make a list of all the windows and doors in your home (including the garage, if you have one). Every evening, check to be sure each is closed and locked, marking it off on your list. Then report "All secure" to Mom or Dad before getting your goodnight kiss.

(↑)(2)(🐾)(💡) Make yourself a [YOUR LAST NAME] Family Security Officer badge with paper, markers, glitter glue—whatever you want!

Investigator Al has always been responsible for investigations and security in every job he's held—starting at the age of fourteen, when he hid in the dusty basement of a meat market to try to catch a thief (he didn't, but he did find out how the criminal was getting into the store). In the forty-seven years since, he's managed two other investigations/security firms, and founded and owns Great Northern Sentry Company.

○ (3)(💬)(🔍)(🐾) Start a Neighborhood Watch program. For inspiration, look in a library book or online. This is not only a great way to promote neighborhood safety, but to become better acquainted with your neighbors.

Investigate Crimes

○ ① 💡 Ask a family member (Big Sis?) to quickly walk through a room you're in, wearing five, six, or seven distinguishing "features" that are different from her regular appearance (only one earring? a dot of mascara on her forehead? cuffed jeans?). Your task is to remember, and report back, two, three, or four of those features. Investigators use tiny details like these to help them solve cases.

⬆① 🎨 💡 Draw a picture of what you remember Big Sis looking like. Then call her back into the room—how many features did you get right?

○ ① 🔍 Learn to tell if a source is not being truthful. Visit the library or the Internet to list two, three, or four ways body language can reveal if someone is lying.

⬆② 💡 🎨 ☀ 🔍 Put your knowledge to the test with someone from an older generation. So, say Grandpa says he took out the trash, but Grandma says he didn't. Sit across a table from Grandpa, asking him questions like "When did you take the trash out?" "How many bags were you carrying?" and "Where did you put them?" While he's answering, watch his body language to determine the truth.

○ ① 🔍 Visit the library or the Internet to report about the purpose of search warrants.

⬆② 🎨 💡 🔤 Create a search warrant to be allowed access into the fridge. (Yes, the fridge! A sample for inspiration is on page 355.) What do you want from inside? What will you do with what you find? Once your warrant has been granted (and you've secured peace), make lunch!

○ ② 💡 🔍 Solve a *victimless** crime by gathering two, three, or four pieces of evidence. So, say, Mom wants to figure

✳Victimless means no one got hurt.

186

out who "stole" the TV remote. You may find Dad's baseball hat on the couch, his favorite bottle of iced tea (half empty) on the coffee table, and his favorite channel on the TV. (Yes, Mom or Dad may have to set this up. For ideas, check out *Encyclopedia Brown* books.)

⬆①💡 Prevent the crime from happening again. In the "Case of the Missing Remote," this may mean tying one end of a string around the remote, and the other end around a leg of the couch.

○ ②🔍 Collect fingerprints from your whole family. There are tons of ways to do this (look in a library book or online), some as simple as pushing your fingers into an inkpad and onto paper. Keep your fingerprints in a [YOUR LAST NAME HERE] Family Fingerprint Log that you create with paper and markers. Be sure to identify whose fingerprints are whose!

⬆②🎨💡 Take prints on paper, shirts, or even hats. Then turn the fingerprints into faces, using markers and pens to add facial features, hair, glasses, all sorts of fun characteristics specific to the prints' owners. You can even give your little Fingerprint People to their owners, as gifts.

CAREER CROSSING

INVESTIGATORS WORK WITH:

Attorneys

Detectives

Electricians

Judges*

Police Officers

Journalist

Grandma doesn't have one foot in the door before you start telling her every detail of your big score: how your teammate set it up, how the opposition didn't stand a chance, how the crowd went wild! Your reporting was so fantastic, she said it was as if she saw the whole event with her own eyes. Look at you: sports hero and Journalist, all in one.

Jump In

○ ① ☻ ⊕ 📖 🔍 Use a library or Internet search to report about America's first newspaper: the *Boston News-Letter*. Include facts about when it was founded, what it originally reported about, and/or how many pages it had.

⬆ ② ⚗ 💡 ☻ ⊕ (abc) 🔍 Create your own *Boston News-Letter* using paper and pens or a computer program. Fill your issue with news relevant to the times (what were the main current events? what did the shops sell? how much was a loaf of bread?).

○ ② ⚗ 💡 ☻ (abc) 🔍 🤝 Grab a local paper. Cut out words from different articles and use tape or glue to put them together as a whole new article, about a socially or environmentally responsible project that's important to you (water conservation? Saving the whales? Supporting local farmers?).

○ ③ ☻ ☀ Take a tour of a local newspaper office or news station—call first to see when tours are scheduled. Afterward, report about the experience.

JOURNALISTS:

- Report about newsworthy events, people, and places
- Write articles, columns, and blog posts for newspapers, magazines, and websites
- Report live on TV, the radio, and the Internet
- Conduct interviews with important people

says Mike Triplett, New Orleans Saints beat writer, *New Orleans Times-Picayune* in New Orleans, Louisiana

I love _writing the kind of stories I like to read._

My biggest on-the-job challenge is _waiting for people to return phone calls._

The number of press passes I've collected is _in the hundreds._

Being in a press box _puts you within earshot of all the fans—you never know what will happen next!_

My most memorable day at work, ever, _was the Saints' first game in the rebuilt, post-Katrina Superdome. It was the most emotional, exciting event I've ever experienced._

If I weren't a Journalist, I'd be _a Teacher, but still a big sports fan!_

○ ③ ⓐⓑⓒ ☼ ◌ Shadow a Journalist. Try calling your local paper or TV station for a direct contact. Maybe you'll get to go on the scene of an exciting event, or watch him interview someone important in your town! After your time together, mail or email a thank-you note.

Research Subjects

○ ① ⓐ ⊕ ⓠ Visit the website www.Wikipedia.com to find a biography of someone you admire (your favorite Author? U.S. President? Inventor?). Then use one, two, or three other sources—like hardcopy or online encyclopedias, a search performed by the Librarian at your school or local library, or official websites about that person—to see if the facts in the Wikipedia entry are correct.

⇧ ① ⓠ ⓑ Define why Journalists would not use the information on Wikipedia in articles they write, without first verifying it elsewhere (try looking on the website's "About" section for clues).

○ ② 💡 🎭 🌐 🔤 🔍 Pretend you're a Foreign Correspondent, reporting from a faraway land. Write an article about a local annual event that takes place while you're in town (like La Tomatina in Spain? Hana Matsuri in Japan?). Research the history of the event, who attends, and why it's exciting—including all of this information in your article helps folks back home get a feeling for what you're experiencing.

○ ② 💡 🔍 Ask a family member to mail you a copy of a photograph of a memorable moment (a vacation? party?). He can even label the envelope: "ATTENTION: JOURNALIST [YOUR NAME HERE]"! Use clues in the photograph to identify when it was taken, who was involved, and what was going on (do Mom's clothes indicate it was sometime in the 1970s? is there a large cake that would indicate a birthday party?).

○ ③ 💡 🌐 🔤 ☀ 💬 🔍 Interview two, three, or four *sources** to create an article about the day you were born. Ask them all the same questions (such as "Where were you when you first heard the news?" "What do you know about my delivery?" "What was the weather like?" "Did you get to see me that day?" "What did I do?" and "What did Mom or Dad say about me?"). Then use everyone's answers to create an article that tells the whole story from lots of perspectives.

> **Journalist Mike** began writing in high school, both for the school paper and part-time for the local newspaper. He later graduated with a bachelor of arts degree in journalism from the University of Iowa, where he worked for the college paper, the *Daily Iowan*. He then earned a summer internship with the *Sacramento Bee* in 1998. Since then he has covered sports—primarily the NFL—for the *Bee* and the *Times-Picayune*.

* A **source** is anyone who provides information for a story.

191

Report the News

○ ① 💡 🔤 🔍 Create a list of interview questions you'd ask someone from an older generation about the most embarrassing thing that's ever happened to her. What do you think matters to readers most: where it happened? Why it happened? Think about what *you* would want to know!

👆 ③ 💡 🌐 🐷 🔤 🔆 💬 🔍 Interview her. Then write an article about her experience, but don't use her real name. Tell your readers her name has been changed to protect her identity (that is, don't give up your source).

👆 ① 🔆 💭 🕐 Keep your source a secret from your family for one, three, or five days straight—even if they try to guess. Real-life Journalists sometimes have to protect a source's identity forever!

○ ① 📚 🌐 🔍 🌍 Visit the library or the Internet to report about censorship.

👆 ② 💡 🔤 🌍 Write an article about the best meal you've ever had—leaving out one, two, or three critical parts (for example, you mention appetizers and dessert, but leave out the main course). Imagine living in a society where your ideas and descriptions were censored. Would your public be getting the whole story? Why would it matter?

> **WHY DOES JOURNALIST MIKE THINK HIS JOB IS AWESOME?**
>
> "I've always loved sports, and I've always loved to write. My job is the perfect combination of the two!"

○ ② 💡 🔤 🔍 Write an article that helps the public make an informed decision on a two-sided debate—one that's going on in your own home. Does Big Sis want a later bedtime? Does Dad think the family outing should be to a ball game, not the zoo? Present facts from both sides, without taking a side yourself.

Adding your opinion turns your article into what's called an "editorial."

(↑) (2) (💡) (abc) (🔍) Rewrite the article, including your point of view. Show both articles to one, two, or three people (not in your family). Which side do these people take? Were they swayed by your opinion?

SO YOU WANT TO...BE A BROADCAST JOURNALIST

○ (3) (💡) (abc) (☼) (💬) (🔍) (🕐) Journalists report what's newsworthy in every way imaginable: via newspapers, radio, websites, blogs, and of course, TV! Broadcast Journalists use video to support the stories they tell.

1. Identify your favorite teacher. Once you've asked if he'd like to participate in your story (and he's said yes), create a list of three, four, or five questions you'd like to ask him. Maybe: "Why did you become a teacher?" Or "What's been your most rewarding experience?" Or "What was your favorite subject as a kid?"

DID YOU KNOW?

Journalists work all hours. So say a game ends at 11 p.m. A Sports Journalist may have thirty minutes to write his story and get it posted online, or to the printer for morning paper delivery!

2. Prepare your video device (a video camera? video phone?)—make sure it is fully charged and you have an extra battery (and/or tape, if your device uses tape) just in case.

3. Interview your subject. You may want to invite a cameraperson (Mom? Dad?) to video while you ask the questions.

4. OPTIONAL: Video extra footage, like the inside of your teacher's classroom, the front of the school, your teacher writing on the blackboard.

5. Go home and watch your reporting.

6. OPTIONAL: Load your interview onto a computer program, where you can incorporate music, edit your footage, even add video of you introducing

your report ("Hi! I'm here at [YOUR SCHOOL'S NAME HERE] to introduce you to [YOUR TEACHER'S NAME HERE] because he's a really, really swell teacher.").

7. Make a copy of your interview and give it to your teacher as a gift.

CAREER CROSSING

JOURNALISTS WORK WITH:

Advertising Representatives

Assignment Editors

Photographers*

Printers

Publicists*

Y our best friend is screaming he should play first. Your *other* best friend is screaming *he* should play first. Then they both turn to you. As a fair Judge who weighs all evidence equally, you calmly announce that while Friend #1 got to the couch first, it was Friend #2 who grabbed the video game control first—so he wins. Case closed!

Jump In

- ① 💡 🎭 🔍 Use a library book or Internet site to report about our three branches of government: executive, legislative, and judicial. Then use an example to define who holds which role in your family: maybe Mom says spring cleaning will take place this Saturday (legislative), Big Bro says it's OK if you need Sunday to finish (judicial), and Dad makes sure everyone does their share (executive).

JUDGES:

- Interpret the law
- Preside over trials
- Decide punishments for crimes

- ① 🎭 🔍 Visit the library or the Internet to report about the roles of two, three, or four of the following: Supreme Court Justices, Court of Appeals Judges, Superior Court Judges, District Court Judges.

  ⬆ ② 🔤 ☀ 🔍 💬 Identify your state's Chief Judge, then mail or email her a letter, thanking her for all her hard work.

- ② 💡 🎭 🌐 💬 Act out your favorite amendment from our Bill of Rights. Let's say you pick the Eighth Amendment (no cruel punishment)—ask Little Sis to demonstrate for Mom or Dad how she's not allowed to tickle you for more than one minute if you borrow her rollerblades without asking. (Yes, you'll need to withstand some serious tickling to act this out!)

says stanford blake, chief judge for the criminal court in miami, florida

I love _making people feel like they were heard and justice was served._

I'm not fond of _Attorneys who don't act professionally and argue with each other._

The first time I sat on the bench I _felt it was where I was destined to be._

My favorite thing to wear under my robe is _a nice tie that makes a nice knot—that's the part everyone can see._

The coolest law is _that everyone arrested is "presumed innocent"—the government must prove guilt before that person can lose his freedom._

If I weren't a Judge, I'd be _a Teacher._

○ ③ 😊 🔍 Visit your city's or town's district traffic court—it's open to the public. Watch a Judge make a decision on one, two, or three cases. Afterward, report about what you saw and learned.

Interpret the Law

○ ① 💡 Ask Mom or Dad to create a new law, for example, "Children's bedrooms must be clean before breakfast." Then, interpret it. So, for example, does this mean all toys must be put away, or that the floor must be vacuumed, too?

　⬆ ① 💡 Interpret the law a second way. Maybe the law could mean the bedroom must be clean

WHY DOES JUDGE STAN THINK HIS JOB IS AWESOME?

"I make sure there's protection against tyranny or a dictatorship by our government. I make sure we uphold the three branches of government our founders created!"

196

before breakfast, but it's OK if it's messy after breakfast. Judges consider laws many times, knowing there's more than one way to interpret their meaning.

(⬆)(1)(💡) Decide which of the two interpretations is most fair by being impartial—this means picking the meaning that works for your whole family, not just you. (So you may *want* to say the "messy after breakfast is OK" interpretation, but you know that's not good for Mom and Dad, who prefer a neat home.)

> *Judge Stan* earned a bachelor of science degree in advertising from the University of Florida and went to law school at the University of Miami School of Law. He started as a Public Defender, representing people who could not afford to hire an Attorney. Later he owned a private practice, where he was paid by his clients to represent them in court. Then, in 1994, he was elected Judge.

○ (1)(💡)(🎭)(🔍)(🐦) List one, two, or three civil responsibilities we have as Americans that are not enforced upon us by law (for example, adults are not forced to vote in political elections, but consider it a responsibility).

○ (2)(✋)(💡)(🎭)(🐦)(abc) Work with someone from an older generation to create the [YOUR LAST NAME HERE] Family Constitution—a declaration of what's important to your family. Write it on notebook paper; use markers, crayons, and construction paper; or even type it into a computer program. An example for inspiration is on page 356.

(⬆)(1)(💡)(🐦) Ask your partner (that someone from an older generation) to create a law he thinks supports your declaration—it's up to you to decide if the law is constitutional. Let's say your constitution states that "Family Activities are to occur a minimum of once a week," and Grandpa says a new law should be "Family Activities take place every Wednesday"— you may declare that law constitutional because Wednesdays happen once a week.

Serve Civilians

- ① 💡 ☀ 🐾 Approve the adoption of a pet, stuffed animal, or even imaginary friend. Ask Mom or Dad to photocopy the Adoption Petition on page 357 (or download a copy at EarnMyKeep.com), then fill it out. When he's done, read over his petition together and sign your name—thereby approving the new addition to your family. Congratulations!

- ② 🎨 💡 🎭 🔤 ☀ 🔍 🐾 Create and sign a (pretend) marriage license. Whether it's for Little Sis's doll and Big Bro's action figure, your pet parrot and your best friend's pet parakeet, or even real-life newlyweds, (1) use a library or online search to identify the key information on a marriage license; (2) use markers, crayons, and paper to re-create one; and (3) deliver it, signed, to its recipients.

If you're adopted, ask Mom or Dad if they filled out a form similar to the one on page 357, and if they remember the Judge who helped your family grow.

DID YOU KNOW?

Some Judges may address as many as forty to fifty cases in one day, every one affecting the life of a fellow citizen. It's a responsibility that requires paying a lot of attention!

Preside over Trials

- ① 💡 🎭 🔍 Dress like a Judge from your home state or even another country. Look in a library book or online to determine what your chosen Judge wears—then use what you find to create your outfit (a sheet as a robe? a bit of ribbon as a collar?).

  - ⬆ ① ☀ Ask everyone in your family to call you "Your Honor" for fifteen, thirty, or forty-five minutes. If someone uses your regular name, hold her in contempt of court. (Fine this person one hug, or something equally silly of your choice.)

- ② 💡 ☀ 🐾 Hear an appeal on a "case" that's been decided by a first Judge (in this example, Dad). So Mom says empty paper towel rolls need to be taken to the recycling bin immediately. Big Bro thinks they can sit on the counter until garbage day. The first Judge to hear the case (Dad) agreed with Mom. But Big Bro thinks this is unfair, and appeals to you. Listen to both sides and make the final decision.

After this task is over, Mom or Dad may reverse your decision, and that's OK.

SO YOU WANT TO...PRESIDE OVER A BENCH TRIAL

o ③ 💡 🎭 🔆 💬 😃 Jury trials are held with a *jury**. At bench trials, however, there's no jury—it's up to the Judge (YOU!) to decide guilt, and perhaps a punishment too.

Why a "bench" trial? Because a bench is where a Judge sits in a courtroom.

✳ A jury is a group of local residents who decide if a person is guilty or not.

1. Think of a case to try, where the plaintiff (Dad? Grandma?) blames the accused (or defendant) (Mom? Little Bro?) with committing a crime: Does Dad think Grandma ate the last cookie in the cookie jar? Does Mom think Little Bro forgot to take care of her houseplants?

2. Ask the accused how she pleads: guilty or not guilty.

3. Ask the plaintiff to present *evidence*** to support the belief that a crime took place, and that the accused is the person who committed it.

✳✳ Evidence can be pictures, alibis (descriptions of where you were at the time of the crime), or even eyewitnesses.

4. Ask the accused to present evidence that proves her innocence.

5. Weigh the evidence and each person's argument. Then use an open mind to decide if the accused is guilty or not guilty.

In real courts, plaintiffs and the accused do not often represent themselves—they typically hire Lawyers to speak on their behalf.

6. Assign an appropriate punishment to the accused, if she is found guilty.

CAREER CROSSING

JUDGES WORK WITH:

Attorneys

Bailiffs

Clerks of the Court

Court Reporters

Judicial Assistants

Congratulations! It took one pile of books, three sweatshirts, and an old bag of popcorn, but you've done it. You've drawn a line between your side and the one belonging to the pesky "other" who refuses to keep her stuff on her side of the car. Great work, Land Surveyor—may your boundary be recognized by all!

Jump In

- ① 🔍 ⚗️ Use the library or an Internet search to learn how compasses work. Report what you discover.

  ⬆️ ① 🧭 🔍 ⚗️ Make your own compass. Get ideas from a book or online. Or try this: put an ordinary sewing needle on top of a small square of paper or cork in a glass of water. See how you can lead the needle with a magnet. Then take the needle out, rubbing its length with the magnet three times in the same direction. Put the needle back on the paper—it should always swivel north.

- ① 🎭 🌐 🔍 Use the library or an Internet search to report about the world's first Land Surveyors. (Hint: They built the pyramids.)

  ⬆️ ① 🎭 🌐 🔍 List two more examples of historical surveying (like Stonehenge).

  ⬆️ ③ 💡 Imagine you're the Land Surveyor for one of your examples, searching out boundaries on an ancient land. Ask Mom or Dad to hide

Land Surveyors:

- Locate and mark land boundaries
- Investigate land boundary disputes
- Develop maps
- Mark the locations for the placement of roads, bridges, and buildings
- Divide parcels of land into smaller parcels

SAYS KURT LUEBKE, PLS, CFEDS, DJ&A, P.C., IN MISSOULA, MONTANA

I love _researching in historical archives and learning about locations hundreds of years old._

My biggest on-the-job challenge is _handling differing county officials' interpretations of state laws regarding land surveying._

The most difficult surveying I've done _took place more than twenty miles from civilization, and involved two to three feet of snow, temperatures in the teens, and a pair of snowshoes._

My favorite piece of equipment is _a high-density laser scanner._

Locating boundaries _is like a treasure hunt. Sometimes I even have to make up the map!_

If I weren't a Land Surveyor, I'd be _a National Park Service Ranger._

boundary stones (pebbles?) in the yard or your favorite room, then hand over "ancient writings" (notepad paper?) that tell of a mysterious, unsurveyed property. The text may read: "Egyptian King Kurt believes there are three pyramids on his land: the jungle gym, the doghouse, and the flower bed. Is this true? Collect all the boundary stones to find out."

○ ③ ⓐⓑ ☼ ◌ Shadow a Land Surveyor. (Try a phone book or Internet search for a local surveying company.) Maybe he'll even give you an on-site demonstration of some of his equipment! Mail or email a thank-you note after your time together.

⬆ ③ ⓐⓑ ☼ ◌ ◌ Accompany your Land Surveyor when he volunteers his services for a nonprofit

WHY DOES LAND SURVEYOR KURT THINK HIS CAREER IS AWESOME?

"I get to travel to new, exotic locations and remote places I never would have seen if I weren't a Land Surveyor."

organization. Remember your thank-you note, too.

Establish Boundaries

- ① 🔍 Visit the library or the Internet to define "deed" and "survey plat."

  - ⬆ ① 🔍 Check out the deed to your home (Mom or Dad should know where it is). If your family doesn't own your property, ask your landlord or County Clerk and Recorder if you can see the plat for where you live.

  - ⬆ ② ♿ 💡 🔍 Create a deed for your bedroom. If you don't have Mom/Dad's deed for inspiration, look in a library book or the Web for ideas. Then use crayons, markers, paper—whatever you want—to make your own.

- ② ☺ Help fellow Land Surveyors conduct future surveys by performing a neighborhood *sidewalk cleanup** (this is the Earn My Keep version of a highway cleanup, often performed on a volunteer basis by local Land Surveyors).

- ② 💡 🏺 Ask Mom to hide a toy or treat somewhere outside, then use a compass to create a list of *bearings*** and distances directing you to your prize (say, *Go N for three steps, then SW for two steps*). Use the compass and her list to find your treasure. Land Surveyors often have to locate a boundary with little more than a list like yours.

Land Surveyor Kurt graduated from the University of Montana with a bachelor of science degree in forest resource management. His education plus on-the-job experience qualified him to take two eight-hour examinations to earn his Professional License. And while he's been in surveying for eighteen years total, he took eight years off early in his career to care for his two girls!

Sidewalk cleanups can involve picking up trash (wear gloves!) and sweeping leaves. You can even recycle what you collect.

Bearings state the direction or course from one object to another. N = North; S = South; E = East; W = West.

○ ② ⊙ ⓐⓑⓒ ☼ Solve a boundary dispute between two family members. Say Big Sis insists the whole family room is hers for a craft project, while Big Bro says it's his spot to hang with friends. Look for clues to help you determine boundaries for each person. (The TV and couch are on one side—perfect for video games? An empty desk is on the other, near the windows—lots of space and light for crafting?) Be firm, but polite, while resolving the dispute.

○ ② ⊙ Mark a legal boundary. Ask Mom or Dad to describe the boundary of the space using furniture and decorations as cues (so, say, "The right side of the couch to the base of the floor lamp, then the base of the floor lamp to the edge of the zebra-striped rug."). Take notes. Then, using masking or painter's tape, mark the boundary described.

Develop Maps

○ ② ⚗ ⊙ ⚗ Make a *planimetric** map of your favorite park. First, visit the park (bring paper and a pencil). Mark your favorite thing to climb on first (the monkey bars? the slide?)—this is your "control point." Then fill in the rest (other play equipment, trees, shrubs, benches, bikes, backpacks, everything!).

⬆ ② ⚗ ⊙ Revisit the park on a different day, marking anything new or different on your map. Are the bikes gone? Has a shrub been added? Land Surveyors know maps are worthless if they do not reflect what's actually there—this requires a lot of updating.

*Planimetric maps show natural and man-made features, and the space between them.

DID YOU KNOW?

Land Surveyors travel wherever, whenever, to get the job done. Imagine getting to survey near the Canadian border one week, near the Mexican border the next!

**Topographical maps note natural and man-made features, the space between them, and their elevation.

○ ② ⚗ ⊙ ⚗ ⚗ Work with someone from an older generation to create a *topographical*** map from your home to his. (Don't live near one of these relatives? Talk on the phone!) Either way, include geographical features like lakes or mountain ranges, as well as man-made features like parks or sports stadiums. Maybe one day you'll spend time together visiting everything on your map.

⬆ ② 🎨 💡 🎲 Add some 3-D elevation to your map—consider creating mountain ranges with crumpled tissue paper and airports with building blocks!

CAREER CROSSING

LAND SURVEYORS WORK WITH:

Architects

Attorneys

County Surveyors

Structural Engineers

Title Officers

Pajamas? Check. Teeth brushed? Yup. Book picked out? Of course. You went through every book in your bedroom and found exactly what you wanted to read. Librarians do this for us every day—helping visitors sift through thousands of books to find the exact match for bedtime, or anytime!

Jump In

○ ③🔍 Visit your local library—report about what you observe. Who goes to the Information desk? How many books do most people return? Are there a lot of people reading?

  ⬆️③🔍 Visit a second public library. List one, two, or three things that are similar to the first. Also list one, two, or three things that are different. Compare their children's sections, movie selections, public meeting rooms—do you prefer the first or second library?

○ ③ⓐⓑⓒ☀️💬 Shadow a Librarian—maybe you'll even be able to help a *patron** find a book! Afterward, mail or email a thank-you note.

LIBRARIANS:

- Access information and books
- Manage library collections
- Host events, like book readings
- Instruct people on the use of library resources and equipment
- Decide where materials are shelved

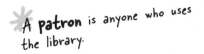

A **patron** is anyone who uses the library.

Manage Collections

○ ①📖 Assign a "new book" shelf (in the kitchen? your bedroom?). Add one, two, or three new or borrowed books to it. Librarians like to preview books

SAYS TERESA SMITH, CHILDREN'S SERVICES MANAGER, EUCLID PUBLIC LIBRARY IN EUCLID, OHIO

I love _seeing the look of wonder on children's faces when I read them a book._

My biggest on-the-job challenge is _people who don't follow the rules._

My favorite book as a kid was _anything fairy tales—I still have my Brothers Grimm Fairy Tales!_

Being around books makes me feel _invincible._

My most important resource is _my staff: Sandra, Carolynne, Monica, Mary, Joyce, Mary Lynne, and Gina._

If I weren't a Librarian, I'd be _working in a craft store._

before they're placed in the regular collection. Now you can, too.

○ ① 🎭 🌐 🔍 Use the library or an Internet search to report about the Dewey Decimal System.

⬆ ② 💡 🗓 Create your own classification system called the [YOUR NAME HERE] Library System. (You'll need a pad of sticky notes and a pen.) First, pull about ten books from your home library. Group 'em into categories (Trucks? Ballet? Sports? History?). Give each category a number (Trucks = 1; Ballet = 2; Sports = 3; History = 4). Then add a decimal point, and one number per book. (Which means the first book about trucks will be 1.1; your second will be 1.2; your third, 1.3.) Give each book a sticky note with its number.

Whether you own three books or three hundred books, the collection where you live is your very own home library!

(↑)(2)(💡)(☀)(🀫) Put the [YOUR NAME HERE] Library System into action. First, write down the titles of the books and their numbers. Post a copy of this list on the wall, while you keep the original. Then shelve your books, in numerical order. Lastly, have family members request a book from the posted list—you'll know exactly where to find it!

○ (2)(✋) Maintain your library's shelves for one, two, or three days. Are they neat? Organized? A soft rag can clear away dust and give your books a fresh look.

(↑)(2)(💡)(✋) Take down all the books on one, two, or three shelves. Are any covers torn or dirty? Pages ripped or bent? Repair the books that can be saved. Then either reshelve them or donate them to your school library.

Librarian Teresa earned her bachelor of science degree in psychology from Clark Atlanta University, and her master of library science degree from Case Western Reserve University. She's been a Librarian for twenty-seven years, which has given her the opportunity to meet some of her favorite Authors—including award-winners Patricia McKissack and Ashley Bryan.

○ (2)(📖) Enhance your home library with one, two, or three books from the public library or bookstore.

(↑)(1)(💡)(📖)(☀) Select your books based on community needs. If your family is going on vacation, pick a destination book. If Little Sis is starting ballet, grab a ballet book. Is Mom loving her new crock pot? A slow-cooker cookbook may be just the thing.

WHY DOES LIBRARIAN TERESA THINK HER CAREER IS AWESOME?

"It gives me access to information, making me smarter. And I get to share the joy of reading with children!"

(↑)(2)(▦)($)(Q) Update your collection while sticking to a budget. (In addition to looking for coupons, you may want to try used bookstores, or websites like Ebay.com or Craigslist.com.) Can you add three new books for $15? Using newspaper or Internet searches, can you find those same books for $10?

DID YOU KNOW?

Librarians lend way more than books. From comic books and magazines to CDs and DVDs—some libraries have more than 120,000 items in circulation, and that's per month!

Provide Information

○ (1)(💡)(☼)(🐾) Answer two, three, or four questions about your home library in a kind, courteous manner. Patrons (like Mom, Dad, or even your Babysitter) can ask you things like: "Where can I find a book about the alphabet?" "During what hours is your library open?" "May I reserve a meeting room?" and "When will the computer be available for use?"

○ (1)(💡)(☼) Arrange to loan a book from your home library to a patron. Slip a sheet of paper into the book that reminds the borrower of its due date. Also inform the borrower of any *fines** he will accrue if the book is returned late—a nickel? A song and dance? A hug?

✳ **A fine is a penalty.**

(↑)(1)(☼)(🕐) Make sure your patron returns his book on time. If he's late, enforce the fine (but be polite!).

○ (2)(⚓)(💡) Set up a book display to promote a theme, like a holiday, subject, or Author. Prop up three, four, or five books on a shelf in an attractive manner. If the theme is, say, swimming, consider adding a pair of goggles for interest.

Organize Promotions

○ ②⊛⊛⊕⊛⊛⊛ Create a booklist (a list of three, four, or five books) you think someone from an older generation may like. Research book titles about his favorite activity, type of food, and place to visit. Give him the list and/or help him go to the library to find the books.

⊕①⊛⊛⊛ Encourage your patron to finish all the books on his list: check in with him the day after your library visit to see if he's started. Maybe call three days later to see if he's having any difficulties—you may have a solution. (You can continue to encourage your patron even after you're done being a Librarian, just for fun!)

○ ③⊛⊛⊕⊛⊛⊛⊛ Invite your family to a book reading. Promote your event with a flyer (handmade or computer-made) that states where, when, and what book you will be reading. On reading day, set out a few chairs and perhaps a plate of cookies. Start your reading right on time, and hold your book up so everyone can see.

⊕②⊛⊛⊛ Write a song or poem to go along with the story, then perform it.

○ ③⊛⊛⊛⊛ Host a book collection party—invite family members and friends over for snacks. In exchange for your tasty treats, request they bring one new or gently used book. After the party, donate the books to a hospital or local children's charity.

CAREER CROSSING

LIBRARIANS WORK WITH:

Authors

Book Salespeople

Musicians*

Publishers

Teachers

Linguist

The nice salesclerk smiled in a friendly way, but you couldn't understand what he was saying. "Ken I hep ya?" he repeated twice. "Hep ya?" you thought. "What's a 'hep ya'?!" Suddenly it became clear: he has an accent! And as any Linguist would do, you instantly struck up a conversation so you could admire his awesome Southern drawl.

Jump In

○ ① 💡 (abc) 🔍 Follow a toddler around for fifteen or thirty minutes. Report the ways she communicates her desires—remember, at this age, not all "words" sound like words.

○ ① 📷 🌐 (abc) 🔍 👁 Visit the library or the Internet to report about endangered languages, including why caring about them is important. List one, two, or three languages in danger of becoming extinct.

⬆ ① 💡 🎭 (abc) Learn one, two, or three words from one of the languages you researched. (Can't find any real words? Create some, based on what you learned about the language). Then teach them to someone from an older generation.

○ ② 💡 📷 (abc) 🔍 Find someone (a family member? neighbor? Teacher?) who is bilingual. Together, compare English to the language she speaks, listing how each language pluralizes and orders nouns and their adjectives (is it "turquoise dinosaur" or "dinosaur turquoise"?). Then list how the other language says "cock-a-doodle-doo"!

LINGUISTS:

- Study the use and history of language, often specializing in particular ones
- Research how the human mind learns language
- Uncover how all human languages are related
- Help machines understand human language

says Steven H. Weinberger, Associate Professor,
Director of Linguistics, George Mason University
in Fairfax, Virginia

I love *listening for interesting pronunciations in people's speech.*

My biggest on-the-job challenge *is staying focused on what people say because I am so absorbed in their particular accents!*

The number of languages I've heard spoken in person by native speakers is *575.*

Human mouths can *make hundreds of speech sounds. English uses about 40. I can make about 250!*

The one English phrase non-English speakers just can't understand is *"Jeet yet?" ("Did you eat yet?")*

If I weren't a Linguist, I'd be *an Electrician.*

○ ③ (abc) (☼) (☺) Shadow a Linguist. To find one, try calling the linguistics department at a local university. After your time together, mail or email a thank-you note.

Study Language Sounds (Phonetics)

○ ① (🔍) (⚗) Use the library or an Internet search to define the organs necessary to produce speech sounds: tongue, lips, velum, and larynx.

(↑) ① (💡) List one, two, or three sounds you make with these organs that are not for communication (like burping!).

Bees may dance. Apes may have specialized calls. But no animal on Earth communicates with language the way humans do!

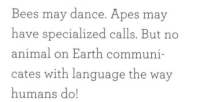

○ ① 💡 🔍 🧪 Learn how to make one, two, or three new sounds with your mouth (water dropping, anyone?). Try looking in a library book, checking online, or asking Mom or Dad.

○ ① 😊 (abc) 🔍 🧪 Visit the library or the Internet to report how many sounds there are in the English language. Then list the language with the most sounds, and the one with the least.

○ ② (abc) 🔍 🧪 Ask a child who is a *native speaker** of English to read a page from your favorite book. Next ask an English-speaking adult who is not a native English speaker to do the same. Report about which sounds seem to be more difficult for non-native English speakers. (Pay close attention to "th," "l," and "r" sounds.)

*Saying that someone is a **native speaker** means he learned the language from birth.

    ⬆ ① 🔍 Use a tape recorder, cell phone, or digital camera to record your speakers' speech.

    ⬆ ② (abc) 🔍 🧪 Ask a second non-native speaker (child or adult) from a third country or region to read the same page. Does she have the same difficulties as your first non-native speaker?

Linguist Steven earned his bachelor of arts degree in anthropology, with minors in East Asian studies and psychology from the University of Pittsburgh. He earned his PhD in linguistics from the University of Washington. When living in China, he taught English. Back in America, he's taught Chinese. He has also been a professor of linguistics for more than twenty years.

Study Words (Morphology)

○ ① 💡 (abc) 📖 🧪 Use a Dr. Seuss book (like *There's a Wocket in my Pocket*) as a brand-new English dictionary—for fifteen or thirty minutes, incorporate the made-up words into conversation as if they were real words. Then discuss why they sound like they could be English words, even though they're not.

o ② 😊 🔤 🔍 🧪 Watch your favorite science fiction movie or TV show. List one, two, or three alien characters whose language sounds like English (uses similar vowel and consonant sounds). Then list one, two, or three characters whose language uses clicks and other sounds not found in the English language.

Study How Sentences Form (Syntax)

o ① 💡 🔤 🧪 Write or say a simple sentence in English that follows the Subject-Verb-Object arrangement (such as "Monkeys peel bananas."). Next, try it in the standard Irish order: Verb-Subject-Object. Lastly, try the usual Japanese order: Subject-Object-Verb.

> **WHY DOES LINGUIST STEVEN THINK HIS CAREER IS AWESOME?**
>
> "I get to study, teach, and write about something every human being uses every day!"

⬆ ② 💡 🔤 💬 Deliver your favorite nursery rhyme as a speech (invite the family to listen), using the Irish or Japanese word order wherever you can.

Study What Words Mean (Semantics)

o ① 🔤 🔍 Use the library or an online search to report about speech recognition. (Hint: it has to do with computers.)

⬆ ① 🔤 🔍 Put speech recognition to the test using the voice recognition feature on a cell phone. Record your voice saying your best friend's name, then see if the phone will dial her. Try it again while whispering loudly, and again with food in your mouth. (You can also try this with an 800-number, like an airline's, that allows you to speak instead of pressing menu buttons.)

o ① 😊 😃 🔤 🔍 🧪 Write or say a sentence in total kid-speak to someone from an older generation (like "That sandwich was sick!"). Ask her what she thinks the sentence means. Repeat the sentence in language she understands (like "That sandwich was incredible!").

(↑) (2) (😊) (🐦) (abc) (🔍) Work with your "older generation" partner, changing the sentence to work for an American region other than your own. (For example, you and your partner may learn that in California, it's a "grinder"; in New Jersey, it's a "hero"; in Louisiana, it's a "po' boy"; and in Delaware, it's a "sub.")

o (2) (abc) (🔍) Use a library or online search to find a joke that's a *pun**— then tell it. Linguists like to study puns because they show how words can be confusing (and funny!). An example? How some words have the same sounds, but different meanings, like "night" and "knight."

(↑) (2) (💡) (abc) Create your own joke, using a pun you make up.

* A **pun** uses a word that has more than one meaning, or sounds like another word, for fun!

CAREER CROSSING

LINGUISTS WORK WITH:
Computer Scientists
Language Teachers
Psychologists
Speech Pathologists
Web Programmers

Marine Biologist

So fast, and so tiny, you almost missed it. But there went that little hermit crab, scurrying across the beach with its little shell on its back. And then—you blinked!—it had left behind its first shell, snuggled itself into a new one, and promptly made its way back into the waves. Lucky Marine Biologists. They get to study the little guy every day.

Jump In

○ ① ⊕ ⊕ Report about what makes the ocean so salty. The library or an online search should reveal the answer. Also list one of the Earth's saltiest bodies of water.

○ ③ ⓐⓑⓒ ☀ ⊙ Shadow a Marine Biologist. Most universities on the coast have a biology department where Marine Biologists work and/or study, or you can try finding one at your local aquarium. Mail or email a thank-you note afterward.

  ⇧ ① 📖 ☀ ⊕ ⊕ Ask your Marine Biologist if he has any journals you can see—they're filled with the latest marine research and discoveries.

○ ③ ⊕ ⊕ ⊕ Visit an aquarium or museum of natural history (one with exhibits dedicated to marine life). Before your visit, make a list of one, two, or three facts you think you know about the ocean. Then, while you're there, find information that proves you right, or teaches you the correct answer.

Marine BIOLOGISTS:

- Study ocean life
- Examine human impacts on the ocean
- Educate the public and the government about how to protect our oceans

says Jarrett Byrnes, postdoctoral associate,
Santa Barbara Coastal LTER, Marine Science Institute,
University of California, Santa Barbara
in Santa Barbara, California

I love *working in the ocean, then putting the puzzles of data back together in my office.*

My biggest on-the-job challenge is *urchin spines in my knee.*

Working underwater is like *flying.*

A typical day in the field starts at *7 a.m.—prep the boat to launch, fill it with gear, and gauge if the weather will cooperate.*

If I could be any ocean-dweller I'd be *a colonial sea squirt because all I'd do all day is filter plankton out of the ocean—how relaxing! Water in, water out, water in…*

If I weren't a Marine Biologist, I'd be *a Chef.*

○ ③ (abc) (☼) (🗩) (🔍) (🧪) Take a tour of a saltwater fish store (some store owners are happy to do this) or a local aquarium (many offer behind-the-scenes tours for kids). After your visit, report about what you learned (you may want to take notes while you're there), and mail or email your tour guide a thank-you note.

Study Ocean Life

○ ① (💡) Define a pretend FIND OF THE CENTURY! Your underwater expedition just revealed a brand new animal, one never seen before by man (or kid). What does it look like? What does it eat? Does it travel in a group, or alone?

○ ① (🔍) (🧪) (🤚) Report about an example of one, two, or three of our coral reef-dwelling friends: *coral**, algae, fish, and sea urchins. Then define "coral bleaching" and what Marine Biologists are doing to help stop it.

corals may look like plants, but they are actually animals!*

220

○ ② 💡 🔍 Spend an afternoon as your favorite ocean animal: eat what it eats (pretend or for real), make your bedroom look like where it lives, even move your body like it's swimming from place to place.

○ ② 🧪 💡 🔍 🧫 Build a cage that will stay in place on the ocean floor (bottom of the bathtub), even when pushed by rough ocean currents (your hands making waves). Use pipe cleaners, clean popsicle sticks, dried pasta—whatever you think won't float away or fall apart. Marine Biologists design cages that hold (or try to hold) any type of ocean animal, in a manner that's safe for the scientist and the animal. As you'd imagine, some animals are easier to cage than others!

> *Marine Biologist Jarrett* graduated with a bachelor of science in biology from Brown University, and a PhD in population biology from University of California Davis, where he worked at the Bodega Marine Lab on the rugged Sonoma Coast (just a hair north of San Francisco). He's been an avid diver since he was twelve.

○ ② 🍽 🌀 Eat some algae (yes, algae) with someone from an older generation. Asian grocery stores sell all kinds, including nori, kombu, and dulse—look in a cookbook or online for ideas on how to enjoy this delicacy. And/or grab a prepackaged seaweed snack from a health store.

○ ③ 🔍 🧫 Spend fifteen or thirty minutes on a beach, reporting about what grows on rocks exposed to waves (like an open shore) and what grows in areas protected from waves (like inside a bay or cove). Their plant and animal communities will be totally different.

○ ③ 🧪 🔍 🧫 Walk along a beach at night for fifteen or thirty minutes (bring a flashlight), describing what the ocean has washed up on shore and the critters that are eating it. Draw or take a picture of one of your favorites—when you get home use a library book or Internet search to define your critter and his meal. (AT-HOME ALTERNATE: Ask Mom or Dad to photocopy two, three, or four pictures of different beach-going night critters and place them around your bedroom, at night. Use a flashlight to collect them all, then report about them.)

Protect Ocean Life

○ ① ⊗ ⊕ ⊕ Use the library or search online to define how oil spills impact marine life and one, two, or three ways people and companies are making a difference.

⊕ ③ ⊕ Join in a beach cleanup. Whether you live near a beach or are just visiting one, participate in a formal, organized event or simply spend fifteen minutes cleaning up with your family—every bit makes a difference.

○ ② ⊗ ⊕ Learn how to use pH strips—ask the owner of a saltwater tank (friend, family member, or local fish store owner) to demonstrate how the strips work, and why they're important. Then give it a try yourself.

⊕ ② ⊕ ⊕ Write an article about your experience, then "publish" it by taping it inside your local paper or a nature magazine, or emailing it to family and/or friends.

○ ③ ⊕ ⊕ Help take care of a saltwater fish tank for one, two, or three days. (If you or a friend or family member don't own one, ask your local fish store owner if you can help her in the store.) Make sure

DID YOU KNOW?

"Marine Biologist" is a general term used when speaking to the public. But people who study interactions between different kinds of sea life are actually called Marine Ecologists!

WHY DOES MARINE BIOLOGIST JARRETT THINK HIS CAREER IS AWESOME?

"I get to spend my life on, in, and around the ocean!"

You could also do this with a freshwater tank.

222

the tank's inhabitants get the proper amount of food and light (usually artificial, from lamps) and that its filters are running properly.

(↑) (2) (🔍) Spend at least five minutes observing the action inside the tank each day you take care of it. Report about what you see—for example, how do the tank's inhabitants react before and after you add food?

(↑) (3) (ⓐᵇᶜ) (💬) (⏱) Present your observations to Mom or Dad as a one, two, or three minute speech.

CAREER CROSSING

MARINE BIOLOGISTS WORK WITH:

Geographers

Oceanographers

Science Writers

Sea Captains

Statisticians

Market Researcher

Tonight's a special night, and the whole family is going out to celebrate. But to where? You ask Mom, Dad, Big Sis, and Baby Bro their preferences and then, hooray! You're ready to present the results of your survey: one vote for seafood and three for a local Italian eatery. Looks like you're a pasta-eating Market Researcher tonight!

Jump In

- ② 💡 ☼ 🔍 Ask five classmates: "What's your favorite ice cream flavor?" (Keep track of their answers.) Then ask five *different* classmates: "My favorite ice cream flavor is [YOUR FAVORITE FLAVOR]. What's yours?" Compare the results—did you notice more people said your favorite flavor if you told them you liked it too? Market Researchers learn how to ask questions in ways that do not influence their respondent's answers.

Market Researchers:

- Collect people's opinions through surveys
- Analyze the results of surveys
- Help clients decide how their surveys' results can better their products or services

- ③ 🔤 ☼ 💬 Shadow a Market Researcher—you'll find market research companies listed in your local phone book or online. After your time together, mail or email a thank-you note.

Uncover "Why?" (Qualitative Research)

- ① 🔍 ☼ Conduct a sniff test. Blindfold Mom, then give her three, four, or five similar things to sniff (spices? bars of soap? cut-up fruit? perfume?). Write down her opinion of each scent (likes? dislikes? reminds her of the first day

SAYS ADAM WEINSTEIN, REGIONAL VICE PRESIDENT, SALES, AUTHENTIC RESPONSE IN NEW YORK CITY, NEW YORK

I love helping clients understand the value of their products and services.

My biggest on-the-job challenge is getting good quality research conducted within rushed timelines.

The farthest I've traveled for research is China, Japan, and Germany—in one trip!

Two way mirrors make focus group participants nervous.

The funniest interviews I ever conducted were for a clinical trial to prove if a new gum could fight bad breath—participants had to blow in our sniffers' faces for hours!

If I weren't a Market Researcher, I'd be a Baseball Player.

of spring?), without revealing the item she's sniffing. When you're all done, review your results—is she surprised she prefers one scent over another?

○ ① 🔍 ☀️ Tear an advertisement out of a magazine (make sure its owner is done with the magazine, first!). Show the ad to someone in your family. Ask what he likes about the ad, what he doesn't like about the ad, and if the ad would motivate him to buy or use the product or service it's selling.

👤 ② 🔍 ☀️ Ask the same questions of everyone else who lives in your home. This is how Market Researchers create a picture of an entire group of people's opinions.

○ ③ 💡 ☀️ 💬 🔍 Run a *focus group** during dinner, about dinner. Your goal? To understand the benefits of dining in and eating out. Use the Moderator's Guide on page 358—this is the kind of

Focus groups allow Market Researchers to ask groups of people their opinions about products, services, issues—just about anything.

script real *Moderators** follow, so they know exactly what to say.

(↑) (2) (💡) (☀) Offer your participants a thank-you for joining in (a family-favorite healthy dessert? a hand-made button that says: I Participated in [YOUR NAME HERE]'s Focus Group? a hug and a "thank-you"?).

○ (3) (😊) (🔍) *Mystery shop*** at your favorite national chain (grocery store? toy store?) with someone from an older generation. Report if the store appears clean and if shopping carts (and/or baskets) are easy to find. Also look for three, five, or seven of your favorite items, reporting if they're displayed nicely and if their prices are clearly marked.

(↑) (1) (☀) (🔍) List how many salespeople you need to ask to find one of your favorite items. (This is one way Market Researchers determine a store's level of customer service.)

(↑) (3) (💡) (🔍) Visit one, two, or three more of the store's locations, reporting the same information. Afterward, compare—is one store run better than another?

○ (3) (💡) (☀) (🔍) (💬) Participate in a socially or environmentally responsible event or activity with your family (cleaning up a local park? volunteering at an animal shelter? donating gently used toys?) Host "in-depth interviews" afterward (doesn't have to be the same day) to determine how your family felt about the experience. Invite each family member, one at a time, into a quiet room. Ask each participant the questions on page 360, recording all the answers on photocopies of the questionnaire, or new pieces of paper. (You can also download the questionnaire at EarnMyKeep.com.)

*A moderator is the person who runs a focus group.

WHY DOES MARKET RESEARCHER ADAM THINK HIS CAREER IS AWESOME?

"Because research is a critical step to bringing out new products and services. I'm part of an important process!"

**Mystery shoppers look like regular customers, but are actually doing market research.

(↑) ② (💡) (abc) (☼) (🔍) Compile all of your research into a report, including what each person thought (but don't name anyone, to protect identities) and an overall conclusion. (An example: "While no one enjoyed picking up trash in the rain, everyone felt good about helping our community.")

Uncover "How Many?" (Quantitative Research)

○ ② (abc) (☼) (🔍) Conduct a telephone survey to determine the most loved book in your class. Call five, seven, or nine classmates, giving each a choice of the same four books. Note each classmate's preference on a list, created either with pen and paper or a computer program.

> (↑) ① (☼) (🔍) Add a follow-up question(s), like "Do you prefer books about friendship, mysteries, or action heroes?" Or "Do you prefer to read at school, in the car, or in bed at night?" Or "Do you prefer reading alone, with a parent, or with a friend?"

> (↑) ② (💡) (▦) Present your results as percentages. You can list them, or go all fancy with a pie chart or bar graph.

Market Researcher Adam graduated from the University of Maryland, College Park, with a bachelor's degree in sociology. For his first job in market research, he asked women in a mall if they'd try on shoes (his payment was soft pretzels!). In the twenty years since, he's conducted interviews, recruited for focus groups, and managed international studies. Now he sells online research for clients like Disney, Microsoft, and Carnival Cruise Lines.

> (↑) ② (💡) (▦) Cross-calculate to determine more complicated percentages, such as which percentage of participants like the same book, action hero stories, *and* reading in the car.

○ ② (💡) (☼) (🔍) Compare two different food brands in a taste test (yum!). First pick two different brands of the same food or beverage (granola with raisins? peach yogurt?). Put samples of each in individual bowls (or cups), next to labels reading "A" and "B." (Important: Secretly jot down which letter goes with which brand so you remember!) Ask participants to taste each and state their preferences. After all participants have tasted, announce the winner. (If you think your participants will identify a brand by how it looks, you can blindfold them prior to their turn to test.)

⬆①☀🔍 Screen your participants before allowing them to participate. For example, if you're testing peach yogurt, ask each potential participant if she even likes the flavor peach—if not, she's not eligible for your taste test.

⬆①💡🔍 Separate your results by type of user: before participants taste, ask them to name their favorite brand of the food you're testing, and how many times a week they eat it. Those who enjoy it three times a week or more are called "heavy users."

DID YOU KNOW?

Market Researchers test products and services months (sometimes years!) before they reach the public. Imagine checking out the latest toy before almost anyone else in the world!

CAREER CROSSING

MARKET RESEARCHERS WORK WITH:

Account Executives

Analysts

Marketers

Product Developers

Publicists*

Meteorologist

I t was the most snow you'd ever seen. In fact, it was the most snow your town had ever seen! And who kept your family in the know before, during, and after the last snowflake fell? You and your on-the-job Meteorologist reporting, sharing tidbits about snow inches, snow plows, and of course—school snow days!

Jump In

○ ①✎🧪 Visit the library or the Internet to report about one, two, or three cloud types: stratus, cumulus, or cirrus.

⬆①✎🧪 Watch clouds form for fifteen or thirty minutes. Simply lay a blanket on the grass on a partly cloudy day and look up—every time a cloud shifts shapes, it's building or dissipating right before your eyes. Can you find examples of what's in your report?

⬆①🎭✎🧪 Ask someone from an older generation to describe the clouds floating above her home—use your report to name what she's seeing.

⬆②🎨💡🧪 Use cotton balls (you can pull 'em apart) and glue to create a 3-D chart of the cloud type(s) in your report. Be sure to label it/them.

○ ①😀🌐✎ Uncover the history of Groundhog Day in a library book or online. Report about what you discover, including whether or not Meteorologists trust the groundhog's weather forecasting.

○ ①✎🧪🌱 Use a library book or online search to report about the ozone layer: include what it is and why our awareness of it is important.

SAYS JAY TROBEC, PHD, CHIEF METEOROLOGIST, KELO-TV IN SIOUX FALLS, SOUTH DAKOTA

I love *that the weather affects everyone, and my forecasts help people plan their days.*

My biggest on-the-job challenge is *making "partly cloudy and 71 degrees" sound interesting—it's a pretty boring forecast for a Meteorologist!*

Perfect weather is *any type of weather that makes people talk about the weather.*

If I were a weather pattern I'd be *a jet stream—you can't see it or hear it, but it affects everything that happens below it.*

During severe weather, I'll work *fourteen hours straight on Live TV without a break!*

If I weren't a Meteorologist, I'd be *a Teacher.*

---

o ①😷🔍🧪 Visit the library or the Internet to learn about hurricanes. Define their five categories and the system Meteorologists use to name them.

①②🎨💡 Draw a picture of Hurricane [YOUR NAME HERE]. Identify your category, where you started, where you're headed, and how long you'll last. (Mom may say forever!)

o ②🔢🔍🧪 Identify the day's high and low temperatures for three,

Meteorologist Jay has a PhD in atmospheric, environmental, and water resources from South Dakota State University. Before becoming a Meteorologist, he worked as a television newscaster and sportscaster. But it's meteorology that has taken him around the world—speaking at weather conferences in France, Spain, the Netherlands, Switzerland, and Slovenia.

four, or five days, converting them into Celsius each day. (You may need to look in a book or online to learn how to convert from Fahrenheit to Celsius.)

o ③ ⓐⓑⓒ ☼ ☺ Shadow a Meteorologist—he may give you a tour of his workplace or teach you a new weather-related fact! After your time together, mail or email a thank-you note.

While in America we use the Fahrenheit temperature system, most of the world (including Meteorologists) prefers Celsius.

Analyze Trends

o ① 💡 🔍 🧪 Use a weather satellite to predict future weather in your hometown. Search the Internet for "weather satellite image" or try NASA's website. Meteorologists use the information gathered by weather satellites in space to help them predict weather all around the world.

o ① 🔍 🧪 Identify the current day's high/low temperature, cloud cover, wind speed, and precipitation percentage (your local paper or its online site will have this information). Then use a weather almanac from the library or the Internet to research the same info for the same day in the year you were born and the year your Mom or Dad was born. (So your report may cover March 3rd this year, March 3, 2004, and March 3, 1969).

⬆ ② 🔍 🧪 Do the same for two, three, or four more days in a row.

⬆ ① 💡 Use the information you've gathered to predict the next day's weather.

DID YOU KNOW?

Broadcast Meteorologists have great memories. Everything they say while on camera is memorized—no script to be found!

WHY DOES METEOROLOGIST JAY THINK HIS CAREER IS AWESOME?

"My job is different every day! (The weather is different every day, isn't it?!)"

Forecast Weather

○ ②🎭😊🔍⚗️ Look in a library book or weather-related online site to find our national weather station symbols—the symbols Meteorologists use to communicate weather patterns. Then write a made-up story (about anything at all), using the symbols in place of words. (See page 361 for an example.)

○ ②🔍⚗️ Collect rain from three different neighborhood locations, at the same time, for five minutes (try asking two friends to put cups out in the rain at their homes or ask Dad to put one outside his office). Use a ruler to measure the amount of rain collected, then compare. Rainfall amounts from the same clouds can be different, even between nearby locations.

⬆①🔍⚗️ Use a library or online search to report about the real shape of raindrops. (Hint: It's not teardrop.)

○ ③🎭💡⚗️ Make your own *barom-eter**. A library or online search will turn up quite a few ways to do this, using items you'll find around your home.

Barometers measure pressure caused by the weight of the atmosphere—lower pressure hints that rain or snow may be on its way.

Broadcast Weather News

○ ②💡abc💬 Deliver a radio report about the weather conditions on an alien planet (yes, you can name your planet and its inhabitants). Ask Mom or Dad to record you with a digital or tape recorder, computer microphone, or cell phone. Include forecasts for today, tonight, tomorrow, and the following seven days.

⬆①💡 Handle a sudden change—Mom or Dad at the "news desk" have just handed you a memo of a last-minute weather update contradicting your weather report!

○ ②💡abc💬🔍😊 Ask Mom or Dad to use a video or digital camera to record you doing an evening TV report. Deliver information you've gathered from your local paper or news channel throughout the day.

🔼 ① ⏱ Use a stopwatch, kitchen timer, or computer clock to time your report—Broadcast Meteorologists have to keep their entire TV forecast to about three minutes.

🔼 ② 🎨 🎭 🔍 Add a map to your report, which you can point to during your broadcast. You can even add official Meteorologist graphics by copying what you see in a library book or online.

CAREER CROSSING

METEOROLOGISTS WORK WITH:

Broadcast Technicians

Climatologists

Graphic Artists

Hydrologists

Journalists*

Mom says "stop fidgeting," but you're not fidgeting! You're drumming, strumming, whistling, snapping—simply playing along to the song in your head, using the best instrument in the world: your body. And once she realizes you're quite the talented Musician, you both start jamming to the "music" you love to make!

Jump In

○ ① 🎭 ⊕ 🔍 Ask Mom or Dad to sing a song he sang to you as a baby (a lullaby? a nursery rhyme?). Why did he decide to sing it to you? Do you remember it? Then visit the library or the Internet to report about it: who sang it first and when? Has it been recorded by more than one Musician?

MUSICIANS:

- Study and listen to music
- Write music
- Record music
- Perform live in shows, concerts, and bands

○ ② 💡 abc 🔍 Keep a little notepad with you for two, three, or four days. List one, two, or three places you hear music, but never realized it before (like in the elevator at the dentist's office? in the grocery store?). Define how the music makes you feel (music played in grocery stores may influence you to buy more!).

○ ② 💡 abc 😊 😃 Show your support for music in schools. Learn more about programs like VH1's Save the Music, then share what you've learned with two, three, or four other people. Or host a fundraiser. Or write a letter to a local legislator about the educational benefits of keeping music in school.

○ ③ abc ☀ 😊 Shadow a Musician. Try a music teacher, local bandleader, or professional at a music camp. After your time together, mail or email a thank-you note.

> ### says Irvin Mayfield, Trumpeter, Bandleader, Professor, and Artistic Director of the New Orleans Jazz Orchestra in New Orleans, Louisiana
>
> I love *connecting with people through jazz music.*
>
> My biggest on-the-job challenge is *flying to performances—I have a fear of airplanes!*
>
> The first time I heard one of my songs on the radio I *smiled.*
>
> Music once inspired me to *go to Istanbul.*
>
> If I were an instrument I'd be *a trumpet because they're cute.*
>
> If I weren't a Musician, I'd be *a Candy Shop Owner.*

○ ③ ⓐⓑⓒ ☼ ☺ Tour a local recording studio. Call first to schedule an appointment—maybe you'll get to see a Musician recording a song! Mail or email a thank-you note to your guide.

○ ③ 🎭 🔍 Attend a music-themed community event, for instance, a music festival or high school choir concert. Report about one, two, or three of the songs or acts you see there.

Play Instruments

○ ① 💡 Play one of your favorite songs as many times as necessary to list the individual instruments in it (listen closely).

WHY DOES MUSICIAN IRVIN THINK HIS JOB IS AWESOME?

"I can alter the emotion of an entire room by the song I select. I can connect with people. I enjoy freedom and creativity. And I get to play with other great Musicians!"

Air bands "play" imaginary instruments—instruments made of air!

👕 ① 💡 ☼ Assign the instruments to family members (Mom on guitar? Dad on drums?), play the song again, and rock out in your own *air band**.

○ ① 🎭 🌐 🔍 Use a library book or online site to report the history and music of one, two, or three of the following: Australia's didgeridoo, Egypt's doumbek, Peru's charango, Russia's balalaika. (Bet you can't say all that ten times fast!)

> 👆 ① 🎭 🔍 Find recordings of the instrument(s) in your report and listen to it/them. Ask your Librarian for help or try online.

> 👆 ② 🎭 🌐 🔍 💬 Pick one of the instruments—dress in clothes from its country of origin (be creative with what you can find in your family's closets)—and present your report as a speech, acting as if you actually play the instrument.

Musician Irvin received his first trumpet in the fourth grade, and went on to graduate from the New Orleans Center of Creative Arts. He continued his studies at the University of New Orleans, Jazz Studies program. Since then, he's launched a music school for elementary students, been appointed cultural ambassador for New Orleans, and even won a Grammy!

○ ② 🎨 Ask someone from an older generation if she plays an instrument—if so, spend some time with her, learning about it and maybe even writing a song together.

Write & Record Songs

○ ① 💡 Use your body as an instrument to play your favorite song. Whistle, hum, snap, clap, knee-slap—even blow kisses. Musicians never know when a song idea will pop into their heads, and they don't need their instruments to get a feel for how it could sound.

Musicians can be your piano teacher, jazz saxophonists, folk guitarists, classical violinists, rock 'n' roll drummers—anyone who creates and performs music.

○ ① 🔍 Define "verse," "chorus," and "bridge." Then print out the lyrics to one of your favorite songs and identify each verse, the chorus, and the bridge. (You can also listen to the song and jot the lyrics down.)

①②💡(abc) Use the formula to write a song about your bedtime routine. First write the words, then hum a tune that fits it. If you know an instrument, you can play along.

①②💡(abc) Turn the song into a duet (maybe Mom has a line about you always wanting a glass of water? or your teddy bear sings about bedtime cuddles?) by adjusting or changing a few lyrics.

①②☼(smile) "Hire" (payment is big hugs) Singers (Mom? Dad? Little Bro?)—give each a lyric sheet and teach them your song's melody. Then use a digital or tape recorder, computer microphone, or cell phone to record them singing your song.

○ ②💡(abc) Write a story about Cream Cheese & Jelly. How did they meet? Did they get along at first? If not, how did they learn to get along? How will the story end? Read your story aloud. Then, *sing* your story aloud—any tune will do!

①①💡 Give your song a title. The titles Musicians choose can influence how listeners feel about a song even before they hear it.

DID YOU KNOW?

Sometimes Musicians write and record a beautiful piece of music in one day. And sometimes it'll take a year to get a song just right!

Perform

○ ②🎨💡(smile)(hand) Define "brass," "string," "percussion," and "woodwind." Then build one, using items from around your home (try using a cut-up cereal box and old shoelaces to make a fun string instrument). Lastly, perform your favorite song (or one you wrote) using your new instrument.

(↑)(1)(💡) Create a pre-performance ritual—something you do before your performance to calm your nerves and get you psyched. Do you take twelve deep breaths? Blink three times and yell, "Bugga, Bugga, Bugga!"?

(↑)(2)(🧪)(💡)(☼)(💬) Make instruments for one, two, or three family members so they can perform with you. Remember to practice first.

(↑)(2)(💡)(🎭) Pull together a costume for your performance—one that reflects your music's style.

(↑)(3)(☼)(💬) Take your act on the road. Visit a local park or a relative's home with your instruments, music, and costume—and give a live performance!

○ (3)(🎭)(🔍) Attend a theatrical performance where music is key, like a musical, opera, or ballet. Report about the role the Musicians played in telling the performance's story.

CAREER CROSSING

MUSICIANS WORK WITH:

Booking Agents

Music Producers

Music Publishers

Singers

Sound Engineers

Nurse Practitioner

You cut your hand, you tell Mom you need a bandage. You feel achy, you tell Dad you could use some chicken soup and a really long nap. Looks like you've got healthcare TLC down to a science! Nurse Practitioners deliver this same kind of service every day—for patients who feel a lot healthier because of it.

Jump In

- ① 😷 🌐 🔍 Report on the history of Nurse Practitioners—yes, they're different from Nurses *and* Doctors.

Evaluate Patients

- ① 🧮 🕐 Calculate how many patients you can see in a day if you start at 9:00 a.m., finish at 5:00 p.m., enjoy an hour for lunch, and each appointment is thirty minutes long. What about if the appointments are forty-five minutes long?

- ① 🔍 Use the library or an Internet search to report on the neurological system.

- ⚕ ① ☀ 🔍 🧪 Examine a patient's (Mom's?) sight by first making an eye chart on a piece of a paper—write a big letter or shape at the top, with three rows of three letters underneath, each row smaller than the last. Ask your patient to cover one eye with her hand—hold the paper a few feet away and see how many letters she can read. Try with the other eye too.

Nurse Practitioners:

- Examine patients
- Educate people on how to get and stay healthy
- Write prescriptions for medications
- Perform procedures like suturing up wounds, delivering babies, and assisting in surgery
- Read and interpret results from tests like X-rays

says Jill Steiner Sanko, MS, ARNP-BC,
University of Miami–Jackson Memorial Hospital
Center for Patient Safety in Miami, Florida

I love _helping people be better off after they see me._

My biggest on-the-job challenge is _patients who think medicine is magic._

I couldn't work without _my stethoscope._

My favorite part of an exam is _listening to my patient._

The most patients I've ever seen in one day is _twenty-four._

If I weren't a Nurse Practitioner I'd be _a Forensic Anthropologist._

⇧ ① ☼ 🔍 ⚗ Examine your patient's hearing with the whisper test. Stand close to her (but not too close) and whisper something. Can she repeat it back to you?

⇧ ① ☼ 🔍 ⚗ Examine your patient's memory with number recall. Recite a few numbers. Ask her to repeat the numbers backward.

⇧ ① ☼ 🔍 ⚗ Examine your patient's balance by asking her to stand on one foot for several seconds. Then repeat on the opposite foot.

○ ① 🔍 Use the library or an Internet search to report on the human cardiovascular system.

⇧ ① ☼ 🔍 ⚗ Examine a patient's (Dad's?) heart rate and rhythm by finding his *pulse**. Place two fingers on the inside of your patient's wrist (try not to press too hard or you won't be able to find it). Count how many times you feel the pulse in ten seconds. Multiply this number by six to determine your patient's pulse rate.

*Your **pulse** is the contraction you feel when blood is pushed through your heart.

⇧ ① ☼ 🔍 ⚗ Examine your patient's *circulation*** by gently

***Circulation** refers to blood's movement throughout your body.

pushing down on any of his nail beds—when you do this, the nail turns white. Let go, and the pink color will return as the blood returns to the fingertip. How many seconds does it take for the color to return?

○ ① 🔍 Use the library or an Internet search to report on the human respiratory system.

🔼①☀🔍⚗ Examine a patient's (Big Sis's?) lungs by listening to her take a breath in and a breath out. To do this, lay your head on your patient's chest while she breathes. Or if you have a pretend stethoscope (some of 'em work pretty well), hold it up to her back in several places to hear all the lobes (sections of the lungs): high near the shoulder, middle of the back, and low on the back near the waistline.

○ ① 🔍 Use the library or an Internet search to report on the human gastro-intestinal system.

🔼①☀🔍⚗ Examine your patient's (Little Bro's?) *bowels** by listening to his stomach. When you put your ear to his stomach, do you hear gurgling and faint pinging sounds? Try this at two different times: when your patient is hungry and when he has just eaten.

Nurse Practitioner Jill graduated with a bachelor of science degree in anthropology—and then realized her dream career was in medicine. So she earned a second bachelor of science degree (this time in nursing) from Rush University, and followed this with a master of science degree (in nursing as well). Twelve years later, she enjoys caring for patients, teaching, researching, and volunteering, all with an eye on patient safety.

WHY DOES NURSE PRACTITIONER JILL THINK HER CAREER IS AWESOME?

"I get to help people feel better every day!"

* **Bowels** are where your body absorbs most of the nutrients from food.

② 😄 🌐 ☀ 🔍 Ask Mom or Dad (your patient) to fill out the questionnaire on page 362 (or download it at EarnMyKeep.com). Review her medical history together. It's important that Nurse Practitioners know everything about their patients' health, in order to take better care of them.

Educate Patients

o ① 💡 🐕 Recommend Mom or Dad (your patient) make one healthy change, and you do it, too. Take a walk around the block, taste a new vegetable, or try a yoga pose.

o ① 💡 List one, two, or three reasons why patients should ask lots of questions, and also listen closely to their health care provider's answers.

DID YOU KNOW?

Nurse Practitioners get the unique opportunity to be a part of a patient's life in ways few others know about— they really value these personal relationships!

o ① 💡 🔍 🐕 List medicine-free ways to lessen pain for one, two, or three ailments, like how taking a warm bubble bath is great for sore muscles, or chewing on a frozen washcloth helps teething babies. Nurse Practitioners prescribe these kinds of treatments because they're inexpensive and easy to do.

o ① 💡 ☀ 🐕 Teach your patient (Dad?) how to take care of himself. Let's say he hurt his arm falling off the monkey bars (ouch!). Wrap his arm in a scarf, handkerchief, or towel, so he can't use it. Demonstrate how he can brush his teeth by using his other hand. Be careful not to get the hurt arm wet. (Make this more interesting by wrapping up his right arm if he's right-handed, his left arm if he's left-handed.)

Promote Prevention

o ① 🔍 🐕 Use the library or the Internet to report on one, two, or three benefits of preventative medicine (also called preventative care).

(↑) (1) (💡) (🐞) (☀) (🧪) Ask someone from an older generation if she's practiced any preventative care (such as visiting a Dentist, staying away from soda, and/or managing stress) that has helped improve her health over time. If she can't think of any, make a suggestion for her to try.

○ (2) (🔍) (🐾) Give a family member one, two, or three preventative care tips that you uncover from a library or online search—then both of you put them into action for one, two, or three days.

CAREER CROSSING

NURSE PRACTITIONERS WORK WITH:

Nurses

Pharmacists

Physical Therapists

Physicians

Social Workers

Outdoor Adventure Guide

Sailing, kayaking, whitewater rafting, fly fishing, horseback riding, mountain biking, *spelunking** (yes, spelunking), rock climbing, bouldering—you name it, the Outdoor Adventure Guide inside you is ready to lead a group deep into the wild outdoors. Although a leisurely stroll around the neighborhood sounds pretty good, too!

*Spelunking is exploring caves for fun.

Jump In

- ② 💡 🔍 Ask Mom or Dad to grab a map of your town from a local gas station (or print one from online) and mark a Point A (starting point) and Point B (ending point). Use the library, the Internet, or your innate map skills to read the map, marking the safest, most efficient route.

  ⬆ ② 🔍 Walk, bike, or drive your route to see if you're right.

- ③ 🔤 ☀ 💬 Shadow an Outdoor Adventure Guide. Check out how he prepares to take a group on an adventure. Mail or email a thank-you note after your time together.

OUTDOOR ADVENTURE GUIDES:

- Create exciting vacations that take advantage of everything nature offers
- Educate travelers about an area's history, plants, and animals
- Keep travelers safe by being experts in first aid and survival tactics

Prepare for Adventures

- ① 💡 🎭 🔍 ⚗ Plan a hiking adventure to the Outback in Australia. List the area's climate, its altitude, and describe the area's terrain. What is the best

SAYS WILLIAM LARRY WEBB, JR.,
DIRECTOR OF EDUCATION, COLORADO OUTDOOR ADVENTURE
GUIDE SCHOOL, INC., IN VICTOR, COLORADO

I love _being in the backcountry, where few people have ever been._

My biggest on-the-job challenge is _cold rain. I can deal with cold and rain, but not at the same time._

The biggest blister I've ever had _went all the way across the back of my heel._

I buy a new pair of hiking boots every _six months to a year._

My favorite time of day to be outdoors is _just as the day is breaking— the woods come alive!_

If I weren't an Outdoor Adventure Guide, I'd be _a Historian._

time of year to visit? Check at the library or online for accurate answers—you may be very surprised.

⚐ ① 💡 🔍 ⚗ List the same information for hiking adventures to one, two, or three other locations, like Canada, Chile, or Zimbabwe.

○ ① 🔍 ⚗ Visit the library or the Internet to learn how to administer simple first aid for blisters, mild bruises, and bee stings.

⚐ ② 💡 🎨 ☀ ⚗ Gather items for a first aid kit (like bandages, tweezers, antibacterial cream, and alcohol pads) and administer first aid on a "traveler" who needs you: someone from an older generation.

○ ① 🔍 🐾 Use the library or the Internet to report about the principles of Leave No Trace—ideals all great Outdoor Adventure Guides take very seriously.

⚐ ② abc 🐾 Write a poem, song, or story incorporating the lessons of Leave No Trace.

- ② 🔍 Look in a cookbook, a library book, or an online site for a healthy trail mix recipe—the kind of snack Outdoor Adventure Guides would likely give travelers to keep them energized. Then make the mix and enjoy it on a short walk around your neighborhood.

- ② 💡🔍 Fill an old school backpack with camping gear (like a pair of socks, flip-flops, sunscreen, and lip balm) and a raincoat and/or rain boots. Ask Mom or Dad to mist you

> *Outdoor Adventure Guide*
> *William* graduated from the University of Mississippi with a bachelor of arts degree, double major in history and anthropology. His passion for the outdoors led him to the Colorado Outdoor Adventure Guide School, where he now combines the things he loves most: cooking, educating, and the outdoors!

with a squirt bottle or garden hose while you try to get your rain gear on and keep the rest of your backpack's contents dry—Outdoor Adventure Guides must be prepared for any emergency!

⬆️① 💡🔍 Have Mom or Dad hide a flashlight in your room. Then find it. In the dark.

- ③ 🧪🧪🔍 Collect safe drinking water with a solar still (a valuable skill if you ever run out of drinking water on an adventure). Look in a library book or online for instructions for how to build one with stuff you've got on hand.

Guide Travelers

- ① 🔍🧪🐢 Visit the library or the Web to report about one, two, or three native flora or fauna that could harm your adventurers. What should you do if someone eats or touches it/them?

- ① 🎴🌐🔍 Use the library, the Internet, even interviews with long-time locals to report about one, two, or three of your town or city's *legends**.

✳️ **Legends** are stories that have been passed down through so many generations, no one knows if they're true or not.

251

Knowing this kind of history helps clients get a full sense of the area in which they're traveling. And Outdoor Adventure Guides do more than take travelers safely from point A to B—they provide a full experience.

(↑)(3)(☺)(⊕)(○) Walk, bike, or drive to where part of your legend's story occurred, sharing the details with your family along the way.

○ (2)(💡)(☼)(○) Go on an adventure in the rain (yes, outside). Pretend you're leading a group (Mom? Dad? Big Bro?) deep into the Amazonian rainforest. Make sure everyone has appropriate gear (rain hats/coats? umbrellas? old sneakers or rain boots?). And while hiking, keep morale up—point out the beauty of the "jungle" as you enjoy a shower from Mother Nature.

WHY DOES OUTDOOR ADVENTURE GUIDE WILLIAM THINK HIS CAREER IS AWESOME?

"I get to share the 'Great Outdoors' with others. The moon and stars are my ceiling, every day is an adventure, and nothing is ever the same."

○ (3)(💡)(○) Lead your family in a campout—anything from an honest-to-goodness overnight at a campsite to a few evening hours lying in sleeping bags in the backyard. List what you'll need (tent? water bottles? ingredients for s'mores?), gather what's on your list, give your family an overview of what to expect, and then camp out. Remember to prepare a ghost story or two!

(↑)(1)(🔍)(⚗)(🕐) Use a library book or an online site to report about one, two, or three nocturnal animals that live in your region. What should you do if you run into one?

(↑)(3)(💡)(🔍) Cook by campfire. Look in a library book or online for a recipe, or try the one on page 363.

DID YOU KNOW?

One of an Outdoor Adventure Guide's most valuable skills is "people skills"—being friendly and informed about news, science, and history is as important as survival and first aid!

SO YOU WANT TO...LEAD AN OUTDOOR ADVENTURE

○ ③ 💡 ☼ 💬 🔍 ✋ ⏰ Take inexperienced travelers on an outdoor exploration they'll remember for a lifetime.

1. First, pick your adventure: Hiking at a nearby waterfall? "Rock climbing" at the playground's jungle gym? Fishing at the water hole? Biking through the "Italian countryside" (the center of town)? Take your group into consideration (does Mom have a bad back? does Little Sis still use training wheels?).

2. Map out your route (on a map from the gas station or one printed from online). Use it to help determine how long the trip will take—include water and bathroom breaks too.

3. Provide group members a list of where they're going, how long they'll be gone, what they should expect to see (yes, it can be imaginary), and equipment needs. Give everyone time to gather/prepare their equipment.

4. Review the map and safety precautions with your group. Check that they have the right equipment.

5. Venture out. Be sure to stay with your group—don't go too far ahead, or lag too far behind.

6. Be respectful of nature. And politely keep everyone on schedule.

7. Bring everyone home safe, on time!

CAREER CROSSING

OUTDOOR ADVENTURE GUIDES WORK WITH:
Division of Wildlife Officers
Forest Service Rangers
Leadership and Confidence Builders
Outdoor Writers
Outfitters

Paleontologist

All you wanted to do was help the dog bury his bone, but a few inches down, your fingers grabbed more than dirt. It was, well, what was it?! It looked like a snail shell…but it was hard, like stone. Your first fossil! Congratulations, Paleontologist—you're on your way to unearthing some of the greatest mysteries on Earth.

Jump In

○ ② 🔍 🎒 😊 Push a toy dinosaur about halfway deep into mud or sand, near water flow (this can be natural, like a stream or river bank, or man-made, as from a garden hose). Watch as the water pushes mud and debris over the dinosaur, burying it. (Once it's buried, remember to take your dinosaur out!) Then use a library book or Internet search to report about how real fossils are preserved—it's very similar to your experiment.

If you use a garden hose, do this where the water's runoff spills onto grass or plants—water is a precious resource!

○ ③ 🔤 ☼ 💬 Shadow a Paleontologist. Many museums have some on staff, or try finding one at a university that teaches geology and/or biology. Come prepared with a question or two, and mail or email a thank-you note right after your time together.

PALEONTOLOGISTS:

- Discover and excavate fossil sites
- Clean, identify, and sort ancient bones and fossils
- Use fossils to study the history of life on Earth

○ ③ 🌐 🧫 🔍 🎒 Invite someone from an older generation to join you in visiting a museum that houses dinosaur bones or other fossils. Before going, discuss your favorite fossils. Then while at the museum, use your inner Paleontologist to report one, two, or three new facts about each.

SAYS ANDREW R. C. MILNER,
PALEONTOLOGIST AND CURATOR, ST. GEORGE DINOSAUR
DISCOVERY SITE AT JOHNSON FARM IN ST. GEORGE, UTAH

I love *discovering animals and plants no human has ever seen before.*

My biggest on-the-job challenge is *protecting fossil sites from fossil thieves and vandalism.*

My most memorable discovery *was a site that revealed two iguanodontians, one terrestrial crocodile, a mammal skull, and the tail of a meat-eating dinosaur!*

If I were a dinosaur, I'd be a *Dilophosaurus because large, meat-eating dinosaurs (theropods) are really cool.*

The one tool I can't work without is *a geology hammer...and a camera... and a GPS unit...and a notebook.*

If I weren't a Paleontologist, I'd be *a Marine Biologist.*

Excavate & Analyze Bones & Fossils

○ ① Visit the library or the Internet to learn about the evolution of birds (dinosaurs' only living relatives). List one, two, or three dinosaurs now believed to have had feathers and what the feathers were used for.

② Collect and dry out a turkey or chicken wishbone, glue it to a piece of construction paper, and then draw the rest of a *Tyrannosaurus rex* or *Allosaurus's* bones around it. (Look in a library book or website for inspiration.)

○ ② Make your own "stone" fossils of "ancient plants." This can be as simple as pressing twigs, leaves, shells, and seeds into store-bought or hand-made play-dough (recipe on page 347) and letting them bake in the sun until they harden. Or search the library or Internet for more complex recipes that use coffee grounds, plaster of Paris—even sand.

○ ②🔍🧪 Ask Mom or Dad to make two, three, or four secret fossils (try the suggestions in the above task), and then bury them as a group (together) in the yard, sprinkling a few fragments on top of the burial site as clues. Your job is to find the fossils by thinking like a Paleontologist: look in the edges of sandboxes, flower or rock gardens, or at the bases of hedges or trees.

Real Paleontologists often start searches for fossils at the bottoms of slopes because fossils tend to shift downward over time.

☝②🔍🧪 Log each of your fossils: list what was found (say, a leaf), what kind of organism it came from (a fern), where it was found (under the rock near the front step), what rock layer it was discovered in (3″ deep in the soil), who discovered it (YOU!), and when it was discovered (2:42 p.m., Sunday).

Excavation sites are what Paleontologists call the places where they dig for fossils.

☝①⏱ Return to your *excavation site**—make sure you've left it as you found it. Refill holes with their dirt. Check to make sure flowers have not been trampled upon.

○ ②💡🧪 Ask Mom or Dad to (1) photocopy or print out a picture of a dinosaur skeleton (look in a library book or online); (2) use a photocopy machine to enlarge the picture; and (3) cut the bones out—without you seeing. Then it's your turn to put the skeleton back together. (If needed, ask for a hint for the type of dinosaur you're reconstructing—you can use a library book or Internet search to find a picture of the skeleton for reference.)

Paleontologist Andrew discovered his first fossil at the age of six. By the age of twelve, he was collecting Ice Age fossils, eventually donating his entire collection to the Canadian Museum of Nature—where he was then offered his first paleontology job. Since then, he's earned a bachelor's degree in geology from Brock University in St. Catharines, Ontario, worked on world-famous fossil localities, and was even the first Paleontologist called in to visit a new discovery of dinosaur tracks in Utah, where he lives and works today.

○ ③ 💡 ⚗️ Pick up a dinosaur skeleton kit from a local or online toy store (about $7) and put it together.

Study Ancient Life

○ ① 🌐 🔍 Visit the library or Internet to report about the parenting habits of Maiasaura ("good mother lizard") from Egg Mountain, Montana or the Oviraptor from the Gobi Desert—two examples of the few dinosaurs that took care of their young.

👕 ② 🧪 💡 🌐 🔍 Make a Mother's Day card from one of your dinosaur's young to his mother, thanking her for the types of food she brought him and what she did to help him survive to adulthood.

○ ② 🌐 🔍 ⚗️ Use a library or Internet search to get to know the Triassic, Jurassic, and Cretaceous periods—report about one, two, or three dinosaur species that appeared in each period.

👕 ② 🧪 💡 🌐 🔍 ⚗️ Draw a picture of your favorite species in his natural environment, doing what he loved best to do (eat? swim? fly?).

○ ② 💡 🌐 🔍 Eat like an herbivore in the Mesozoic era. Visit a farmer's market or specialty food store to research the kinds of edible plants local

---

WHY DOES PALEONTOLOGIST ANDREW THINK HIS CAREER IS AWESOME?

"Because major discoveries are made not only during excavations, but also while looking through old museum collections and in the lab while the fossils are being prepared—I never stop learning new things!"

DID YOU KNOW?

Whether in the bush, the desert, or the freezing arctic, Paleontologists can just look at a landscape's rock formations to get a good hunch if fossils are buried inside!

About 65 percent of dinosaurs ate plants, not meat.

to your region. Then include a few of these plants with every meal for one, two, or three days.

○ (2) (💡) (🔍) Walk, bike, or drive around your neighborhood, paying particular attention to what you see. Are the trees especially tall? Is it raining? Is your community hilly? Describe and name the kind of prehistoric animal that would have thrived in your environment (*Neckalashafootasaurus*: a long-necked dinosaur that ate leaves from tall trees, had long lashes to keep water out of its eyes, and walked on wide, flat feet that were stable on hilly terrain!).

CAREER CROSSING

PALEONTOLOGISTS WORK WITH:

Biologists

Climatologists

Geologists*

Government Officials

Paleontology Artists

Photographer

I t's a big birthday for Dad this year, and your family's pulled out all the stops: his favorite meal, his favorite cake, his favorite friends and loved ones all gathered to toast the Big Guy. And there you are, camera in hand, snapping shots of everyone and everything to capture the kind of memories only a Photographer can deliver!

Jump In

○ ①🎨🎭🌐🔍 Visit the library or the Internet to report about a famous Photographer (your Librarian or an online search can help you find one who photographs subjects that interest you, like wild animals, sporting events, or foreign cities).

🎩②🎨💡 Shoot some pictures that mimic your Photographer's style. Use pictures from your report for inspiration.

○ ①🎨🔍⚗️ Take a photograph of Mom or Dad with a digital and a cell phone camera—compare the two shots. Then use a library or Internet search to uncover what technology makes one better than the other.

○ ②💡🎨🔍 Ask someone from an older generation for a picture of herself when she was young. Study the photo and report about what you see—is it in color or black-and-white? Does it have a postcard-like border? Are the corners rounded? Is it grainy? Are the colors rich and vibrant, or muted? How does the quality of the photo compare to the photos Mom and Dad take now?

PHOTOGRAPHERS:

- Create images for websites, magazines, newspapers, and advertisements
- Take pictures that capture the action at events

SAYS RICHARD GREENHOUSE, OWNER, RICHARD GREENHOUSE
PHOTOGRAPHY, INC., IN ROCKVILLE, MARYLAND

I love *the smile on my clients' faces when they see their finished product.*

My biggest on-the-job challenge is *how heavy my equipment can be— sometimes I think I need a Mack truck to carry it all!*

The best outdoor shooting conditions *are different for people (overcast so they don't squint) and architecture (beautiful blue skies).*

To get the perfect shot, I once found myself *in a very dangerous place with a circus lion.*

The most difficult subjects I've ever photographed *were ballet dancers. They work so hard at being perfect, the picture is either perfect or it's no good.*

If I weren't a Photographer, I'd be *a Teacher.*

① ① ⑫ ⑭ ⑭ Ask if she has any film negatives or slide negatives to show you—they're pretty cool. (If there are none to be found, research film and slides at the library or online, together.)

② ⑭ ⑫ ⑭ ⑯ Take eight, ten, or twelve pictures of a socially or environmentally responsible subject of your choice (Dad installing a low-flow toilet? Big Sis turning the A/C off and opening the windows to let nature cool your home?). Before shooting, create a list of different angles and/or different times of day, to ensure each of your pictures is unique. Print out your photos.

Just use your home printer— you don't even need fancy photo paper.

① ② ⑭ ⑫ ⑯ ⑭ Select five favorites. Use tape or glue to attach each to five pieces of black or white poster board or construction paper. Then prop each board on a window ledge, or tape up on a wall—invite family members to a viewing of your work, just like real Photographers do.

○ ③ (abc) (☀) (☺) Shadow a Photographer. Maybe you'll see him retouch a photo or set up for a shoot. Mail or email a thank-you note right afterward.

> **WHY DOES PHOTOGRAPHER RICHARD THINK HIS CAREER IS AWESOME?**
>
> "I get to take pictures and get paid for it! Pictures that, ten years from now, will make people smile because they bring back a great memory."

Photograph Events

○ ② (⚓) (💡) (☀) (⏱) Ask Mom or Dad for a shot list—a list of three, four, or five pictures he wants taken at dinner.

For example, Shot #1: Mom, Dad, and Big Bro; Shot #2: Mom serving Brussels sprouts; and Shot #3: Dad enjoying Brussels sprouts.

Discuss the shots so you know what he's looking for, then at the event—take them! Print out your pictures and review them together.

○ ② (⚓) (💡) (☀) Take one, two, or three *portraits** about a half-hour before a family event. Then during the event, take one, two, or three *candids*** of the same people. After the event, print out your pictures. Compare the shots—which style do you prefer?

Portraits *are posed photos, with subjects looking directly at the camera.*

Candid *photos are unposed, informal shots.*

○ ② (⚓) (💡) (☀) Shoot an everyday event (Little Bro brushing his teeth? Mom coming home from work?) in a

Photojournalism *tells a story with pictures.*

*photojournalistic**** style—this means capturing the event from beginning to end, without posing or directing any of your subjects.

(⬆) ② (⚓) Tape or glue printed pictures into an album (one picture per page). The album can be either handmade with construction paper and a stapler, or one you buy from a craft store.

Photograph for Commercial Use

○ ① 🚲 💡 🔍 Take close-up shots of two, three, or four different textures in nature: a flower's petal, a blade of grass, an earthworm's wormy body. Print out your pictures and examine how the camera captured the subject's texture and color.

⬆ ① 🔍 Ask a family member to identify your subjects in three guesses—no hints!

If you don't have free access to a camera, pick up a single-use camera (about $13) from a grocery, convenience, or drug store.

○ ① 🚲 🔍 🧪 Manipulate light with a camera's flash. First take a picture of a person (Mom? Dad? the Newspaper Delivery Boy?) with his back to the sun, flash OFF. Take another picture, flash ON. (The camera's instruction book will say if you can manually shut the flash on and off.) Then compare the two shots. This is how Photographers work around the sun's changing light, depending on time of day or weather.

Photographer Richard graduated with a bachelor's degree in business and public administration twenty-five years ago—and promptly decided to make his life's passion his work instead. He taught himself the art of photography and opened the company he still runs today, taking pictures of folks like Tom Hanks, Mariah Carey, every President since Jimmy Carter—even Elmo and Kermit the Frog!

○ ② 🚲 💡 🔍 Take a picture of an inanimate object (your flute? your soccer cleat?) in an interesting setting (on a fireplace mantle? sticking out of a toy box?). Then shoot your object in one, two, or three other settings. Compare your pictures: which setting shows off your subject best? Photographers will shoot sometimes hundreds of pictures to get the one that works.

○ ② Ⓐ Ⓨ Ⓠ Ⓘ Photograph one, two, or three of the following foods, using food-styling tricks: your favorite fruit sprinkled with drops of water to make it look morning-fresh-from-the-garden; your favorite green veggie microwaved a minute or two to bring out the brightest green color; a bowl of your favorite cereal in heavy cream instead of milk to prevent sogginess; your favorite juice mixed with water to allow more light to filter through (looks more refreshing).

Ⓣ ② Ⓐ Ⓨ Ⓠ Ⓘ Ⓒ Photograph pictures of the food(s) without the tricks, allowing each food to sit at least a half-hour before shooting. Which photo makes each item look tastier?

DID YOU KNOW?

Photographers need to know more than photography to get a great shot—capturing the moment a bird learns to fly means knowing at which age that bird is likely to fly!

CAREER CROSSING

PHOTOGRAPHERS WORK WITH:

Art Directors

Graphic Designers

Hair Stylists

Lab Technicians

Magazine Editors

Mom wants to shoot a video of you "being you" (something about "growing up so fast she can't stand it"). So you suggest visiting the park after school (when it's not so sunny) and then grabbing some ice cream (when it's not so crowded) so you can make practice by 4:00 p.m. Thanks to your Producer skills, she got her video, and you got to practice on time!

Jump In

○ ③ⓐⓑⓒ☼☺ Shadow a Producer. Call a local production company or a local television channel to find one. After your time together, write or email a thank-you note.

Prepare for Productions

○ ①💡🔍 Find a picture of an exotic location in a travel magazine. Then do a location scout—look for a place in your own home that could be used to re-create the scene (could the bathroom be turned into a rainforest waterfall? the garage into a desert?). List what you'd need to add to make the location look more real.

⬆②🎨💡 Create your location. Add some of Mom's potted plants and a construction paper rainbow and ta-da! A bathroom rainforest it is. Producers often help turn regular places into magical spots using techniques like these.

producers:

- Find Directors and production companies
- Establish schedules and budgets
- Organize casting auditions (to find just the right Actor)
- Look for the best locations for a production
- Coordinate every detail, including travel arrangements and wardrobe decisions

Location scouts can take Producers anywhere around the globe.

> ## says Angela Edwards, owner,
> ## Twin Productions in Silver Spring, Maryland
>
> I love _bringing a story to life using a script and a budget as my guides._
>
> My biggest on-the-job challenge is _keeping track of all the details._
>
> The most dangerous shoot I've ever managed _took place in a helicopter. We almost crashed because the Director was on the throttle!_
>
> I once worked on a set _in front of the White House. All our equipment had to be sniffed by security dogs._
>
> I never go to a shoot without _my cell phone._
>
> If I weren't a Producer, I'd be _a Publicist._

(↑)(1)(🏠)(💡)(🔍) Take a digital picture of your scene so you can get a feel of what the camera will see. Make adjustments as needed.

○ (2)(💡)(☀) Request headshots of Actors to play members of your family. Ask Mom to take digital pictures of Dad dressed up like Little Sis. Or Big Sis dressed up like Baby Bro. Or even Grandma dressed like Uncle Harold! Study the headshots—are there ways your Actors can be made to look even more like the part they're playing?

(↑)(1)(☀) Get all of your Actors to sign a (pretend) _release*_. Photocopy the one on page 364, download it at EarnMyKeep.com, or make up your own.

*A **release** is a document that allows someone's words and/or image to be used by someone else.

○ (2)(💡)(🔍) Find a Director to direct a movie about your life story. You'll find Directors' names listed at the end of movies or shows, or on online databases. Want a funny flick? Research Directors from shows that make you laugh.

Want a horror film? Find a director from something spooky. Some Producers keep DVD libraries of Directors' work to help them find just the right one.

⬆②💡🎬🔍 Do the same for a life-story movie about someone from an older generation, presenting her with two, three, or four Director choices. To help her decide, describe the Director's style and a few of the movies or shows he's shot.

○ ③🧮💲🔍 Budget a shoot for a great scene: the day you were born. First, list the number of "Actors." (Mom, of course. Dad? The doctor? Remember to include yourself!) Then list how you'll get to the hospital (plane? taxi?) and how many nights you'll need to stay in the area for your shoot (one night? two nights?). Then use the Internet or your imagination to find and calculate your costs. So, how much would it cost, say, for four Actors to travel to the hospital's location (airfare? taxi fare?), and stay in a nearby hotel overnight?

⬆②🧮💲🔍 Add in meals too. Where will your team eat breakfast, lunch, and/or dinner, and how much will it cost?

⬆②🧮💲🔍 Beat your budget. Can you find a less expensive way to get there? Less expensive hotel? Less expensive restaurant? Coupons or discounts?

Producer Angela graduated with a bachelor of science degree in journalism from the University of Maryland, College Park, and has been a Producer for fifteen years. To really understand everything that goes into production, she's worked on every level, from Production Assistant to Executive Producer—she's even taken screenwriting classes!

Producers work in theater, television, radio, movies, even commercials—anywhere there's an idea or program that needs to be brought to life.

○ ③ 💡 🔤 📖 Build a storyboard. Buy or borrow (from the library or a friend) a comic book of your choice. Photocopy one page. Cut out each frame. Tape or glue each frame, in order, onto a piece of white poster board. Then describe what you'll need to bring the scene to life: the number of Actors, their genders and ages, the location(s), the costume(s), and any special requirements, like roller skates or Bengal tigers.

Producers give storyboards to Directors to help them plan how to shoot each scene.

Produce

○ ① 💡 ☀ Help a family member with a wardrobe malfunction in a moment of stress. (This will take a bit of pre-planning.) Maybe Mom tucks her skirt into her pantyhose before work? Or Big Bro puts a (washable) "stain" on his favorite shirt right before a date? Producers often save the day from mishaps like these.

○ ② 💡 ☀ Use a video, digital, or cell phone camera to shoot a baby or pet doing a favorite trick. What can you do to get your Actor to act on cue? How many takes before he gets it right?

○ ② 💡 Shoot a commercial for sunglasses—when it's raining. (Producers can control many things, but the weather is not one of them.) Assuming your original intent was to describe how sunglasses block the sun, think of a quick change to account for the cloudy weather. Then

> **WHY DOES PRODUCER ANGELA THINK HER CAREER IS AWESOME?**
>
> "No matter how many times I've produced, it is never, under any circumstances, the same thing. The team, the technology, the rules, the scripts—every project keeps me interested and engaged!"

DID YOU KNOW?

Producers use the same steps to produce a thirty-second television commercial as they would a three-hour Academy Award-winning film!

march outside and shoot your Actors (Little Sis? Grandpa?) while holding an umbrella over your Director (Mom? Dad?) to protect her video equipment.

⬆️②💡☀️💬⏰ Set a timeline for your shoot, and stick with it. Brief all your Actors about the schedule prior to shooting. Is wardrobe fitting from 4:30 p.m. until 4:45 p.m.? Rehearsal from 4:45 p.m. until 5:00 p.m.? Actual filming from 5:00 p.m. until 5:20 p.m.? A great Producer (YOU!) knows to keep an eye on the clock, politely keeping the production moving so it stays within its timeline.

⬆️①💡 List how you'd plan differently for next time. Even if you stuck to your timeline, is there something you wish you had mentioned? Something you could've left out?

o ③💡☀️🕐 Organize *craft service** for a socially responsible reality show (the cameras will be imaginary, but what your family does will be real). First determine the activity (neighbor-

*Craft service provides buffet-style snacks and drinks for the crew on a movie, TV, or commercial set.

hood cleanup? donating gently used toys?), create a list of what will energize each participant (trail mix? fresh fruit?), and then provide it to your Craft Service Representative (Mom? Dad?). The day of your "taping" (read: doing the activity), make sure your food order is filled properly.

CAREER CROSSING

PRODUCERS WORK WITH:

Art Directors

Copywriters*

Directors

Sound Engineers

Video Editors

Project Manager

Project name? Back-to-school shopping. Supply list? Teacher-provided. Wish list? Metallic backpack with remote control zipper. Budget? Nine-dollar highlighters are out of the question. Schedule? Dinner starts in an hour. Challenges? The store's out of rulers?! Your inner Project Manager handles it all with ease—project completed!

Jump In

- ① 💡 (abc) ☼ Practice *delegating** at a meal your family eats together. So if it's breakfast, kindly direct one person to make the pancakes, another to set the table, and a third to clear the dishes afterward. Remember to give yourself a task, and take care to do it well. And keep in mind: good manners count.

> **Delegating** is the act of assigning tasks to others.

- ③ (abc) ☼ 💬 Shadow a Project Manager. Maybe he'll give you a tour of his office, or take you to a project's site. Either way, write or email a thank-you note after your meeting.

Plan Projects

- ① 💡 ▦ 🕐 Create a project plan for a very busy woman: the Tooth Fairy! Let's say every member of your class loses a tooth on the same day (what a coincidence). How do you recommend she handle such a big collection? Define her timeline (how many kids per minute? per hour?), how she'll carry all those under-the-pillow gifts—even a Plan B in case a bedroom window is stuck and she needs an alternate entrance!

PROJECT MANAGERS:

- Create project plans
- Establish budgets and oversee spending
- Organize and lead project team members

SAYS DAVID BECHLER, PE, MBA, PMP, CONTRACT/BUSINESS MANAGER, CH2M HILL IN MILWAUKEE, WISCONSIN

I love *pulling together people of all cultures, personalities, and abilities to accomplish extraordinary things.*

My biggest on-the-job challenge is *making sure my team members work well together, in order to get the job done.*

The best day to start a project is *immediately after completing the last project.*

Budgets make me *happy, tense, agitated, elated—it all depends on my team's performance!*

To complete a job on time, I once *chased a moose off a project site.*

If I weren't a Project Manager, I'd be *running my own business.*

○ ① 💡 Define the activities necessary to complete a project (Mom or Dad's choice). List them in sequence. So say you're wrapping a present: (1) Gather wrapping paper, scissors, and tape; (2) *This could be planning a family reunion, a science fair experiment, the house-training of a new puppy, even a low-budget summer vacation.* Cut the paper to size; (3) Wrap it around the present; and (4) Tape it shut. Ta-da! (Mom or Dad may even give you a project that requires library or Web research to define.)

○ ① 🔍 Use a library or Internet search to define "deliverables," "scope of work," "risk management," "resource plan," and "safety plan."

⬆ ② 💡 🖩 💲 🔍 ⏱ Photocopy the Project Delivery Plan on page 365, or download it at EarnMyKeep.com, and use it to organize an imaginary project of your choice. Want to turn your bedroom into the ultimate skateboard park? Get to planning!

Oversee Project Executions

o ① ⓥ ⓒ Establish, in writing, start and end times (or dates) for a project of your choice. Add alternate end times (or dates) that account for potential challenges. When your project is completed, see if you kept to your schedule.

⬆①ⓥⓒ Keep an eye on your schedule while your project is in progress. If you're going to miss your deadline, try shortening or eliminating a task (without compromising the quality of the final result).

o ②ⓥⓔⓢ Monitor a project of your choice that costs money (even as little as $5). First make an itemized list of what you expect the project to cost (*estimate*). After project completion, compare your estimates to what you really spent (*actual*).

> *Project Manager David* is a certified Project Management Professional. He earned his bachelor of science degree from the University of Wisconsin and a master of business administration with honors from the Keller Graduate School of Management. For more than twenty years he has served several management leadership roles, while volunteering his time to mentor students interested in project management, science, technology, and engineering careers.

⬆②☀ⓢ Dole your money out to those who need to buy resources for your project. Request receipts. File the receipts in an envelope marked: [YOUR NAME HERE]'s Project Expense Receipts.

o ②ⓥⓑ Add a socially responsible aspect to a project of your choice. For example, if you're cleaning out the garage, donate gently used items your family no longer needs to a local organization or charity.

o ②ⓥ☀ Handle a surprise change calmly and politely. First start a project of your choice. Ask Mom or Dad to incorporate a surprise challenge. Were you supposed to organize all your board games' pieces into little baggies, but there are none left? Use your Project Manager skills to come up with an alternate solution.

⬆ ① 💡 List one, two, or three recommendations that may help reduce unwanted surprises next time.

○ ③ 💡 ☼ Assemble and oversee a team for a project of your choice. First, define your project and its tasks. Next, list who would best help you execute your plans, politely request their assistance, then get the job done together.

⬆ ① 💡 🔤 Distribute information to your team by reading, emailing, or handing out a memo with the project's goals and each team member's roles.

⬆ ② 💡 🌀 ☼ Include someone from an older generation who doesn't live in your home (or even your city). Assign a task he can do from his location (researching the best way to handle a challenge, for instance?). Project Managers often oversee team members who work in distant locations.

⬆ ① ☼ Perform *quality assurance**—check in with your team members to ensure they're handling their duties. Kindly encourage those who need help, and commend those who are working hard. (Remember to check in on long-distance team members too.)

DID YOU KNOW?

Project Managers have been known to manage projects larger and more complex than many small and mid-sized businesses!

* **Quality assurance** is the system of checking a project's level of excellence.

⬆②💡☀ Thank your team for their participation and support after completing your project. Make a card, deliver a healthy sweet treat, or— and perhaps most importantly—offer a sincere thank-you with a smile and a hug.

CAREER CROSSING

PROJECT MANAGERS WORK WITH:

Accountants*

Construction Managers

IT Specialists

Technicians

Transportation Engineers*

W ho knows about the wildest water park? And the latest pop sensation? You, of course. So who do you tell? Every one of your friends! Sounds like you've got the makings of a great Publicist—a person who encourages interest in new products, exciting people, even great causes like recycling. And who wouldn't love to spread the scoop on that?!

Jump In

○ ① 🎭 🌐 🔍 Visit the library or Internet to report about the first time in American history the phrase "*public relations**" appeared. (Hint: It has to do with railroads.)

What Publicists do is called "public relations," or PR for short.

○ ③ 🔤 ☼ 💬 🔍 Tour a local public relations firm. Call and ask first to set up your appointment. Before visiting, report about one, two, or three of the firm's current or past clients. After visiting, mail or email a thank-you note to whoever gave you the tour.

○ ③ 🔤 ☼ 💬 Shadow a Publicist. Maybe she'll invite you to join her at a publicity event! After your time together, mail or email a thank-you note.

Inform the Media

○ ① 🔍 Use the library or an Internet search to report about the purpose of a

PUBLICISTS:

- Create public interest in people, places, products, or events
- Write press releases, articles, and website content
- Set up media interviews to promote what their clients are doing
- Update social media pages like Facebook and Twitter on behalf of their clients

SAYS KAREN EINISMAN, FREELANCE PUBLICIST IN MINNEAPOLIS, MINNESOTA

I love making _a real difference for my community._

My biggest on-the-job challenge is _training spokespeople who have never been in front of a camera._

Researching information for a press release can take as little as _one hour_ or as long as _a few days!_

My most rewarding PR moment was _when two women called in during a TV news segment I placed for the American Heart Association. The information they received saved their lives._

The first time I trained a spokesperson I _didn't know what I was doing._

If I weren't a Publicist, I'd be _a Nutritionist._

press release. Also list two, three, or four pieces of information included in a typical press release.

(↑) (2) (abc) (🔍) Write a press release about the latest and greatest game. (Yes, video games count. In fact, check out the sample on page 366 for inspiration.) Include information about the game's manufacturer, its release date, the age of its target audience, how much it costs, and where it can be purchased. Oh, and what makes it the latest and greatest!

Publicist Karen graduated from the University of Maryland with a bachelor of arts degree in journalism. She's been working in public relations for fifteen years, specializing in nonprofit communications. This means she gets the word out about organizations that help others.

o ② 🔍 Pick up Mom or Dad's favorite section of the newspaper (main? local? sports? entertainment? business?). Make a **A byline** is the reporter's name.

list of every article's title and *byline**, every day for three days. After three days, compare your lists—do you see some of the same Reporters' names repeated? If so, can you identify the subjects that most interest each one? Publicists share their gotta-know-it news with the Reporters who would be most likely to report about it.

⬆①💡 Name what you think each of these Reporters is going to write about the next time their articles appear—kudos to you if you're right! (It's OK if a few of the Reporters don't contribute to the paper within your time of being a Publicist.)

o ③ ☼ 💬 🔍 🕐 Learn about a local charity: What is its mission? How big is its organization? How can the community get involved? Who is the main contact for more information? Then get in touch with the teacher in charge of your school newspaper or newsletter, pass along what you've learned, and suggest one of his Reporters write a story about it.

Conduct Crisis Communications

o ② 💡 ☼ 💬 Correct a family member's public image by holding a press conference. Let's say Big Sis neglected her trash duties. The public (your family) thinks she's being irresponsible. Your client (Big Sis) tells you she knows that if the garbage goes out too early, raccoons will get to it. Invite members of the press (Mom? Dad?), introduce your client, and tell the story to set the record straight.

⬆② 💡 💬 ☼ Answer one, two, or three questions from the press. Before your press conference, prepare with your client—make sure you know the whole story and how she feels—because you will be answering for her.

Promote People, Products & Services

○ ②(abc)(📖)(🔍) Promote the Author of your absolute favorite book. Learn about where he's from, his professional background, if he's written other books, and a few interesting facts about him. Share what you've learned with one, two, or three friends.

(⬆)①(💡)(🔍) Coordinate your promotion with his birthday or the anniversary of the publication of one of his books. This gives your story a nice *hook**.

*A **hook** is information that entices people to learn more.*

○ ②(🎨)(💡) Create a baby announcement for a doll, action figure, pet, or, yes, real baby. Use markers, crayons, and paper, ribbon, sequins—whatever you fancy—on an announcement that lists the baby's name, weight, length, parents' and siblings' names, and place of birth.

> ### WHY DOES PUBLICIST KAREN THINK HER CAREER IS AWESOME?
>
> "I have always loved sharing news about the things that excite me (from new bands to new stores to new causes). Now I get to do that every day, and get paid for it!"

○ ③(☀)(💬)(🔍) Promote your favorite *Mom-and-Pop*** shop. First visit the

***Mom-and-Pop** shop refers to local, small businesses.*

Owner (call to see when she'll be available). Prepare questions to ask her, like "When was your store established?" "What do you sell?" (you clearly already have a good idea), "What are your hours of operation?" and "What is your business's phone number, address, and website?" Then promote the store to two, three, or four of your friends.

(⬆)②(🔍) Track your success. Give each person you tell a word to say when he goes into the store. The Store Owner can report to you how many people came into the store (over the course of, say, three days) because of your promotion.

Train Spokespeople

○ ① 🔍 Use the library or an Internet search to report about the role of a spokesperson. Publicists make sure spokespeople know their stuff.

⬆ ② 💡 🎨 🔤 ☀ Turn someone from an older generation into a spokesperson for your favorite after-school activity. Prepare her by developing three, four, or five key message points: one reason why your after-school activity is fun, plus two, three, or four benefits it provides. Then help your spokesperson practice delivering that information.

DID YOU KNOW?

Publicists get a firsthand view of what goes on behind the scenes at TV and radio stations when one of their spokespeople goes on the air!

⬆ ② 💡 🎨 Watch your spokesperson deliver the information to a brand-new audience (Big Sis? your Aunt? your Mail Carrier?). Does the audience understand the message from the information you gave your spokesperson? Did you leave something out that could be added? Did you give too much information?

⬆ ② 💡 🎨 ☀ Video your spokesperson, then review the video together. Does your spokesperson deliver her key messages clearly, so her audience "gets" what she's saying? Should she use fewer "umms"? And what about her body language? Kindly suggest ways your spokesperson could improve her performance. (It helps if you first compliment your spokesperson on something she did well.)

CAREER CROSSING

PUBLICISTS WORK WITH:

Event Planners*

Fundraisers

Journalists*

Media Personalities

Newspaper Editors

I t's why you bring an extra canned good to school every fall. And why you donate a present to the toy bin every winter. The Social Activist in you wants to help change the world to be a better place—and here's how you can devote your career to making that happen!

Jump In

○ ②🔆📺🌐🔤🔍😃 Be one of the world's most effective Social Activists. First, do some research on Mahatma Gandhi, Martin Luther King Jr., Gloria Steinem, Nelson Mandela, or a Social Activist of your choice. Dig through closets to put together a costume. Then become your Activist, delivering a short speech about where you come from, what you believe in, and what positive changes you affected.

⬆②🎨🔆😃 Make a poster that supports your Activist's cause and display it for your family to see.

○ ③🔤☀💬 Shadow a Social Activist. To find one, try asking your local community center, place of worship, or State Capitol. Or scan your local newspaper for issues that interest you, then call the organizations mentioned in the article. Mail or email a thank-you note after your big day.

⬆②📺🌐🔍 Research your Social Activist's cause before meeting her. Use the library or an Internet search to learn about its history, your Social Activist's position, and the opposition's view.

SOCIAL ACTIVISTS:

- Inspire social change by educating the public on issues and causes
- Research issues
- Give people simple solutions to solving important problems
- Lobby for new laws that protect American citizens

SAYS MARI ANNE GEST, SOCIAL ACTIVIST
IN PORTLAND, OREGON

I love _the excitement of a campaign for change._

My biggest on-the-job challenge is _chasing the money to carry out a campaign for change._

I've been known to work _eighty-hour weeks._

An issue that did not go my way (but should have) _was trying to save the Tillamook State Forest from over-harvesting and clear-cutting._

My letters to President Kennedy and Premier Nikita Khrushchev resulted in _my parents receiving a call from the U.S. Defense Department._

If I weren't a Social Activist, I'd be _no longer living—it's just part of my being!_

○ ③ 💡 🔍 ⏱ Use the library bulletin board or an Internet search to find an activist meeting about a cause that affects your community—attend, and discuss your experience.

Research Issues

○ ① 💡 🔍 ⏱ Look through the newspaper to identify an issue meaningful to you. Visit the library or the Internet to report about it: why is the issue important? Has anything been done in support of it? If so, were changes implemented? Could more be

WHY DOES SOCIAL ACTIVIST MARI ANNE THINK HER CAREER IS AWESOME?

"I get to make the world a bit better every day. I get to live in the solution, rather than the problem. Solutions give us hope and energy!"

This could be local parks that need cleaning, school programs that need funding, even endangered animals that need protecting.

286

done? Social Activists like to know everything they can about the issue they're representing.

(↑)(1)(💡) Define one, two, or three opposing viewpoints, as well as ways you could counter-argue them.

(↑)(2)(💡)(☼)(💬) Host a Q&A (a question and answer session) about your issue. Have Mom or Dad ask you two, three, or four questions, using your report as background material. If you do not know an answer, always be honest. Say something like, "I do not know, but I will find out and get you the answer." After your Q&A, make sure you do!

> Social Activist Mari Anne spent three years in college taking a variety of classes that inspired her. Life experiences led her to work at a labor organization, where she began a twenty-four-year (and counting) career in social activism. You know those stop signs that swing out from school busses (protecting kids as they get on and off)? Thanks to Mari Anne, they're legally required on every school bus in Oregon.

o (2)(🎨)(☼)(🔍) Interview someone from an older generation about an issue that's important to him. Come to your interview prepared with questions (do your research first). You can even use a video or digital camera to capture your discussion.

(↑)(3)(💡)(🎨)(🐾) Act on it together. Pick a task from the *Persuade Audiences* section (below) and do it for his issue, with him.

Persuade Audiences

o (1)(🎭)(🌐)(🔍)(🐾) Use the library or an Internet search to list one, two, or three songs that have brought attention to great causes. Use the same resources to find the songs, and listen to them.

(↑)(2)(💡)(abc) Write a song about an issue that's important to you—rewrite lyrics to an existing tune you like, or create something brand-new.

○ ② 💡 🔤 👣 Inspire your family to change something at home by creating an *emotional hook*: start with a fact ("We kids aren't fond of meatloaf"). Then offer the emotional tie-in ("When we don't enjoy our food, we don't enjoy dinner time as much"). The emotional hook evolves from that ("Change 'meatloaf night' to 'fish stick night' for happier dinner conversation!").

⬆ ② 🎨 💡 🔤 ☀ 💬 👣 Put your emotional hook into action. Post a flyer on the fridge, hand out handmade, safety-pin-able buttons, deliver a speech—whatever you'd like to spread the message.

○ ② 💡 🔤 ☀ 🔍 👣 Write a letter to the editor of your local newspaper in support of a cause (your choice). Start by describing your cause. State two or three facts in your favor. Then explain why you believe in your issue. Consider offering a way others can help. Social Activists make their letters even more effective by mailing or emailing them right after an article on the same issue has run. A sample letter can be found on page 367. (But remember that every newspaper has its own rules for submitting letters that must be followed if you want your letter published.)

○ ③ 💡 ☀ 🗓 💲 💬 👣 🔔 Organize an event—a bake sale, a dance-off, a sit-in—in support of an issue (your choice). Include five friends or family members in your effort. Make a list of responsibilities and delegate the work, remembering to be very polite. Social Activists know there is greater strength in numbers, and the best way to keep those numbers up is to be nice to volunteers.

○ ③ 💡 🗓 💬 👣 🔔 Use your talents to make the public think about a cause (your choice). Are you a good jumper? Tell friends and family that you'll donate one minute of time to a worthy cause for every jumping jack you can

DID YOU KNOW?

When it comes to their issues, Social Activists stay on top of the latest news and developments—making them the first to know what concerned Americans need to know!

do in thirty seconds. (So if you do twenty jumping jacks in thirty seconds, you'll volunteer for twenty minutes at your local animal shelter that weekend.) Invite everyone to cheer you on, then get jumping!

Lobby for Causes

○ ① 🔍 Use the library or an Internet search to list one, two, or three facts about lobbying. (Does Mom or Dad say you never take "no" for an answer? This task is perfect for you!)

○ ② 💡🔤☼🔍👐 Convince a *government official** (Mom? Dad?) to see your side of an issue important to you. List three, four, or five reasons why, say, your family should recycle. (You may need to research these first.)

*Government officials include State Representatives or Senators, school district Superintendents, or Town Mayors.

⬆ ① ☼ Dress appropriately for your audience. To be taken seriously by government officials, Social Activists wear things like clean pants or a dress, a tucked-in shirt, no hats—clothing that says, "I respect you. Please listen to my concerns."

CAREER CROSSING

SOCIAL ACTIVISTS WORK WITH:

Campaign Consultants

Graphic Designers

Lobbyists

Pollsters

Printers

Toy Designer

There are no legs. Or marbles. Or chutes and ladders. And yet, that toy is the one you pull out first, every rainy day. And why not? With a few creative change-ups (licorice legs, anyone?), it's just like the original—only better. Now imagine being a Toy Designer every day, rainy or otherwise!

Jump In

○ ① Examine your favorite toy. List one, two, or three things that you like about it ("It features my favorite cartoon character."), what other children may like about it ("It's small enough to fit in Big Sis's pocket."), and what parents may like about it ("It has a low price.").

○ ② Stop by a toy store—list two, three, or four different toys or games made by the same company.

① Use a library or Internet search to report about the toy company that makes the toys (or games) you found. Include when the company started and what kinds of products it makes (toys made of wood? games for toddlers?). Do you own any of them? Are you surprised to find out the company makes one of your favorites?

○ ② Ask someone from an older generation about his favorite toy when he was a kid—when did he get it? Who gave it to him? Did he share it with anyone special? Use the library or the Internet to research the toy's creation date, manufacturer, and if it's still being produced.

TOY DESIGNERS:

- Keep up with what kids are doing, watching, and wanting
- Draw new toy ideas
- Build models of what their toy ideas look like, sometimes using computer software
- See their ideas through, from idea presentation to the manufacturing of the final product

SAYS ANTHONY MONZO, SENIOR PRODUCT DESIGNER—
CRAYOLA OUTDOOR AND COLOR WONDER PRODUCT LINES,
CRAYOLA, LLC, IN EASTON, PENNSYLVANIA

I love _turning something I imagined into a real product._

My biggest on-the-job challenge is _removing features I believe add to a toy's quality, visual appeal, and play value._

My favorite toy as a kid was _good old-fashioned wooden blocks!_

The first time I saw one of my designs in a store I _almost shouted, "Hey, I designed this!"_

The toughest design limitation is _package size._

If I weren't a Toy Designer, I'd be _a Photographer._

① ② ⊕ ⊕ ⊚ Re-create the toy using stuff you find around your home, then give it to him as a gift.

① ② ⊚ ⊞ ⑤ Buy the toy at the cheapest price around (try secondhand stores or websites, or borrow for free), and play it with him.

○ ③ ⊕ ⊕ ⊕ Visit a toy museum—use the phone book or do an Internet search to see if there's one nearby. Report one, two, or three cool facts you didn't already know about toys.

Develop Concepts

○ ① ⊕ ⊕ Come up with an idea for a toy. Use pencil and paper to sketch your idea. And think about if it's battery-operated or not. Battery-operated toys

WHY DOES TOY DESIGNER ANTHONY THINK HIS CAREER IS AWESOME?

"I get to turn whatever I dream into something that brings great joy to children: a brand-new toy they may grow up and remember as one of their favorites!"

get sound and lights. Manual toys get cool gears and mechanics.

⬆①💡 Modify your toy idea to please both children *and* their parents. Super Slinky Silly Slime sounds great to kids, but messy to adults. (Maybe use a special material that doesn't stain clothes?)

⬆①💡 Fit your toy idea within current trends. Is your action figure from last year's hit movie? Your marketing department

Toy Designer Anthony graduated with his associate's degree in industrial design from the Art Institute of Philadelphia. He's been creating toys for the past fifteen years with companies like Mattel, Tyco, and Crayola. In fact, you can thank him for Crayola's Rainbow Rake, Color Wonder Magic Light Markers, and 3D Chalk Sets!

may say it needs to be an action figure from *this* year's hit movie.

○ ①💡🔍✏️ Report about the importance of safety in toy design. Then list one, two, or three features that make toys safer (like lead-free paint).

○ ①💡 Imagine a new toy for boys, ages five to eight. Now define a modification that would make that toy appeal to girls of the same age. What about toddlers? Teenagers?

⬆①💡✏️ Add an educational twist—does it help a child spell? Teach environmental awareness? Incorporate math skills?

○ ②💡🔍 Watch some children play with a toy (your siblings? cousins? kids at the playground?). List one, two, or three changes you could make to the toy that would make it more fun for them.

Present Ideas

○ ①✏️💡🔤💬🔍 Think quick! Sometimes Toy Designers have only one day to dream up and present a new toy idea. Can you imagine a toy, draw a picture of it, and explain how it works, all in fifteen minutes?

○ ② 🎨 💡 Create a presentation drawing for a toy idea. This is a fancy drawing that you'll mount on cardstock or construction paper with glue or tape, so it has a border (makes your drawing look very professional).

⬆① 📊 List your toy's measurements: height, length, and width. Toy Designers are precise—even to the hundredth of an inch.

⬆② 🎨 💡 📊 Develop a *scale** drawing of how the toy looks from the side, top, and front. Each view displays the overall shape and details

*Drawing something to **scale** means the paper version has the same proportions as the 3-D version.

of the product—essential when determining the product's size and how it will fit into a package.

Make Prototypes

○ ② 🎨 💡 Build a *prototype*** of a toy idea using clay or store-bought or homemade play-dough. (For a recipe, see page 347.) Use a variety of tools to

Prototypes bring a toy to life: its function, design, and basic shape and size. Prototypes are also called models.

sculpt your prototype, such as toothpicks, butter knives, wire, sandpaper, or popsicle sticks.

⬆② 🎨 💡 Build your prototype with a material other than clay—try foam core, paper, cardboard, or Styrofoam.

○ ② 🎨 💡 Use an existing toy as inspiration for a new toy—build a model that looks similar to one you have, then add new features or modify existing ones to create something unique.

SO YOU WANT TO...SELL YOUR TOY IDEA

○ ③ 🎨 💡 🔤 ☼ 📊 💲 🔍 Get ready to impress—upper management (Mom or Dad) has the final say on whether your toy proposal becomes a toy reality.

1. Present a presentation drawing (see the *Present Ideas* section, page 293). Mention the toy's cool features and consumer benefits. (You may want to practice your presentation first.)

2. Display a prototype of your toy.

3. Define how much will it cost to produce your toy. Even the simplest products can cost $100,000 to manufacture. (Base your figures on amounts you find online, or just enjoy making them up.)

DID YOU KNOW?

Yup, Toy Designers get to buy toys. LOTS of toys. Anything to inspire the next big thing. And the best part (can you believe it gets better?!): the company pays for what they buy!

4. List what you expect the price of your toy to be and how many you'll need to sell to cover the cost of making it.

5. Finish your presentation by suggesting the perfect packaging option—this is what your toy comes in (closed box? open box? clam shell? blister card?). And sometimes, the product IS the package! Look in a toy store, a library book, or online for fun options.

CAREER CROSSING

TOY DESIGNERS WORK WITH:

Marketers

Mechanical Engineers

Model Makers

Packaging Engineers

Project Managers*

Translator

While your babysitter can't understand Mom's list of instructions, it's all perfectly clear to you. So when she reads: *Sunshine's at the bottom; Ladybug's set to 7*, you tell her it means: "My 'Good Morning Sunshine' pajamas are in the PJ drawer at the bottom of my dresser and my nightlight will turn on at bedtime." Thank goodness there's a Translator like you in the house!

Jump In

○ ① Use the library or an Internet search to report about the purpose of the United Nations and the six official languages it uses. Why do you think those six were chosen?

○ ③ Shadow a Translator. She is likely to show you very cool books in different languages. She may also teach you new facts about words—did you know Eskimos have more than one word for snow? After your time together, mail or email a thank-you note.

Know Cultures & Languages

○ ① Find one, two, or three examples of words that American English has adopted from other countries. (A hint of one example? This French pastry is buttery and flaky and tastes awfully good filled with chocolate.)

① Report about why sharing cultures is good for global relations.

Translators:

- Change words from one language into another
- Know how to speak and read two languages, often more
- Immerse themselves in other cultures

says claudia h. engle, translator in washington, dc

I love *being a communication bridge between people.*

My biggest on-the-job challenge is *tight deadlines.*

The hardest text to translate is by *Authors who don't get to the point. If text isn't clear in its original language, imagine having to say it in a different one!*

My native tongue is *Spanish.*

The best way to learn another language is to *live in another country and learn its culture.*

If I weren't a Translator, I'd be *dreaming of becoming one.*

○ ① 🔤 🔍 Use the library or the Internet to report about the differences between American English and British English (those folks who live over the *pond**), including one, two, or three words American English uses but not British English, and vice versa.

✳ *In Britain, the **pond** is the Atlantic Ocean.*

⬆ ① 🔤 🔍 Add one, two, or three Australian English words to the mix. (Shrimp on the barbie, anyone?)

○ ② 💡 🔤 🔍 Create a dictionary of five, ten, or fifteen words used only in your family's language (is dinner called "din-din"? is bedtime called "lockdown"?). Include the spelling and definition of each word, as well as a sample sentence of its use. For examples of dictionary-style entries, look at a dictionary at home, at the library, or online.

○ ② 💡 🔤 🔍 Learn Pig Latin. (It's as fun to speak as the name is to say!).

> **WHY DOES TRANSLATOR CLAUDIA THINK HER CAREER IS AWESOME?**
>
> "I help people who may otherwise find it difficult to get their messages across."

If Mom or Dad aren't familiar with it, look in a library book or online. Then use it in regular conversation for fifteen, thirty, or forty-five minutes.

(⬆️) (2) (💡) (ⓐⓑⓒ) Ask Mom or Dad to write a short, silly story in Pig Latin for you to translate into English.

Translate

○ (1) (🎭) (🎭) (ⓐⓑⓒ) List two, three, or four accepted cultural phrases and their translations. (An example? How "Get out!" means "I can't believe what you're saying!")

○ (1) (🎭) (ⓐⓑⓒ) Ask Mom or Dad to text you a sentence or two—using text jargon. (If you don't have a cell phone, she can write it on a piece of paper. And if Mom or Dad isn't familiar with text-style phrases, there are online sites that can tell her what to type/write.) Your task is to translate the sentence into plain English.

○ (2) (🎭) (🎭) (🌐) (ⓐⓑⓒ) Ask Mom or Dad to write a *haiku** about your favorite meal, game, or place to visit, using language found in your family's ancestral or religious culture (*I love fresh bagels/A cream cheese schmear brings mazel/Oy! I kvell at lox*). Translate it into plain English, keeping the

Translator Claudia earned a bachelor's degree in English from George Mason University, studied translation and interpretation at Georgetown University, and specialized in French translation at Universidad de Los Andes in Bogotá, Colombia. She has close to twenty years' experience as staff translator at an international organization, and volunteers time to translate materials that help non-English-speaking parents communicate with their kids' teachers.

What's the difference between a Translator and an Interpreter? Translators translate the written word. Interpreters translate the spoken word.

Haikus are three-line Japanese poems: the first line has five syllables; the second, seven; and the third, five.

same meaning, rhythm, and word count as the original. (Poems and songs are fun challenges for Translators.)

○ ② 💡 🎭 (abc) Photocopy from a rule-book (or print from a website) how to play your favorite sport. Translate it for someone from an older generation who's never played. After he's read your transla-tion, ask him to tell *you* the rules—that's how you'll know if your translation is right. (So instead of "Dribble down the court," you'd write "Bounce the basket-ball with alternating hands as you move forward toward your basket.")

DID YOU KNOW?

Translating ultra-long books makes Translators very happy—that's because many are paid by the word!

○ ② 💡 🎭 (abc) Ask someone who is bilingual (a family member? a Librarian? a Teacher?) to write down a joke that's funny in her language. Use a [HER LANGUAGE HERE]-to-English dic-tionary to translate it to English. Is the joke still funny? Does it even make sense?

Translation doesn't always work word-for-word because cultures use the same words differently. We say "time flies." Other cultures may think we mean a clock flying out the window!

⬆️ ② 💡 🎭 (abc) Use the dictionary to write a joke that's funny in both languages. Try it out on your bilin-gual expert. It's OK if your ideas don't exactly work out—even the best Translators are challenged by humor.

○ ③ 💡 🎭 (abc) 📖 Translate a passage from a Shakespeare play (try a comedy: *As You Like It, The Taming of the Shrew,* or *A Midsummer Night's Dream*) into our modern-day English—without *slang**. (A Librarian or English Teacher can point you in the right direction for this task.)

*Slang is informal language.

⬆️ ② 💡 (abc) Add slang to your translation, then read the version to a friend. Surprised to learn Shakespeare was so cool?

○ ③ 💡 (abc) 📖 Back-translate one, two, or three paragraphs from your favorite story or magazine. First, work with someone who's bilingual to translate the English version into a second language. Then give the translated version to a different person who speaks your second language. Ask him to translate the version back into English. Now compare your two English versions—how similar are they? Where are their differences?

CAREER CROSSING

TRANSLATORS WORK WITH:

Authors

Graphic Designers

Proofreaders

Revisers

Terminologists

Transportation Engineer

Y ou're trying really hard to keep a positive attitude, even while sitting in bumper-to-bumper traffic. So while you've got the (unplanned) free time, you start dreaming a Transportation Engineer's dream—the one where a new road pops up and over your current stuck position, providing a free-and-clear route to everywhere you want to go!

Jump In

o ① 🎭 🌐 🔍 🧪 Use the library or an Internet search to report about one, two, or three amazing achievements in transportation engineering: the Big Dig (Boston's Central Artery/ Tunnel Project); the Channel Tunnel (the Eurotunnel Rail System); Kansai Airport (Osaka Bay, Japan).

o ① 🔍 Use the library or an Internet search to describe one or two different types of pavement markings and the colors used for them. Also describe one or two different sign shapes and the colors used for them.

🔼 ① 🐾 💡 🔍 Grab some sidewalk chalk and mark your sidewalk or driveway (and/or use paper and markers to make signs). Follow the guidelines set by the U.S. Department of Transportation, or create some new ones (like "Driveway for Mom Only!").

o ② 🔍 🚲 Walk, ride a bike, or drive through your neighborhood, identifying one, two, or three examples of safety measures incorporated by a

Transportation Engineers:

- Plan new transportation systems
- Oversee building of trails, roads, bridges, railroads, harbors, and airports
- Estimate the size and costs to build transportation facilities (like railroad stations)
- Modify existing systems and facilities to operate more efficiently and safely

I love *seeing my piles of maps and calculations constructed into something I can drive on!*

My biggest on-the-job challenge is *project delays.*

The coolest project I have ever worked on is *the Hoover Dam Bypass.*

I move *1,300,000 cars every month (1,500 to 2,200 passenger vehicles fill one lane per hour!).*

The first time I ever drove on a road I designed, I felt *excited, proud, and relieved it was constructed the way I designed it.*

If I weren't a Transportation Engineer, I'd be *a Writer.*

Transportation Engineer. Look for speed bumps; curves in a long, straight road (to prevent drivers getting bored and losing focus); signs; pavement markings; even medians.

- ③ ⓐⓑⓒ ☼ ☺ Shadow a Transportation Engineer. You'll find one by contacting your local city or county Public Works Department. After your time together, mail or email a thank-you note.

- ③ 🎭 🌍 🗺 🔍 Visit a railroad museum or train station with someone from an older generation—look in the phone book, call your state or county's visitor center, or look online to see if there's one near you. Read about the museum's highlighted exhibits, or the station's history, before visiting. Then while there, see if you can find examples of what you read.

Develop Plans

- ② 💡 Create a plan to improve passenger travel to and from the bathroom in your home (ever knock over the person coming out of the bathroom while you're trying to get in?!). List how many people use the bathroom each day, how many times they use it, and the path(s) they take to get there. Then define a new way to get to the most-used room in your home (through the roof? a secret path under the floor?).

○ ②⑨⊞◎ Ask two family members to name the first two items that pop into their heads (bunny slippers? pipe cleaners? laundry detergent bottles?). Measure your bedroom (ten feet?). Then calculate which of the two items would make a cheaper road. (How many of each item do you need to reach ten feet, and how much does each item cost?) Then determine which item would need to be replaced more often—pipe cleaners may be cheaper than bunny slippers, but bunny slippers are thicker and would therefore last longer. This is the kind of "thinking ahead" Transportation Engineers put into everything they build.

Transportation Engineer Pam graduated with a bachelor of science degree in civil engineering from Iowa State University. She's been a Transportation Engineer for twenty-three years. She is a registered Professional Engineer with licenses in the states of Arizona, Iowa, and Nevada, as well as a Certified Traffic Control Supervisor.

Oversee Construction

○ ①◎ Visit the library or Internet to report about two, three, or four of the big dogs of construction equipment: grapple, crane, bulldozer, excavator, loader, dump truck, grader. Compare how they're used differently.

⬆②◎◎ Draw a brand new piece of equipment (dreamed up by you). Or make a 3-D version using recycled stuff from around your home. Keep your equipment's purpose in mind: scooping? lifting? digging? hauling?

○ ②⚗ Be a concrete mixer. (Typically, this work is done by enormous trucks. You'll be using a spoon and some elbow grease.) Start with cement (brownie or cake mix). Add some rocks (chocolate chips and/or nuts) and some sand (coconut flakes). Add some water (oil, applesauce, and/or eggs, as per your mix's instructions). Let your concrete cure (bake in the oven, as per your mix's instructions). Then eat!

🔼①🔍🐾 Visit the library or Internet to report about concrete recycling—it's super cool.

Move People & Goods

○ ①🏛️🔍⚗️ Test a sloped area of your driveway or neighborhood sidewalk for steepness. Use three different items, like a grape, a marble, and a toy car. Which one goes down the slope fastest? When building things like roads and bridges, Transportation Engineers must know how steep a surface can be and still be safe.

🔼①🔍⚗️ Alter the surface for different results. Try laying down a towel or a piece of paper, or sprinkling the surface with sugar or sandbox sand.

○ ②🎨💡🎭🔍 Visit the library or the Internet to report about subway systems. Then ask Mom or Dad to grab a map of your city or town from a Realtor's office, government office, or visitor center, or print one from online. Use markers or pens to draw in a new subway system, with trains running to your favorite local destinations.

○ ②💡🔍 Ask Mom or Dad to use backyard dirt to build a mound about the size of a toaster. Your task is to cut through that "mountain"—without it collapsing during *excavation** and after your new road is constructed. Use tools (a butter knife? a spatula? your fingers?) to excavate the mountain. Then use twigs, bark, or leaves to create the road

> **WHY DOES TRANSPORTATION ENGINEER PAM THINK HER CAREER IS AWESOME?**
>
> "I help thousands of people every day move across something I designed. My designs could last one hundred years. And my projects are built with really cool machines!"

Excavation is the act of making a hole—in this case, in your mountain.

that runs through it. You can even line your excavation with rocks or boards to keep it standing, or add a tube for a tunnel. Test it out with toy cars and trucks.

- ⬆①💡🐾 Decorate your mountain so it blends in with its surroundings—maybe by adding grass clippings or planting a flower on top.

o ②🐾💡 Create a detour to your kitchen. Pretend there's "construction" (dinner-making) in progress, blocking the path you usually use to get to the fridge. How would you direct traffic to get there safely? First determine your new path (around the back door? underneath the kitchen table?). Then create signs (with construction paper and markers) and cones (with rolled and taped or stapled construction paper) to bypass the construction.

- ⬆①💡☀ Ask Mom, Dad, or Big Bro to give your detour a try. Consider making changes if necessary.

DID YOU KNOW?

Transportation Engineers design pathways, bridges, tunnels, and ramps for animals too—such as tortoises, lions, elk, deer, sheep, moose, horses, cattle, and even alligators!

CAREER CROSSING

TRANSPORTATION ENGINEERS WORK WITH:

Civil Engineers

Economists

Geologists*

Land Surveyors*

Technical Writers

Travel Agent

The day is here! It's really here! You and your family are finally headed to your favorite amusement park. And you know the whole plan by heart: where you're staying, how you're getting there, and exactly which attractions you'll hit first. Everything a Travel Agent needs to know for the perfect vacation!

Jump In

○ ① 🎒 (abc) 📖 🔍 Buy or borrow an issue of *National Geographic Traveler*. Report about one of the featured destinations in a way that would make it appealing for a family vacation.

⬆ ② 💡 🐢 Repurpose the pictures in the magazine for a school assignment, thoughtful card, or craft project—Travel Agents donate outdated brochures to schools for this purpose. (You can only do this **Up It!** if you own the magazine, or borrowed it from someone who says it's OK.)

TRAVEL AGENTS:

- Make arrangements for travelers
- Negotiate prices with airlines, hotels, and car rental services
- Help customers apply for passports and visas
- Create itineraries for travelers' trips

○ ① 💡 🎒 Promote one of the world's greatest travel destinations: Casa a la [YOUR LAST NAME HERE]! List what makes it a great place to visit (bunk beds? in-home library?), native customs (Saturday morning omelets? bedtime pillow forts?), and the best time of year to stay (autumn because there's lots of family birthdays, which means tons of cake?).

⬆ ② 🎨 💡 (abc) Create a brochure for Casa a la [YOUR LAST NAME HERE] that includes details from your list. Consider adding a picture or two.

SAYS PEGGY O'NEAL PEDEN, INDEPENDENT TRAVEL ADVISOR, CWT VACATIONS IN NASHVILLE, TENNESSEE

I love _planning exciting trips, then imagining my clients enjoying them!_

My biggest on-the-job challenge is _making changes to airline tickets._

The most exciting trip I ever planned _took a Tennessee high school football team to play an Alaskan team. The kids saw glaciers and seals and learned Native American dances._

I can book an entire vacation in as little as _half an hour._

My favorite places in the world to travel _are Ireland and Norway._

If I weren't a Travel Agent, I'd be _a Teacher._

○ ③ⓐⓑⓒ☼☺ Shadow a Travel Agent—she may show you the computer booking system only Travel Agents are allowed to use! After your time together, mail or email a thank-you note.

Coordinate Logistics

WHY DOES TRAVEL AGENT PEGGY THINK HER CAREER IS AWESOME?

"It lets me explore the world!"

○ ①🏢🔍 Calculate how long it would take a traveler to get from Washington, DC, to Los Angeles by land on cheetah. (Look up how many miles it is, and how fast a cheetah runs.) Next calculate by air on a racing pigeon, and (imagining the United States is all water) by ocean on killer whale.

○ ①☺🏢$🔍 Visit the library or the Internet to report about how exchange rates work. Then calculate how much US$1 would be worth today (right now) in one, two, or three of the following: Beijing, Brussels, Brazil. Travel Agents help their clients develop budgets that will cover their spending, no matter where they're going.

⬆①🎭🖩💲🔍 Calculate how much your favorite restaurant meal costs in your hometown and how much it would cost in Paris, France.

⬆②🎭🖩💲🔍 Visit a local bank and ask to see some foreign currency. You can even bring US$1 with you and exchange it for foreign money.

Design Itineraries

Itineraries are travel schedules that list things like flight numbers and tour reservations.

○ ②🎭💡🌐🔍 Create a personalized Web page for someone from an older generation's dream vacation destination, using white paper, markers, and pens. First confirm the destination with your traveler. Then research location highlights: is it known for its architecture, theater, and/or outdoor adventures? Then draw a home page with the information she would love most. Use other destination websites for inspiration.

⬆①🎭 Tape the page to the front of a computer (imaginary or real) so she can pretend to "click" on it. (If you can't do this in person, mail your Web page to her, and listen on the phone while she "clicks.")

○ ②💡🔍 Please two traveling companions with opposite travel preferences (Mom and Dad? your Art Teacher and your P.E. Teacher?). First pick a U.S. state capital (your choice), then list one, two, or three days' worth of activities (meals included) to satisfy them. For example, Boise, Idaho, has great museums *and* great hiking.

○ ②💡🖩💲🔍 Plan an extravagant trip to your dream location. Include costs for transportation, hotel, and a rental car for seven days, six nights. Then create the same experience for half the budget. Can you find comparable hotels? Less expensive airfare?

○ ②💡🌐🔍 Be a Travel Agent for folks who could've surely used one: Daniel Boone, Lewis and Clark, or Robert E. Peary. After using the library or the Internet to research where he (or they) traveled, report one, two, or three ways good planning would have made the voyage easier (yes, you can use your imagination!).

Prepare Travelers

○ ① 🎭 🔍 Report about the latest dress codes for security lines at United States airports (try www.FAA.gov).

　　⬆ ② ☼ 🔍 Dress two family members (or friends) in layers and layers of clothes (make sure the number of layers is equal on each person). Walk them to an open area in your home (so they have room)—then yell GO! Who will get their outer clothes off fastest at the airport security line?

Travel Agent Peggy studied English at Lipscomb University, then earned a master's degree from the University of Kentucky. Her interest in travel inspired her to open her own travel agency. She's taken classes in travel management and traveled the world to learn about the places her clients might want to go. She's also written three mysteries, in which the main character is (you guessed it) a Travel Agent!

○ ① 🎭 🔍 Prepare a zippered plastic bag of liquids and gels allowed on airplanes. (Again, try www.FAA.gov, or your local airport's website.) Then throw it into your luggage for the next time you travel by plane.

○ ③ 🎭 🌐 🔍 Take a walking tour of your hometown, to become familiar with "off the beaten path" sites. To find a tour, call your local Chamber of Commerce or try online—your city may have its own website with suggestions.

　　⬆ ① 🏆 🔤 Report about one, two, or three of your favorite stops in a way that would be enticing for a traveler.

○ ③ 🎭 🌐 🔍 Try out one, two, or three local customs: is there an annual street fair you've never visited? A restaurant with the best [LOCAL FOOD HERE] you've never tasted? Travel Agents familiar with an area's customs are better able to help their clients get to know the local culture.

○ ③ 🔍 Test out two, three, or four local playgrounds. Report about each park, including: the type of equipment, what age kids would like it the most, and its proximity to a snack shop.

SO YOU WANT TO...ARRANGE A FAMILY TRIP

○ ③ 💡 😊 🔤 ☀️ ▦ $ 💬 🔍 ⏱️ Whether you're going out of the country for one month or around town for one day, this is your chance to put your Travel Agent skills to work.

1. Present your family with two destination options. Let them decide which wins.

2. Research options for transportation, hotel/motel (if applicable), and rental car (if applicable). Present two, three, or four. (OPTIONAL: Include cost information.) Let your family pick.

3. Create one or two activity and meal itineraries, based on information you learned at the library or online about your destination location. (OPTIONAL: Include cost infor-mation.) Once you have family agreement, make necessary reservations.

DID YOU KNOW?

Travel Agents stay on top of the news around the world—surprise weather conditions and other events may affect their clients' travels, and they need to be ready to help!

4. Three days prior to departure, con-firm your reservations by calling your *suppliers**.

Suppliers are the providers of things like airlines, hotels, rental cars, and restaurants.

5. Two days prior to departure, present your travelers with a memo in-cluding ideal clothing to pack, any new transportation regulations, and predicted weather.

6. The day of departure, confirm your travelers have their necessary docu-ments, including reservation information. Leave a copy of the itinerary with a friend or relative.

7. Enjoy your trip!

CAREER CROSSING

TRAVEL AGENTS WORK WITH:

Airline Reservation Agents

Bus Operators

Hotel Concierges

Hotel Reservation Agents

Rental Car Agents

TV Writer

Think your life would make a great TV show? Of course it would! You've got the star (you), the parental figures (Mom, Dad, and the like), the best friend, the cool teacher—everything a TV Writer needs to come up with a new show or change up the story on an existing one. So, TV Writer, let's get writing!

Jump In

○ ① 🎭 🌐 🔍 Look in the library or online to report about America's first television broadcast in 1927 (maybe even before your grandparents were born!).

⬆ ① 🎭 🌐 🔍 Identify the country's longest running children's show. (Hint: It involves a clown.) Also find out how long your favorite show has been *on the air**.

○ ① 💡 🎭 🌐 🔍 Ask someone from an older generation about her favorite show when she was a kid. List one, two, or three ways it's the same as your favorite show. Then list a few ways it's different.

⬆ ② 🎭 🌐 🔍 🔍 Find an *episode*** of her favorite show online, or on VHS or DVD at the library. If you can, enjoy it together.

○ ③ 🎭 🔍 Visit a local TV station. Call first—many offer tours. After the tour, report one, two, or three new facts you learned about the station and the shows it produces.

> **On the air** means the show is being broadcast.

TV WRITERS:

- Create and develop characters
- Invent new worlds and explore alternate realities
- Write scripts, which include the dialogue that Actors say
- Develop a series of scripts to tell a bigger story

> An **episode** is one show of a series of shows that, combined, tell a story.

says stefan wallach, tv writer, owner, HIT BY THE PITCH productions, LLc, in Los Angeles, california

I love the creative process.

My biggest on-the-job challenge is making sure nothing goes wrong if parts of a script are changed—like an Actor could say the wrong line or a major prop could get left out!

My all-time favorite TV character is Homer J. Simpson.

I do my best writing late at night.

The most bizarre change I've made to a script is removing the word "butt" because we had exceeded our allotted limit of three "butt"s per script.

If I weren't a TV Writer, I'd probably be an awful Musician.

○ ③ⓐⓑⓒ☼◯ Shadow a TV Writer. Mail or email a thank-you note after your time together.

○ ③☺⚲⚲ Visit a museum of television or broadcasting. (Use online searches to see if there's one in your area.) While there, identify one, two, or three facts about TV you never knew before.

Reality TV does not employ a writing staff. Instead, camera crews are sent out to follow the show's participants. The show's content is created by using whatever footage was captured.

Pitch Ideas

○ ①💡ⓐⓑⓒ☼◯⏰ Sell a show idea to a Network Executive (Mom or Dad). First, create your idea (is it a show about kids who travel in outer space? dogs that like X-treme sports?) Then present your idea. Be passionate. Get the *network** excited about your idea quickly—Network Executives are busy so you have to draw them in within the first few minutes.

Networks are stations or groups of stations, like the Food Network or PBS.

(⬆)(2)(💡)(☀) Answer questions about your idea. In preparation, think about what a Network Executive may say about your show: does it take place in a location that's too expensive (maybe Hawaii)? Are there too many characters (which means too many Actors on the payroll)?

> **WHY DOES TV WRITER STEFAN THINK HIS CAREER IS AWESOME?**
>
> "I have unlimited possibilities at my fingertips, to create wherever I want viewers to go!"

Answer the questions thoughtfully and politely. (Maybe you'll create a fake set locally, to save money. And maybe your show is as interesting with fewer cast members.)

(⬆)(2)(💡)(𝑎𝑏𝑐) Sell your idea to two different Network Executives, but not at the same time. Would you use

A pitch refers to your idea.

the same *pitch***, or take their individual personalities into consideration? For example, how would you try to sell your idea to Disney Channel versus Discovery Kids?

Develop Scripts

The cast are the Actors.

○ (1)(💡) Invent a *cast**** of three characters. List their gender, age, place of residence, and occupation (yes, for a kid, "school" is an occupation). And give each a name.

(⬆)(1)(💡) List two, three, or four facts that further develop each character. Does one of your characters have an allergy to peanuts? Another loves to fly kites? Including interesting tidbits about your characters makes them feel more real.

○ ② 💡 Create a *story arc**. First, imagine a main character. Now list what happens to her in two, three, or four episodes in a row. Do new characters show up? New adventures? New lessons?

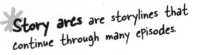

⬆️ ① 💡 Incorporate a current event into one of your scripts. Say, the hottest-selling pop star does a musical number at the school dance (where one episode takes place).

*Story arcs are storylines that continue through many episodes.

DID YOU KNOW?

On average, ten to twelve TV Writers collaborate in the writers' room for hours on end to make the best possible product: a TV show you and your family will love to watch!

Write Scripts

○ ③ 💡 🔤 Write a script. First you'll need to list your characters, their location, and what happens. Next you'll put this information into script format (check out the example on page 368), which you can do with pen and paper or a computer program.

⬆️ ② 💡 🔤 Let your first draft sit, unread, for a full day. Then revisit. (Real TV Writers do this with their own scripts all the time.) Do you notice anything that could be changed? Maybe you want to make the script funnier, more dramatic, or scarier?

○ ③ 💡 🔤 😊 Influence your audience's interests. Write an episode for your favorite TV show that focuses on an environmental or social

TV Writer Stefan graduated with a bachelor of science degree in marketing from the University of Florida in Gainesville. He has been working in television for the past eleven years. He wrote for Bill Maher on *Politically Incorrect,* as well as NBC's *The Weakest Link.* He has also been a Freelance Writer for Nickelodeon.

issue that's important to you. Maybe your favorite character forgets to recycle, needs to be more polite to strangers, or holds a fundraiser for a deserving cause.

○ ③ 💡 🔤 Write a script about an everyday occurrence (customer orders food at a restaurant? kid learns how to ride a bike? traveler takes a train trip?). Then, rewrite your script as a comedy (the waiter trips over a banana peel, sending food flying everywhere!). Adding just a bit of humor can change the entire story.

⬆ ③ 💡 🔤 Rewrite your script one, two, or three more ways. Try a drama, a Western, or even a mystery.

CAREER CROSSING

TV WRITERS WORK WITH:

Actors

Directors

Producers*

Set Designers

Stage Managers

Picnicking in the park was great—until clean-up time. Your arms were filled with empty baggies, dirty napkins, and sticky juice boxes, but no trash cans could be found! Your mind kicked into overdrive: who do I call to get trash cans installed? How long will it take? And will there be recycling ones, too? It's Urban Planner to the rescue!

Jump In

○ ① 🎭 🌐 🔍 Look up your home-town's census records at the library or online (try www.census.gov). List two, three, or four things that have changed since you were born. Urban Planners use census information to learn about communities' needs. (New kids filling the neighborhoods? New schools may be built. More people leaving their cars at home? More public transportation options may be introduced.)

⬆ ② 🎭 🌐 🏠 🔍 Join someone from an older generation in looking up census records for where they grew up. Do they remember filling in census forms every ten years?

⬆ ② 💡 🎭 🌐 🔍 Create your own census. Use the photocopy-able census work sheet on page 371, or download it from EarnMyKeep.com, to list statistics from the year you were born, and corresponding stats from the year it is now.

URBan PLanneRs:

- Work with communities to identify their wants and needs
- Collect and analyze data about places to learn how they function
- Make maps to show what communities look like, and what they could look like
- Plan for streets and side-walks in new neighborhoods
- Assist in the development of new or remodeled com-munity buildings

Earn It, Learn It

says shannon yadsko, urBan pLanner ii, parsons Brinckerhoff in washington, DC

I love *planning better communities for the next generation.*

My biggest on-the-job challenge is *accepting how long it takes to implement some plans—many take twenty years!*

I spend a lot of my day *answering the needs of a diverse group of people.*

Public meetings often *open my eyes to completely new viewpoints.*

My transportation maps *change twenty times before they're perfect.*

If I weren't an Urban Planner, I'd be *an Urban Studies Professor.*

○ ③ ⓐⓑⓒ ☼ 💬 Shadow an Urban Planner. Try finding one at your local planning department (every county in the United States has one, and many cities and regions have their own). After your time together, mail or email a thank-you note.

Evaluate Needs

○ ① ☼ 🔍 Interview Mom or Dad about what she likes (and doesn't like) about your neighborhood. Is it easy to get around or is there too much traffic? Are there plenty of parks or not enough sidewalks? Take good notes (or have Mom or Dad take them for you).

⬆ ① 💡 🙂 Consider the needs of people who are disadvantaged, like those who use wheelchairs

Urban Planner Shannon earned both a bachelor's degree and a master's degree in urban planning from the University of Virginia and has been a planner for five years. She realized urban planning was the right career for her when she tried both architecture school and engineering school, but neither was the right fit—urban planning was the perfect balance!

or don't speak English. List two, three, or four things in your neighborhood they'd find difficult to navigate.

⬆③☼💬🔍 Expand your list to represent the needs of other community members. Interview two, three, or four of the following: a Teacher, a Shop Owner, a resident of more than ten years, a resident of fewer than ten months, a kid your age.

○ ②🌐💡 Create a 3-D map of a city's transportation system—with recycled materials, food, toys, whatever you want—on the floor. First think about how people get from place to place (like railroads, public transportation, even bike paths). Then create your system. Does the railroad circle the town (toy train tracks)? Are there bus stations (shoe boxes)? Roads (strips of construction paper)?

⬆②🌐💡 Make little townspeople (popsicle sticks? pipe cleaners?) or use toy people to double-check your system. Can they get from point A to point B easily? Is there a glitch in your system that needs to be addressed?

⬆②🌐💡 Use more around-the-house materials to fill in your town. You could add a community center, playground, school, theater, hospital, even a place of worship—think about your favorite places in your neighborhood for inspiration.

> ## WHY DOES URBAN PLANNER SHANNON THINK HER CAREER IS AWESOME?
>
> "I get to help create great places for people to live, work, and play. I feel like I'm helping to make the world a better place!"

Urban planners use the terms *space, area, neighborhood, community,* and *place* interchangeably.

Plan Projects

○ ① 💡 Plan a community of the future that answers future-you needs. Will future-you be a Journalist who zips around town in a car that flies? Sounds like your community will need floating traffic lights and buildings with fast-acting garage doors (for you to zip right on to the news scene!). List two, three, or four improvements that Urban Planner-you can do for future-you.

DID YOU KNOW?

Urban Planners learn how to better their own community by traveling to lots of other communities—when you visit a new place, it's easy to see what works and what doesn't!

○ ① 💡 👀 Establish a community-centered goal (like "Have a clean, safe park for all the neighborhood families") and two, three, or four projects that can meet it (like posting signs reminding everyone to pick up after themselves; installing new trash cans; and encouraging *patrols** to make sure the area stays clean).

Patrols could be extra police officers or even watchful community members.

⬆️ ③ 👀 Make it happen. Or at least, get the ball rolling (some projects will continue long after you finish being an Urban Planner).

Municipal Officials govern a local city or town.

○ ② 💡 ⓐⓑⓒ ☀️ Convince a *Municipal Official*** (Mom? Dad?) to add a project of your choice (amusement park? swimming pool? rocket ship launching pad?) to her capital investment program—a program used to prioritize investments in community facilities like libraries and town centers. Give her two, three, or four reasons to sway her in your favor.

Implement Ideas

○ ① 💡 🧮 💲 ⏱️ Develop an implementation plan for a project that could make life better for your family (clean out the mudroom so it's faster to get inside on wet, muddy days? set up an arts center in a corner of the family room?). List whose help you'll need to get the job done, how much you think it will cost (can you do it for free?), and how long you think it will take.

⬆②ⓐⓑⓒ☀️💬 Present your plan, and why it's important, to your "community members" (your family) at a public meeting (over dinner). Share your intention and how the public will benefit from it. Be polite because you may need their help with your plan!

⬆③💡☀️💬⏰ Work with your family to complete your project.

⬆①ⓐⓑⓒ☀️ Keep the "public" informed of your project's progress. Post a flyer in the kitchen or send a brief email when you're about halfway done, and again after project completion.

CAREER CROSSING

URBAN PLANNERS WORK WITH:
Architects
Cartographers
Elected Officials
Public Facilitators
Transportation Engineers*

The coolest part of the new DVD player is its teeny-tiny remote. However, tiny remotes come with tiny buttons. And when Mom tries to hit "play," it fast-forwards! So you ask Dad to try. Then Grandma. And Grandpa. And suddenly you're a UX Researcher on a mission to find out what's so not cool about the new DVD player's coolest part!

Jump In

○ ① 😊 🌐 🔍 Try one, two, or three of the following: boil water without a microwave; send a letter without email; find the definition of "onomatopoeia" without the Internet; report about what's going to happen on the next episode of your favorite show without an onscreen cable guide or a website.

⬆️ ① 😊 🔍 Try the same activity(ies) using technology, then report about the differences in your experience(s). This is a great example of how UX Researchers uncover what updates people want made to the things they use every day.

○ ② 💡 🔍 Turn on the TV and the radio—loud. Then read aloud from your favorite book. While doing so, have Mom or Dad give you a directive, without shouting, from across the room (such as "Find the keys I hid in the sleeve of my green T."). Successfully complete

UX Researchers:

- Analyze electronics to identify how they could be made easier and more enjoyable to use
- Run experiments to see how people use computer programs and websites

What's the "UX" stand for in "UX Researcher?" User Experience—"U" for "User" and "X" for the "Ex" sound in "Experience!"

SAYS SABINA ALTERAS, PHD, OWNER/PRINCIPAL, ALTERAS CONSULTING IN SEATTLE, WASHINGTON

I love *seeing my recommendations incorporated into an improved product.*

My biggest on-the-job challenge is *making sure each research study reveals just what's needed to make a product better.*

The funniest test I ever ran was for *a video game with characters called "meeples." Imagine creating a professional-sounding report while referring to "meeples!"*

End users that are fun to observe are *kids because they're very honest and enthusiastic.*

My favorite childhood video game *was my Atari (loved Space Invaders and Pac-Man!).*

If I weren't a UX Researcher, I'd be *an Architect.*

their task (it may take a few tries). UX Researchers know it's hard for people to understand messages with everything that competes for their attention.

- ② 💡😎🌐🔍 Visit the library or the Internet to report about the Atari 2600 (yes, there were video games before X-Box and Wii). Then compare a photocopy or printout of the Atari's joystick to a current game system's joystick. List one, two, or three changes that were most likely recommended by a UX Researcher.

- ③ 🔤⚙️💬 Shadow a UX Researcher. Find one by calling a local college's psychology, computer science, or engineering department. Or try searching online for a large software company. After your time together, mail or email a thank-you note.

Research & Analyze Products

○ ① 💡 🔍 Look around your home to identify one, two, or three examples of unfriendly electronics product design (too hard to figure out which DVD player cord goes where? buttons too close together on a clock radio?).

Make this "official" by creating a homemade research laboratory: a quiet spot with a table and chair for your participant.

○ ② ☼ 🔍 Watch an "end user" (Mom? Little Bro?) use an electronic gadget (cell phone, iPod, handheld video game) she has never used before (like selecting a player on a video game). Start and end with the gadget off, so you can witness the full experience. Ask your end user to talk out loud while using the product ("I am turning it on now by pushing the ON button on the side."). Do not respond to the user's comments (one of the hardest parts of researching!). Write down what you hear and see, including facial expressions.

⬆ ① 💡 List one, two, or three recommended changes that could improve user experience.

UX Researcher Sabina earned her PhD in industrial/organizational psychology from the University of Connecticut. She specializes in "engineering psychology"—meaning, she studies how people think, remember, and learn. She then uses this information to recommend designs that make electronic products easier for us to use!

○ ② 🔍 Research your favorite video or online game—list a description of the product, what makes it different from similar products, and its *user profile**.

⬆ ① 💡 🔍 Identify one, two, or three problems with the game (for example, "Items are hard to move with a mouse.").

User profiles include information about a product's typical user, like age, gender, and amount of experience with the game.

○ ② 🎨 💡 🔍 Test a website on paper. Draw a brand-new website home page

Look at real-life home pages for inspiration.

for your favorite musical artist, predicting what users will want to do when they first get there. (Do you feature her new album, assuming people will want to hear a sample? Do you list tour dates, hoping people click to buy tickets?) Then draw a second page—the one you hope people will click.

⬆ ① ☼ 🔍 Test your website. Place your home page in front of a family member, and don't say a word. What does he like? What does he think is missing? Does he "click" (point his finger) where you want him to click? If he does, show him the second page and see how he does there too.

○ ② 🧪 💡 🐛 ☼ 🔍 Turn a household task into an icon game. Pick your task (say, feed the dog). Create icons (symbols) to explain each step, drawing each on individual pieces of paper (a closet = "open the closet doors"; a bag = "get the bag of dog food"; a bowl = "put the food in the bowl"). Give your icons to someone from an older generation, one at a time as she completes each step—do *not* tell your user what each icon means. If she does one wrong, that's OK. Your job is to observe and report about her experience.

WHY DOES UX RESEARCHER SABINA THINK HER CAREER IS AWESOME?

"I get to study all types of people as they try to use all different types of electronics, software, and websites—and the final product is something that's easy to use, easy to learn, safe, and so much more enjoyable than it would have been without UX research behind it!"

DID YOU KNOW?

To make electronics better, some UX Researchers learn how to do things like activate police equipment or fly planes—anything that gives insight to how a product will be used!

(↑) (2) (💡) Review your report. Remove any icons that weren't necessary. Combine those that can be combined. If need be, create a new icon (or two).

(↑) (2) (☼) (🔍) Repeat the game with a new participant to see if your changes result in a smoother, faster experience.

Make Recommendations

o (1) (💡) Define a redesign of Mom's or Dad's car dashboard that makes it easier (and more fun!) for *you* to use. So say, instead of their fuel gauge, it could be a counter of how many more times you can get to practice without running out of gas.

o (2) (⚓) (💡) (🔍) (🖐) Find an electronic gadget or website that would be unusable for someone who is visually impaired (like the type is too small on the TV remote, or the *navigation** on your favorite website is too complicated). Then draw a more user-friendly version.

Navigation refers to tabs on a graphic bar that tell users where they can go.

CAREER CROSSING

UX RESEARCHERS WORK WITH:

Computer Programmers

Graphic Designers

Industrial Designers

Product Developers

Subject Matter Experts

Zoologist

You did more than beg for that puppy. You researched his favorite type of kibble. How often he naps. The best age to house-train. And then, when you finally brought him home, you were all about the feeding, bathing (yes, even the walking). Why? Because the Zoologist in you can't get enough of those sloppy puppy kisses!

Jump In

○ ① 🔍 🧪 Use the library or an Internet search to define two, three, or four of the following: kingdom, phylum, class, order, family, genus, species.

⬆ ① 🔍 🧪 List the kingdom, phylum, class, order, family, genus, and species of your favorite animal.

○ ① 💡 🧪 Imagine a new animal for fellow Zoologists to study. (Maybe it has an elephant's body, platypus's bill, and snake's skin.) Name your animal (an Eleplatysnake!) and define its *habitat**, diet***, and *behavior****.

⬆ ② 🎨 💡 Draw a picture of your animal.

○ ② 🎨 🔍 🧪 🐾 Ask someone from an older generation to identify her favorite endangered animal. Report about its natural habitat and why it is threatened.

ZOOLOGISTS:

- Study animal behavior to better understand and care for them
- Care for animals, including feeding them and keeping them clean
- Educate people about the importance of protecting animals

Habitat is where an animal lives.

Diet is what an animal eats.

Behavior is what an animal likes to do (swim? climb trees? juggle?).

says TIM THIer, ZOOLOGICAL Manager, SAINT LOUIS ZOO IN ST. LOUIS, MISSOURI

I love _working with endangered animals in the wild, like the Grevy's Zebra._

My biggest-on-the-job challenge is _caring for animals in the extreme cold._

The most bizarre thing an animal did to me at work was _vomit on me! (It was pretty gross.)_

If I were any animal, I'd be _a giraffe because they're graceful. And they get to see the world from high up._

The worst animal poop to clean up is from _an elephant because it's so heavy._

If I weren't a Zoologist, I'd be _a Firefighter._

① ② 🐾 🔍 🐾 "Adopt" an endangered animal together. Ask about these programs at your local zoo, or do an online search. Even the smallest donation helps protect our endangered animal friends.

○ ③ abc ☀ 💬 Shadow a Zoologist. Call your local zoo to see if someone on staff is able to show you around. Many larger zoos offer tours for kids. Afterward, mail or email a thank-you note.

○ ③ abc 🔍 🌡 Visit a zoo, then write an article about an animal you saw there. (This is extra fun if a new animal is being loaned from another zoo, or if a baby animal was recently born.) Include facts like size, native habitat, and status (threatened? endangered?)—you'll find this kind of information in the graphics posted near the animal's zoo home.

Not all zoologists work at zoos. Some study animals in laboratories. Others follow animals in their natural habitats, spending months living outdoors!

(↑)(1)(abc)(👁) "Publish" your article by mailing or emailing your article to one, two, or three friends or family members. Zoologists share their research with other Zoologists by publishing articles like these—then everyone can benefit from what they learned.

Take Care of Animals & Habitats

○ (1)(💡)(🔍) Create a list of three, four, or five maintenance tasks for your favorite zoo animal's habitat (you may need to use the library or an online search to complete your list). Let's say it's the hippos: you'd need to plant ferns and fill the moat.

(↑)(2)(👁) Maintain an animal's grounds for two, three, or four days. (So for your neighbor's turtle, this may include changing the cage liner and fixing a broken bell.)

○ (2)(🔍)(🧪) Use the library or an Internet search to report about your favorite animal's dietary needs. Try to uncover why those foods are important for that particular animal (for example, lions eat meat because meat's proteins help build strong muscles).

Zoologist Tim has been working with animals for fourteen years, and is currently pursuing a master's degree created specifically for employees of zoos and aquariums through George Mason University and the Association of Zoos and Aquariums. He has also visited zoos around the country to gain more experience with different ways to care for animals. His very first job at the Saint Louis Zoo was giving leaf cutter ants fresh leaves every day, so they could create their gardens!

(↑)(2)(🧪)(👁) Fulfill the dietary needs of an animal (your iguana?) for two, three, or four days.

○ ② 💡 🔍 Report about the proper way to clean and groom your favorite land animal *and* your least favorite land animal. List one, two, or three ways the processes are the same and how they're different.

Why a land animal? It'd be awfully hard to clean or groom a fish!

 ① ② 🕑 Clean and groom an animal (neighbor's Chihuahua?) for two, three, or four days.

○ ② 🔍 🧪 🕑 Keep a record of an animal's behavior for three, four, or five days, at the same time(s) every day. So, for example, you'd record the behavior of the class guinea pig on Tuesday, Wednesday, and Thursday at 9:00 a.m. and 11:30 a.m. each day.

 ① ① 💡 🔍 🧪 Review your re-cords—report on any changes in the animal's behavior.

 ① ③ 🕑 Pack your record with the animal if he is being transferred.

So if that guinea pig is going to the class next door, your records will help that teacher take better care of her.

○ ③ 💡 🔍 🕑 Arrange care for an animal in its owner's absence (is your cousin taking care of Grandma's tabby cats while she's out of town?). Prepare a list that includes things like what/when to feed,

This can be for a real-life animal or a pretend one, and a real-life absence or a pretend one.

when to water, when to bathe, when to walk, what the animal likes to do (your list may vary depending on the type of animal). Then make sure all supplies are ready and clearly marked. And remember to leave the Veterinarian's phone number!

DID YOU KNOW?

Zoologists sometimes play Mommy and Daddy to animals in their care. So if a new gazelle mom doesn't know how to care for her babies, zoo staff will help raise the calves!

Manage Programs

○ ② 💡 🖩 $ 🔍 Use paper and pen or a computer program to establish a budget for the care of an animal of your choice (yes, you can use your own pet). Determine the costs for one month of cleaning, feeding, and habitat upkeep. Add extra money for surprises like veterinary visits and lost dog collars.

⬆ ② 🖩 $ ⏱ Track your spending for five, six, or seven days. Report if you are on-track to stay within the month's budget.

> **WHY DOES ZOOLOGIST TIM THINK HIS CAREER IS AWESOME?**
>
> "I get to work with very rare animals every day, and play a small part in helping endangered species survive in the wild."

○ ② ⚙ 💬 ⏱ Delegate one, two, or three animal care assignments to your staff (Mom? Dad? Little Sis?). So, say you assign Mom "feeding duty," Dad

Could even be a pet you're pet-sitting.

"pooping duty," and Little Sis "grooming duty" for one day of a pet's care. Make sure the tasks are completed. And be sure to be polite when requesting your staff's services.

CAREER CROSSING

ZOOLOGISTS WORK WITH:
Curators*
Horticulturists*
Nutritionists
Veterinarians
Welders

Create-Your-Own!

Whats so great about this world of ours? That the sky's the limit—especially when it comes to what you can do when you grow up. In fact, this book's forty-nine Earn My Keep careers are just the tip of the iceberg. There are zillions of career possibilities waiting for you, and Create-Your-Own! is your chance to try 'em all out.

To get started, first pick a career. Then:

o Use a library book or Internet search to learn a little bit about your career of choice, or if you're lucky enough to know one, ask an Expert about it. Then brainstorm a task that re-creates part of the job. Remember, Earn My Keep is not about trying to do it all. It's about exploring one tiny aspect of a career at a time. For example, let's say you want to be a Personal Trainer—these folks help better people's health through fitness. You could report about how muscles work. Or create a music playlist (on iPod, CD, or simply written on paper) that Mom could listen to while exercising. Or ask Dad to do as many sit-ups as he can in one minute, every day for three days. Record his results, noting if he can do more repetitions as the days go by.

   ⬆ Try to do it all (yes, I know I said you shouldn't, but this is a great exception) by creating your own **So You Want to…** This is the mega-task that follows a career process from start to finish. For Personal Trainer, this may mean asking Mom which part of her body she'd like to make stronger; researching a good exercise for that muscle group (no weights!); teaching Mom how to do that exercise; and recording how many repetitions she can do, while you politely encourage her to try her best!

o Look at ideas in activity and craft books, parents and kid magazines, and on your favorite TV shows the Earn My Keep way. Find the instructions for "How to pull a rabbit out of a hat"? You're a Magician! Come across the ingredients for "Fruit Pizza"? You're a Pastry Chef! Yes, you'll better guarantee your authenticity if you ask a real-life Expert for task tips, but sometimes a little imagination works just fine.

o Interview an Expert. You can ask questions like those in the Earn My Keep interviews (such as "What do you love about your career?" "What's your biggest on-the-job challenge?" and "If you weren't a [CAREER NAME HERE], what would you be?") and/or create your own list of questions. You can interview in person, on the phone, or via email.

The Expert can be someone you know or someone you don't. Check the phone book and/or Internet for resources.

⬆ Turn your interview into a written report, an oral presentation, or both!

⬆ Include Career Crossing in your interview—ask your Expert which other professionals he works with to get his job done.

⬆ Ask your Expert for a **Did You Know?**—that cool little fact that makes you say, "Wow! I didn't know that about [INSERT CAREER NAME HERE]s!"

o Build on Career Day. Ask your school's Guidance Counselor if she can share the contact information from a favorite speaker. Perhaps he'd have a little time to help you create a task, participate in an interview, or even give you a tour of where he works.

o Ask Mom or Dad to create your own "Bring Me to Work Day." (Seeing what your parents do all day is a great way to Earn My Keep!) If a full day isn't an option, consider just an hour or so after school.

o Teach someone something you're good at doing. Experts are often tasked with passing their skills on to up-and-coming Experts. So if you love to draw characters (like a real Cartoonist!), teach Mom how to draw your favorite. Or if you've earned a new karate belt (like a real Karate Instructor!), teach Dad how to do a jump axe kick. It may seem, at first, like you're not learning anything new, but the act of teaching is a great way to reinforce your skills and practice good manners.

MORE THINGS TO CONSIDER

o Involve someone from an older generation. Together you could do anything from brainstorming a task idea to actually performing the task.

o Add a Social Responsibility twist to any task—this can be any positive social or environmental act. Remember, even the smallest actions add up to a big impact that betters our entire planet and the people who live on it.

PART 3

THE BONUS STUFF

Photocopy, then cut out your new EMK Cash bills.

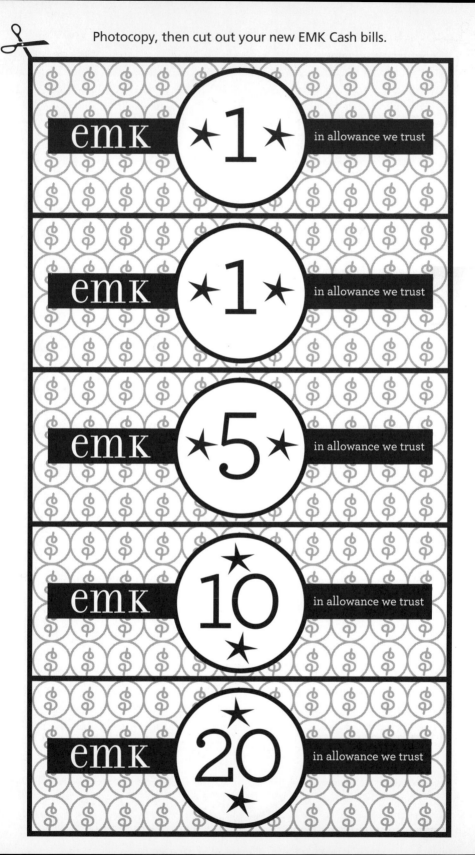

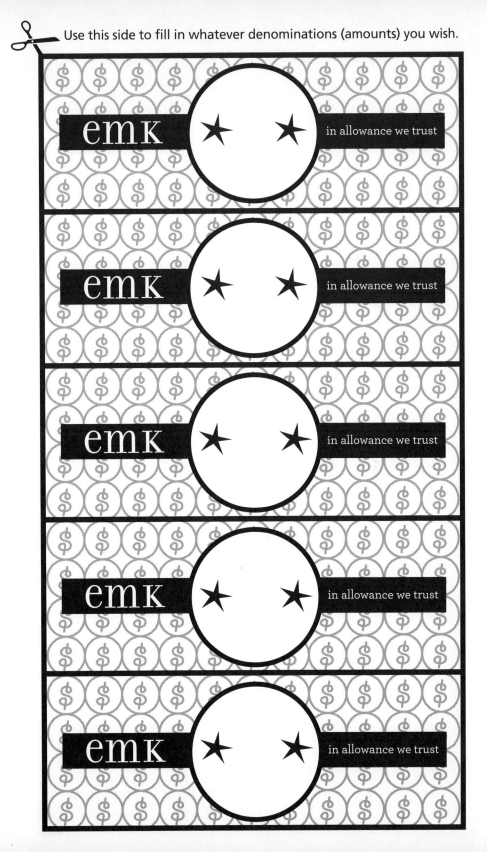

Sample Thank-you Note

(From page 29)

So for a glorious hour (or half-hour or entire afternoon), you shadowed an Expert, seeing firsthand what a real professional does and maybe even acting the part with a task or two. But your experience hasn't ended yet!

In the real world, real professionals express gratitude with a mailed or emailed note. Now you can too. This is your opportunity to thank your Expert for his time, and share something about the experience you really enjoyed. If you handwrite your letter, consider including a drawing of something you and your Expert did together. If you email, maybe attach a photo. Either way, here's an example for inspiration.

Dear Mr. Cavasin,

Thank you for taking the time to show me how to be an investigator. It was very nice of you to spend your lunch hour with me. I really liked learning how you use cameras to solve cases and keep our town safe. Now I can be an investigator at home helping my Mom find things around the house!

Sincerely,
Shane Kullen

Astronomer, Contractor, Paleontologist
& Toy Designer: Play-dough Recipe

(From pages 63, 89, 256, and 294)

Making your own play-dough is fun. Making your own play-dough is creative. Making your own play-dough is a great way to throw out an elbow or shoulder, so I highly recommend asking Mom or Dad if you've got an electric mixer for the recipe here. Otherwise, look online or in a book for a stovetop version—I've heard they're equally quick and easy.

- Mix 3 cups flour, 1/3 cup salt, and 2 Tbsp. vegetable oil.
- Add 1 cup water, 1/2 cup at a time.
- Mix with a spoon (or electric mixer).
- Knead the dough (or use that mixer)—it'll be crumbly for a bit but will eventually blend into that familiar doughy consistency.
- Separate the dough into sections, add a bunch of drops of food coloring (a different color or combination of colors per section) and knead again. (Or throw back in that mixer! Though, typically, after a bit of electric mixing, we'll pull the dough out and knead by hand. It's cool to make the marble colors blend to solid.)
- And then...ta-da! Homemade play-dough that's safe to eat (though quite icky-tasting!).

Store your play-dough in resealable baggies and it'll stay soft for a week or more.

Accountant: Income Tax Return

(From page 47)

Department of the Earn My Keep Allowance Program – Internal Revenue Service | **YEAR:**

Income Tax Return for Adorable Single Filers

Your first name	MI	Last name	Your birthday

Home address		Apt no.	

City, town, or post office	State	Zip code

Income 1. List how much you've earned doing Earn My Keep... 1

Credits 2. List how much of your Earn My Keep earnings you've donated to charity.............................. 2

3. Subtract the amount in line 2 from line 1 3

Tax 4. Use the amount on line 3 to find your tax in the tax table below 4

Amount you owe 5. Multiply the number on line 4 by the amount on line 3.. 5

Tax Table

0–$20	½%
$20.01–$30	1% + 10 cents
$30.01–$40	1½% + 20 cents
$40.01–$50	2% + 35 cents
Over $50.01	3% + 55 cents

Sign here

Under penalties of not being honest, I declare that I have examined this return, and to the best of my knowledge, it is true, correct, and accurately lists all amounts and sources of income I received doing Earn My Keep.

Upon signing, I will give Mom or Dad a HUGE hug for not making me pay taxes like they have to pay every year!

▶ Your signature	Date
Your occupation	
Daytime phone no.	

348

Accountant: Budget Plan

(From page 48)

Event name _____

Start date: _____ **End date:** _____

BUDGET _____ **ACTUAL** _____

Location $ _____ $ _____

Food $ _____ $ _____

Decorations $ _____ $ _____

Entertainment $ _____ $ _____

Transportation $ _____ $ _____

Favors $ _____ $ _____

Special clothing $ _____ $ _____

Other $ _____ $ _____

Other $ _____ $ _____

Other $ _____ $ _____

TOTAL $ _____ $ _____

Copywriter: TV Script

(From page 96)

Most TV spots are thirty seconds long.

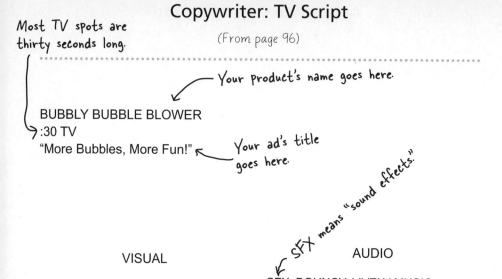

Your product's name goes here.

BUBBLY BUBBLE BLOWER
:30 TV
"More Bubbles, More Fun!"

Your ad's title goes here.

SFX means "sound effects."

VISUAL	AUDIO
Boys and girls, about eight or nine years old, run around a backyard, where bubbles are everywhere! Bubbles in all shapes and sizes—round ones, long ones, animal-shaped ones, even spaceship-shaped ones—all coming from the Bubbly Bubble Blower machine.	SFX: BOUNCY, LIVELY MUSIC SFX: NEIGHBORHOOD SOUNDS (CARS DRIVING BY SLOWLY, A SPRINKLER, AN ICE CREAM TRUCK) **Kids: (LAUGHING AND CHEERING)**
One of the kids rides around on the back of a horse-shaped bubble.	SFX: GALLOP OF HORSE
It POPS and he falls softly to the ground, laughing.	SFX: POP! OF EXPLODING BUBBLE VO: **What's so great about the big, bubbly bubbles from the Bubbly Bubble Blower?**
Another kid wears a bunch of bubbles like muscles, flexes and stretches his arms and legs like a circus strongman.	SFX: CIRCUS MUSIC VO: **Everything!**
A little girl "plays" a bubble shaped like a giant trombone. The bubble POPS and she takes a bow.	SFX: TROMBONE TUNE SFX: POP! OF EXPLODING BUBBLE
SUPER: More Bubbles. More Fun! BUBBLY BUBBLE BLOWER Logo	VO: **Get more bubbles and more fun! Buy your own Bubbly Bubble Blower today!**

VO means "voice over" (or announcer).

A "super" is words on-screen.

A logo appears at the end.

350

Copywriter: Radio Script

(From page 97)

This is how long the spot is.

Where you want people to visit.

COUNTY FAIR

:60 RADIO

"Funnel Cake"

Your spot's name.

SFX means "sound effects."

SFX:	CARNIVAL SOUNDS (FERRIS WHEEL MUSIC, ARCADE GAMES, PEOPLE LAUGHING)
MAN:	(DEEP BREATH IN) Yesserree, spring is in the air. How do I know? Because I'm here! I'm hot! I'm crunchy! I'm covered in powdered sugar!! Ahhh, yes, it's me—your mouth-watering, County Fair–going funnel cake. Is there anything better? No, not me (but thank you). The FAIR! Rides…
SFX:	ROLLER COASTER WHOOOSH!
MAN	:…games…
SFX:	DING-DING-DING-DING!!!
MAN:	…animals…
SFX:	MOOOOOO…
MAN:	…yes, they're a bit stinky and they lack a certain powdered-sugary-ness about 'em—but they're all here! Check out poetry and science projects from kids all over the county. Get woozy on the swings…no, the coasters…no, the swings…no, that big BOAT that turns you upside down…
SFX:	ROLLER COASTER RIDERS, SCREAMING
MAN:	…(seriously?? Who rides that?!). All I know is this HERE's the place to be THIS WEEKEND AND NEXT WEEKEND ONLY!
SFX:	BOUNCY, HAPPY MUSIC
VO:	Don't miss the County Fair! Grab advance tickets at convenience stores across town. And join in for food, fair, and FUN!
SFX:	BACK TO CARNIVAL SOUNDS
MAN:	I don't know why folks say I'm fattening. The more you eat, the thinner I get.

SFX can also be music!

VO means "voice over," and is typically used for important information.

Costume Designer: Pieces List

(From page 102)

Actor's name:	
Character's name:	

Scene	Item	Description	Quantity
#1 Kitchen	T-shirt	Stripes, blue	1
	Shorts	Cargo, khaki	1
	Sock	Ankle, white	2
	Sneaker	Lace-up, white with blue stripe	2
	Watch	Dark green jelly band, white face	1
	Hat	Floppy, striped, khaki/white	1
#1			
#2			
#3			

Guest Relations Manager: Feedback Card

(From page 163)

··

_____ HOTEL
GUEST RELATIONS MANAGER'S LAST NAME

GUEST SATISFACTION SURVEY

Please tell us how you learned about the _____ Hotel:
MANAGER'S LAST NAME

○ **Family member**   ○ **Friend**
○ **Friend of family member**   ○ **Flying elephant**
○ **Other (please list)** _____

Please rate the following:	GOOD	REALLY GOOD	REALLY, REALLY, REALLY GOOD
Staff greeting upon arrival:	○	○	○
Cleanliness upon arrival:	○	○	○
Comfort of bed:	○	○	○
Comfort of pillows:	○	○	○
Fluffiness of bath towels:	○	○	○
Late-night snacks:	○	○	○

Did you visit any local sites? If so, which one(s)? _____

_____

Please rate our staff on overall service:

○ GOOD   ○ REALLY GOOD   ○ REALLY, REALLY, REALLY GOOD

How likely are you to recommend the _____ Hotel to others?
MANAGER'S LAST NAME

○ LIKELY   ○ VERY LIKELY   ○ VERY, VERY, VERY LIKELY

Including this visit, how many times have you stayed with us?

1 (FIRST TIME)   **2–4**   **5–9**   **10+**

Are there any staff members you'd like to mention for outstanding service during your stay? If so, please share your reason for mentioning them.

_____

_____

_____

THANK YOU FOR YOUR FEEDBACK AND FOR STAYING AT THE _____ HOTEL!
MANAGER'S LAST NAME

Human Resources Manager:
Wellness Program Enrollment Form

(From page 173)

Employee's name: _____

Date: _____

This Wellness Program is developed to strengthen _____.
<small>EMPLOYEE'S NAME</small>

in three key areas: mind, body, and spirit. Participants signing this Enrollment Form

agree to try the listed recommendations, and they may choose to report their

experiences to Human Resources Manager _____ when
<small>HUMAN RESOURCES MANAGER'S NAME</small>

they've completed the program.

FOR THE MIND
Recommendations: _____

_____

_____

_____

> **Example:** *Use the library or an Internet search to create a booklist on subjects of interest to your employee.*

FOR THE BODY
Recommendations: _____

_____

_____

_____

> **Example:** *Provide a recipe for a healthy dinner.*

FOR THE SPIRIT
Recommendations: _____

_____

_____

_____

> **Example:** *Recommend a stress-relieving hobby, such as knitting or bird watching.*

SIGNED _____   _____

<small>EMPLOYEE'S NAME</small>   <small>DATE</small>

_____   _____

<small>HUMAN RESOURCES MANAGER'S NAME</small>   <small>DATE</small>

United States District Court

STATE OF MARYLAND

SEARCH WARRANT

CASE NUMBER: 5801

TO: Any Authorized Family Member of the Inman Family WHEREAS Investigator Cole has reason to believe the Honey is trying to get the Mustard into a sticky mess; AND WHEREAS I, Judge Adelle, find sufficient probable cause has been presented (a sticky Mustard cap) in order to allow for this search warrant to be issued.

THEREFORE YOU ARE HEREBY COMMANDED to proceed without unnecessary delay to the suspected place (the Kitchen Fridge) and conduct a search of said suspected place to see if a crime has been committed.

IF YOU FIND THAT FOR WHICH YOU SEARCH, YOU WILL TAKE IT AS EVIDENCE and secure it from destruction as in such cases provided by law. BUT you will also use the sticky Honey bottle, pouring a bit over some freshly cut apples, which you will then enjoy as a snack.

ISSUED THIS DAY ___September 26, 2011___ AT ___7:12 pm___.
DATE   TIME OF DAY

Judge Adelle
_____
JUDGE MOM OR DAD'S NAME

We the people

of the Sohn Family, in order to form a more loving Family do ordain and establish this Constitution for the United Sohn Family.

Article 1.

Section 1.

All kids will respect decisions set forth by adult(s).

Section 2.

Adult(s) will respect and validate concerns, issues, and opinions brought up by all kids, and will take them into consideration when making decisions.

Concerns, issues, and opinions will be brought forth at biweekly family meetings. Healthy treats and beverages are mandatory.

Section 3.

Family activities are to occur a minimum of once a week. These include, but are not limited to, neighborhood walks, game nights, movie matinees, county fairs, scavenger hunts, and stargazing.

Judge: Adoption Petition

(From page 198)

⋅⋅

1.   Petitioner's name: _____

       Address: _____

       _____

       Length of time the petitioner has lived in his/her city/town: _____

2.   Date pet/stuffed animal/imaginary friend was placed in the home

       of the petitioner: _____

3.   Pet/stuffed animal/imaginary friend's name: _____

       Date of birth: _____

       Place of birth: _____

4.   Three reasons why named pet/stuffed animal/imaginary friend
       would be happy in the petitioner's home:

       1. _____

       2. _____

       3. _____

The petitioner declares that he/she will be able to nurture and care for the pet/stuffed animal/imaginary friend, and that he/she will welcome the pet/stuffed animal/imaginary friend into his/her home with love. Therefore, the petitioner asks that this adoption be made so.

_____ Petitioner's name	_____ Petitioner's signature
_____ Date	_____ Judge's signature
_____ State of	_____ County of

Market Researcher: Moderator's Guide

(From page 226)

You don't have to read this word-for-word,
but this script includes all your important points.

I. INTRODUCTION

Thanks very much for joining us and sharing your opinions about dinner. Our goal is to understand the benefits of eating in and dining out. My name is [YOUR NAME], and I will be moderating our focus group this evening. This means I will not be giving my opinion—doing so may influence your answers.

A few important things to know:

First, there are no right or wrong answers…just YOUR answers.

Second, please talk one at a time, so we can clearly hear what each of you has to say.

Third, if we go off-topic, I may ask you to wrap up your thoughts so we have time to get to everything.

And now, let's begin!

II. PARTICIPANT INTRODUCTIONS

I'd like to go around the table and invite each of you to take thirty seconds or so to tell us your name, what you like to do for fun, and your favorite thing to eat for dinner.

(Proceed with introductions)

III. IMPRESSIONS OF THE DINING EXPERIENCE

(1) Let's start out by seeing who prefers to eat in, and who prefers to dine out. If you prefer to eat at home, please raise your hand *(count the number of hands)*. If you prefer to eat at a restaurant, please raise your hand *(count the number of hands)*.

Now I'd like to hear why you prefer one more than the other.

(2) Now I'd like to explore the costs of eating in and dining out.

First, the money costs: I'd like each of your best guesses at how much it costs to prepare your favorite home-cooked meal, and how much the same meal would cost at a restaurant. (*Can also encourage your family to include the prices of things like gas and gratuity.*)

Next, let's talk about the health costs. What's the difference, health-wise, between meals you eat at home, and those you eat in restaurants?

(3) Next I'm interested in how you feel about sharing dinner together as a family. Is it important to you? If so, why? If not, why not?

Now I'd like to know if you think it's better to share dinner at home or at a restaurant, and why.

(4) And our last question of the evening: after participating in this research study and listening to your family members' opinions, have you changed your preference for eating in or dining out?

IV. SUMMARY

This wraps up our questions about eating in and dining out. Thank you very much for participating in our focus group!

Market Researcher:
In-Depth Interview Questionnaire

(From page 227)

Each person you interview gets her own sheet.

....

PROJECT NAME: _____

DATE: _____

PARTICIPANT BEING INTERVIEWED: _____

1. **In which event did you participate?**
   (Example: A race to raise money for a local charity.)

2. **What were your responsibilities?**
   (Example: I handed water to runners as they raced by.)

3. **How did the experience make you feel?**
   (Example: Good. I felt like I was making a difference.)

4. **Do you think it was time well spent?**
   (Example: Yes, because otherwise those racers would be thirsty!)

5. **Would you recommend the experience to another person?**
   (Example: Yes! It was fun.)

6. **Do you think there could be improvements to the experience?**
   (Example: I wish I had checked the weather first—I wore jeans, and it was hot!)

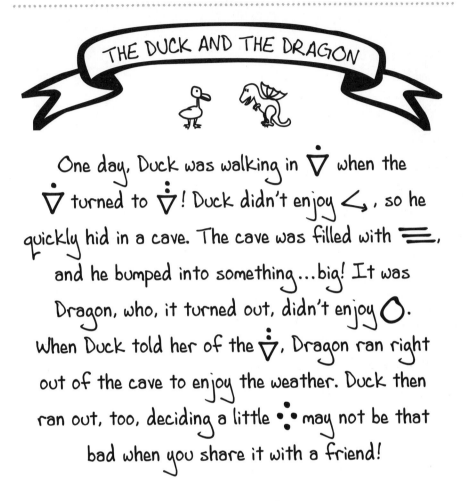

THE DUCK AND THE DRAGON

One day, Duck was walking in ∇̇ when the ∇̇ turned to ∇̈! Duck didn't enjoy ⟨, so he quickly hid in a cave. The cave was filled with ☰, and he bumped into something...big! It was Dragon, who, it turned out, didn't enjoy ◯. When Duck told her of the ∇̈, Dragon ran right out of the cave to enjoy the weather. Duck then ran out, too, deciding a little ⋮ may not be that bad when you share it with a friend!

THE END!

Key for "The Duck and the Dragon"

∇̇ slight rain showers   ☰ thick fog

∇̈ violent rain showers   ◯ clear skies

⟨ lightning   ⋮ heavy rain

Nurse Practitioner: Medical History Questionnaire

(From page 246)

Identification

Patient name: _____ Gender: _____ Age: _____

Place of exam: _____ Date of exam: _____

Patient's chief complaint *(if applicable)*: _____

_____

Does anything hurt you now? If so:

When did it start hurting? _____

What do you think caused it? _____

Does it affect day-to-day activities? _____

Does a kiss make it feel better? _____

Does frozen yogurt make it feel better? _____

Does patting your head and rubbing your belly make it feel better? _____

Past Medical History

Childhood Illnesses *(Example: Mumps? Measles? Chicken pox?)* _____

_____

Hospitalization History *(Have you ever been in the hospital?)*

If so, for what? _____

If so, did you get a cast that all your friends could sign? _____

Habits

How many hours do you sleep per night? _____

Are you exercising at least 3 times per week? _____

Do you eat 5-9 servings of fruits and/or vegetables per day? _____

If no, are you aware of how nutritious these foods are for the body? _____

Do you laugh at least 3 times per day? _____

If no, are you aware of how wonderful laughing is for the body? _____

Social History

Occupation: _____

Religion: _____

Cultural/ethnic background: _____

Favorite outdoor activity to do with friends: _____

Outdoor Adventure Guide: Campfire Recipe

(From page 252)

– Makes one meal

WHAT YOU'LL NEED:

Hamburger meat (1/2 lb.)

Potato (1 small to medium-sized)

Carrots (1 regular-sized or small handful of baby carrots)

Onion (1/2 medium)

Bell pepper (optional)

Salt and pepper to taste

Shredded cheese (1/3 to 1/2 cup)

Jalapenos (optional, but Outdoor Adventure Guide William loves 'em!)

WHAT YOU DO:

– Shape hamburger meat into a patty (remember to wash your hands after shaping your patty—raw meat germs can make you sick!). Place on a sheet of aluminum foil, about 12"x12". Add the rest of the veggies to the meat. Season with salt and pepper. Wrap the foil around the meat and veggies and place next to a campfire. Rotate every 10 minutes. Cook until done (typically 45 minutes to an hour, depending on the fire's temperature and your elevation. You can check for doneness the old-fashioned way—opening up the foil and looking—or with a meat thermometer.) Sprinkle on cheese, let it melt, then top with jalapenos (if you'd like). And lastly, enjoy!

Stay safe! Never go near a fire without an adult's supervision.

Producer: Consent and Release Agreement

(From page 268)

I hereby allow the use of my name, photograph, voice, and/or likeness by

Producer _____ for the Earn My Keep "Pretending to Be Members of My
PRODUCER'S NAME

Family" task only. Producer _____ shall own any and all photographs and
PRODUCER'S NAME

recordings of me pretending to be _____, but he/she
FAMILY MEMBER ACTOR IS PRETENDING TO BE

is not allowed to use any of the photographs or recordings without asking me first. I

don't want surprise pictures showing up online or on posters at my birthday party!

Producer _____ is not allowed to use these photographs or recordings in
PRODUCER'S NAME

any new way in the future either. One day I might run for president and I don't want to

have to answer to Diane Sawyer about this project.

I have read this release before signing my name below, I agree that I fully understand

its content, and I look forward to working with such a talented, fabulous, wonderful

Producer like _____.
PRODUCER'S NAME

_____   _____
Name   Signature

_____   _____
Date   Address

_____   _____
Witness

_____

Project Manager: Project Delivery Plan

(From page 274)

Project name:	Start date:	End date:

Location:

Project purpose:

Deliverables:

Scope of work:

Project team:	Risk management:

Resource plan:	Safety plan:

Team Member	Task	Budget $	Actual $	Start time and/or date	End time and/or date

I agree to take responsibility for managing this project in order to complete the work on budget and on schedule, while treating my team members (if applicable) with respect and maybe even to some fresh fruit or lemonade.

SIGNED _____

PROJECT MANAGER'S SIGNATURE

Publicist: Press Release

(From page 280)

FOR IMMEDIATE RELEASE

Media Contact: Publicist Karen

407-555-0930

Start with the date, where the news is coming from, and what the big announcement is.

DARIO'S DANCE DAZE HITS STORES IN TIME FOR HOLIDAY SHOPPING

August 8, 2011, Minneapolis, MN—Minneapolis-based White Picket Fence Entertainment Company announced today the November 26, 2011, release of Dario's Dance Daze, the fourth game in its wildly successful Dario video game series.

Dario's Dance Daze takes Dario into the underground world of Daze Land. Players wind their way through 24 levels of dancing fun in search of the magic dance-step shoes. The object of the game is to capture the shoes and do the Daze Land Dance before time runs out.

Finish with any other important information, including where the media can learn more.

Dario's Dance Daze will be compatible with Nintendo DS and Wii gaming systems and will retail for $29.99 and $49.99. For more information, visit the White Picket Fence Entertainment Company website.

About White Picket Fence Entertainment Company

Founded in 1994, White Picket Fence Entertainment Company creates video games for children and adults. White Picket's Dario series, first released in 2001, is the best-selling game series in the United States, Japan, and England.

###

These little "pound" signs mean there's no more to read.

OPTIONAL: Give a little info about the company that manufactures your game.

Social Activist: Letter to the Editor

(From page 288)

The name of the newspaper to which you're writing.

The Oregonian

Remember to check your local paper's rules for letter submission!

Letter to the Editor

January 31, 2011

Re: Article: School district may cut funds for arts programs in elementary schools

My brother and I are students at Vineland Farms Elementary School. We don't want our arts programs taken away. Art is my favorite subject in school. I like to draw and use clay. Someday I want to be an artist. My little brother likes music. He loves to play the recorder. My Mom and Dad liked watching him at his recital. If the government stops paying for these programs, we will both be very sad, and miss our teachers.

Sincerely,

End your letter with something polite. "Sincerely" is very professional.

Amy and Scott Vaughn

You don't have to write a Letter to the Editor in response to one of the newspaper's articles, but if you do, be sure to mention it.

. . . .

STARCHY & HUSK

← The title of the show.

OPEN ON:

INTERIOR. THE OFFICE—DAY   *Where the story takes place.*

FRED STARCHY, A FUN, EASYGOING POTATO, SHOOTS JUMP
SHOTS AT A MINIATURE BASKETBALL HOOP, ATTACHED TO A
TRASH CAN.

THOMAS J. HUSKOWITZ, AKA HUSK, A BRAINY, INTENSE EAR
OF CORN, IS READING OFFICE PAPERWORK.

                                        CUT TO:

ANIMATORS NOTE: STARCHY IS IN FRONT OF PACKED BASKETBALL
STADIUM WITH THE WHOLE CROWD CHEERING HIS NAME.

This means a change of scene ("cutting" to a different scene).

                    STARCHY
                (announcer voice)
    Idaho down by one point...time running out.
    All-American point guard Starchy has the
    ball. LeBron defending.

LEBRON JAMES POPS INTO FRAME TO DEFEND HIM.

                    STARCHY
    No wait, Michael Jordan...

LEBRON DISAPPEARS AND MICHAEL POPS IN TO GUARD STARCHY.

                    STARCHY
    No wait, Melo...

MICHAEL DISAPPEARS AND CARMELO ANTHONY POPS IN.

No, LeBron is better…

CARMELO POPS OUT AND LEBRON IS STANDING THERE
FRUSTRATED WITH HIS HANDS CROSSED AND TAPPING HIS
FOOT IN DISGUST.

CUT TO:

THE ANNOUNCER TABLE WITH AL MICHAELS.

AL

It looks like Starchy could blow this completely implausible fantasy.

STARCHY GIVES A LOOK TO THE ANNOUNCER.

STARCHY

He fakes left, goes right…shoots…

STARCHY LETS A BEAUTIFUL JUMPER FLY…OFF THE RIM!

STARCHY

Ugh! No. Wait. The rebound…

ANIMATORS NOTE: THE CROWD CHANTS.

Starchy…Starchy…Starchy…Starchy…

STARCHY TAKES IT ALL IN AS HE COMES OUT OF HIS HAZE.

BACK TO:

HUSK

Starchy, Starchy…

STARCHY

Huh, what? Did we win?

HUSK

No. And if you wouldn't mind coming back to Earth, we've got some real problems here. If we don't get another job soon, it will be our final game.

STARCHY

Okay. Okay. Give me a minute. Let me think… Let me think.

STARCHY AND HUSK PACE THE FLOOR IN UNISON. STARCHY STOPS. AHA!

STARCHY

I've got it! We'll win "American Idol."

Urban Planner: Census Form

(From page 321)

START HERE

The left side of this census form counts every person living in your household on the day you were born:

Month   Day   Year of birth

1. How many people were living or staying in your home on the day you were born?

2. List the ages and genders for each person living in your home on that day.
(M for male and F for female)

3. At that time, adults living in your home got to work by:
Mark box(es) with an X
❏ Bike
❏ Bus
❏ Cab
❏ Car
❏ Flying elephant
❏ Foot
❏ Roller skates
❏ Scooter
❏ Subway
❏ Train

4. What time did your family typically eat dinner?

5. What did your room look like?

_____

_____

_____

The right side of this census form counts every person living in your household today. Provide your age now:

Age

1. How many people are living or staying in your home today?

2. List the ages and genders for each person living in your home today.
(M for male and F for female)

3. At this time, adults living in your home get to work by:
Mark box(es) with an X
❏ Bike
❏ Bus
❏ Cab
❏ Car
❏ Flying elephant
❏ Foot
❏ Roller skates
❏ Scooter
❏ Subway
❏ Train

4. What time does your family typically eat dinner?

5. What does your room look like?

_____

_____

_____

Acknowledgments
(aka My Eternal Gratitude)

When my Agent (the fabulous Stephanie, to be thanked in a minute) was explaining how and why Publishers determine a book's allotted word count, I learned it had to do with paper: the number of words dictates the amount of paper the Publisher needs to print the book. (She also mused it has to do with weight, as in: I was not to create a book that gives kids hernias when they pick it up.)

Since the number of words (and amount of paper) required to thank everyone who has been a part of Earn My Keep far surpasses the weight four out of five Pediatricians would recommend to their patients who read books about allowance, you'll find a full list of folks at **EarnMyKeep.com/THX2U**. In the meantime, allow me to pay homage to the high-stakes players without whose collaboration none of this would be possible.

(In order of appearance, as it pertains to the book, backward-ish. If there's more than one person, in alphabetical order.)

To Graphic Designers/Web Developers Peter Grillot and Shelley Kirby: For EarnMyKeep.com. (Ever built a website? If so, you know how big a thank-you this is.) And to UX Researcher Sabina Webb: For testing said website!

To Copyeditor Sabrina Baskey-East, Managing Editor Sarah Cardillo, Production Designer Angela Cardoz, Editor Regan Fisher, Designer Ashley Haag,

Proofreader Barbara Hague, Art Director Mallory Kaster, Designer Sarah Krzyzek, Publisher Dominique Raccah, Publicist Heather Moore, Production Coordinator Tina Silva, Editorial Director Todd Stocke, Production Designer Danielle Trejo, everyone in Sales and Marketing, and the entire Sourcebooks family: for pulling out all the stops for an unknown (and incredibly appreciative) Author.

To Make-up Artist Atalie Abranovic, Hair Stylist Dana Comanda, Photographer Richard Greenhouse, Publicist Louisa Hart, Wardrobe Stylist Cendy Jovel, Media Consultant Jacki Schechner, Musician Rob Tryson, TV Writer Stefan Wallach, Niece-of-the-Year Meg Weinstein, and Musician Todd Weinstein: for reminding me why Copywriters shouldn't write their own key messages, take their own pictures, shoot and edit their own videos, write their own theme songs, pick their own clothes, or (heaven forbid) do their own hair and make-up.

To Parent Educator Linda Jessup: For a lovely foreword, of course. But also for gracing Earn My Keep with your experience and expertise.

To Art Directors Tracy Kordon and Cheryl Sohn: For the most adorable "Part 3: The Bonus Stuff" in history.

To Social Worker Melissa Antonucci, Parenting Educator Patricia Cancellier, Clinical Psychologist Allison K. Chase, Teacher Jamie Dobbs, School Counselor Eden Godfroy, Teacher Jason Godfroy, Developmental Psychologist Les Halpert, Rabbi Joui Hessel, Teacher Kerry Hoch, Child Developmental Specialist Eileen Trop Shimony, Teacher Christine Terrill, and Parenting Program Director Sue Yulis: For being my Education + Child Development Review Team. And for jaw-dropping insights and input now infused in every page of this book.

To Market Researchers Bobbie Kirkland, of the web opinion: For crafting the perfect research survey for our national program testing; and Reena Nawani, of Authentic Response: For making sure we actually had participants to take the survey!

To Lawyer Gerald M. Levine: For exceptional service in the line of trademarks, releases, and all sorts of law-related things I never knew about before.

To Graphic Designer Rhonda Weiner: For spot-on, absolutely stunning brand design. And for the cutest little icons I have ever had the pleasure of meeting.

To each and every Expert: For loving what you do for a living. For jumping into this with me blindly. For opening your lives (professional and otherwise) to create the perfect picture of your world. For exemplifying what it means to be generous with your time. Working with all of you has been such a gift. A truly wonderful, enlightening, educational, many times roll-on-the-floor-laughing gift I would never, ever trade.

To ★Acquisitions Editor Extraordinaire Shana Drehs★: For making me feel like I was your only Author (still don't know how you do that). For answering every one of my novel-length emails. And for allowing me to keep my promise of putting ★s around your name.

To Lawyer Sheila J. Levine: For infinite kindness, professionalism, generosity, and enthusiasm, wrapped in lawyerly expertise.

To Accountant Gerry Solis: For being the first person to officially welcome Earn My Keep, LLC, into the world.

To Agent Stephanie Kip Rostan: For turning a good proposal into one heck of a book. For calming me down and lifting me up. And for this simple statement, "I know this great Editor at Sourcebooks who would love Earn My Keep."

To Producer Angela Edwards: For giving kids everywhere two weeks' paid vacation.

To Once-Upon-A-Time Acquisitions Editor Bruce Katz: For reviewing the query letter of a complete stranger. And for telling her to rewrite it.

To Creative Directors Bruce Campbell and Christine Slingerman: For (oh so patiently) teaching me everything I needed to know to pull this whole thing off.

To my family by blood, my family by marriage, my friends from the junior high bus, and every friend thereafter: For pushing for me, cheering for me, and allowing me to do the same for you.

To Kessem Winger: For saying, "I love how Mia used manners when she was being a Market Researcher." And not laughing when I answered, "This would make a really cool book."

To Mike Rodin: For a Stepdad's never-ending support, guidance, and use of the phrase, "I'll see you at the top!"

To Avi Tryson: For being "The-Most-Amazing-Brother-Turned-Starter-of-Earn-My-Keep's-Facebook-Fan-Page." Ever.

To Michael J. Tryson: For being my Dad, always. And, while I miss you every day, for helping me appreciate the magic of quality over quantity.

To Susan Abby Halpert Tryson Rodin: For thirty-eight years of Mom-things. For not having any edits to the manuscript except a typo ("How could a mother find anything wrong with her own daughter's work?!"). And for buying a dress to wear on Oprah, the day I got an Agent. (She claims she was kidding, but Mike and I are really not so sure.)

To D: For holding my hand. For telling me you're not my "Big Boy" but my "Little Man." For being proud of who you are.

To Adam: For showing our children that you can be as passionate about your family as you are about your career. For tackling the kids' breakfasts (all the time) so I could grab an extra hour of sleep. For knowing as soon as this gargantuan project was done, I'd probably take on another. And for, yes, being a darn good softball hitter. Go #12!

And finally, to the one who started it all, Miss Mia: For loving lip balm. For reading our book. For doing our book! For making me want to be a better person for you and your brother. The world is a better place because you're both in it (how do I know? I'm Your Mother!).

About the Author

SAYS ALISA T. WEINSTEIN, AUTHOR, FOUNDER, EARN MY KEEP, LLC, IN POTOMAC, MARYLAND

Photo by Richard Greenhouse

I love *that I get to work with amazing people I would have never otherwise met.*

My biggest on-the-job challenge is *burning the midnight oil to make my deadlines.*

I do most of my writing *at the nightstand in my bedroom.*

The first thing I did upon finishing *Earn It, Learn It* was *the laundry.*

I became an Author at age *thirty-six (any age is a good age to try out a new career!).*

If I weren't an Author I'd be *a happy Copywriter, still!*

Icon Legend

ART

CREATIVE
THINKING

CULTURE

HISTORY

INTER-
GENERATIONAL

LANGUAGE

LITERATURE

MANNERS

MATH

MONEY
MANAGEMENT

PUBLIC SPEAKING

RESEARCH

SCIENCE

SOCIAL
RESPONSIBILITY

TIME
MANAGEMENT

UP IT